The Strength Not to Fight

The Strength Not to Fight

An Oral History of
Conscientious Objectors
of the Vietnam War

James W. Tollefson

Little, Brown and Company

Boston   Toronto   London

First Edition

Library of Congress Cataloging-in-Publication Data

Tollefson, James W.
  The strength not to fight: an oral history of conscientious objectors of the Vietnam War / James W. Tollefson
     p.   cm.
  Includes bibliographical references.
  ISBN 0-316-85112-4
  1. Vietnamese Conflict, 1961–1975 — Conscientious objectors —
United States.   2. Vietnamese Conflict, 1961–1975 — Personal narra-
tives, American.   I. Title.
DS559.8.C63T65   1993
959.704'31 — dc20   92-36335

Page 201 of text: "O Bird" originally appeared in *Fine Madness*, 1991. Used with permission of the author.

Pages 213–14 of text: "You Don't Have to Carry a Gun" appeared on the album "One World" performed by Just Us. Used with permission of the songwriter.

10   9   8   7   6   5   4   3   2   1

RRD-VA

Designed by Barbara Werden

Published simultaneously in Canada by Little, Brown & Company (Canada) Limited

Printed in the United States of America

Acknowledgments

This book is dedicated to the individuals interviewed for this project. These men opened their hearts and their homes to me. It is literally true that, without them, this book would not have been possible.

The first task was to find COs to interview. For help in that process, I am grateful to: Mary Steuben and Steve Ratzlaff of the Mennonite Church; Nan McMurray of the Fellowship of Reconciliation; Jonas Davis and Ellen Cooper of the American Friends Service Committee; Len Shriner of the Church Council of Greater Seattle; Herman Will of the Commission on World Peace of the Methodist Church; and the staff of the offices of the Central Committee for Conscientious Objectors, the Mennonite Central Committee and the General Conference of the Mennonite Church, the War Resisters' League, Earthstewards, and the Educators for Social Responsibility.

Richard Dunn, Susan Williams, and Rob Weller at the Department of English at the University of Washington provided indispensable help.

For their support and encouragement, I am grateful to my agent, Edward W. Knappman, and to Ray Roberts, Michael Pietsch, and Betsy Pitha at Little, Brown.

Greg Boehme, JoAnn Boehme, Bob Jacobs, and Bob Tollefson

Acknowledgments

read and commented on the manuscript. Sheri Herndon assisted in typing.

David Ortman, Tom Snyder, Mike Stern, and John Williams provided valuable material that might not otherwise have been available to me.

I am especially indebted to two people who worked on this project from the beginning: Maureen Jackson, who used her remarkable ability to decode hour after hour of taped interviews to produce several thousand pages of typed transcripts; and Elisabeth Mitchell, my research assistant, who conducted some of the interviews and gave generously of her never-wavering enthusiasm and belief in the project.

Finally, I am grateful to Bob Withington, who read parts of the manuscript and talked with me about it nearly every week for two years; and Suzanne Bade, who commented on every sentence as I read the manuscript aloud and tenderly edited every page.

Contents

The Strength Not to Fight

▬▬▬▬▬▬

"My father wouldn't talk about it. Even when the letter from my draft board arrived. Not a word. I felt very alone." I looked again at the photograph Carl had taken from the shoebox, long hidden in the hall closet. The photo was from his high school graduation in 1964. Standing next to the smiling, lanky adolescent in the black robe were his proud parents. High school sweethearts in 1942. Married in 1945. Carl came along a year later.

"My father was in World War II and fought in Europe. After I refused induction in 1967, I went home to visit. I was there four days. But he wouldn't talk to me. He was ashamed that his oldest son wouldn't go to war."

The older man in that photo had his arm around his son. Carl's mother stood slightly to the side, smiling. Within four years after that photo was taken, Carl and his parents had come to see each other as the enemy.

"We don't fight now. We're more like strangers. We talk every few weeks on the phone. But I haven't been home in four years. They've never met my three-year-old daughter. All they have is a picture of her I sent them last Christmas."

Slowly putting the photo back into the shoebox, Carl almost whispered. "I think I understand now why my father felt as he did. The Nazis were the enemy of his generation. To him, war was a way to save humanity. But the Vietnamese were not my enemy. So I refused to fight. I felt I had no choice. Despite the cost, I would do it again."

I

In the years since the end of the war in Vietnam, newspaper columnists, filmmakers, scholars, and millions of other Americans have studied and argued about the antiwar movement. To some, it was a source of enormous pride when ordinary people forced their government to turn away from an immoral war. To others, it was one of the main reasons for America's most humiliating defeat.

Largely ignored in this debate are the people who made principled stands against the war in Vietnam, those whose conscience required that they refuse to fight: the conscientious objectors to the Vietnam War.

I was one of them. At nineteen, I got my CO deferment easily by writing a persuasive application to my draft board. I was one of the privileged few. But there were many others who didn't find the easy success of a quickly granted deferment, but instead the grinding struggle of confrontation. Faced with family rejection, exile, arrest, and imprisonment, they nevertheless continued to stand firm in their opposition to that war. Who were they? Who were their parents? What forces drove them to such extremes of self-sacrifice and isolation? How did it feel to live a life of sustained and principled pacifism? And what were the consequences for themselves and their loved ones? Could I have done what they did? These were the questions that I carried inside myself for twenty years. And these were the questions that I sought to answer as I began this project.

I started with a handful of names. I posted notices on bulletin boards. I visited the traditional peace churches and the CO organizations. But mostly, I made my way by word of mouth from one CO to another. "I know a guy who was a CO back East. I'll tell him about you. Maybe he'll call." Late-night, cross-country calls from strangers ended with appointments for taped interviews. One by one, I turned up a lawyer, a judge, a fisherman, a farmer, a truck driver, a doctor, a carpenter, students, teachers, and the unemployed. One was my neighbor two houses away, his front porch visible from my living room window. Others were from New York, California, Maryland, Indiana, Connecticut, Alaska, and other

4

states across the country. Some live in Canada. So this is not a scientific sample. The truth of the stories in this book rests not in statistics, but in the ability of these COs to sweep aside the abstract philosophical debate over war and peace, and instead reveal the hearts and the minds of young men whose lives were changed forever by Vietnam.

When I came calling, asking them to tell their stories, most were eager to talk. The interviews lasted two to four hours each, some as long as six. I was one of the few in the past fifteen years who seemed interested. Most COs felt obligated to tell their stories honestly and completely, for the sake of accurate history and their own personal sense of responsibility. Some were cautious and wanted to know what kind of book I planned to write. I told them I did not want to do a political book. I was not interested in praising them or condemning them or apologizing for them. My goal was to understand and to accurately convey their experiences.

So these are personal accounts of the war at home. There is the uncertainty of chronology, due to twenty years of forgetting. There also may be exaggeration and even outright lies. I excluded some stories that just didn't ring true in the telling. But there is also ultimately the profound truth of forty solitary individuals talking about their lives during one of those rare moments in history when an entire generation was forced to answer the question, where do I stand?

The war at home was more than street demonstrations. It was arguments over the dinner table, late-night calls from pay phones near safe houses, tearful goodbyes in courtrooms and prison visitors' centers, and silent anger that — for some — has lasted a lifetime. This book is about intensely personal and passionate responses to the war in Vietnam. Draft board hearings and secret passages to Canada and lonely prison cells and the horrors of combat were the exceptional settings in which these ordinary people lived their lives. In a few short months, many were transformed from high school students to eighteen- or nineteen- or twenty-year-old draft resisters, refugees in exile, and federal prisoners.

Read together, their collective stories seem contradictory. Some speak with obvious pride in what they did, while others express profound confusion or remorse. In interviews across the United States, I found that there is no single truth of the conscientious objectors' story during America's war in Vietnam. But perhaps this book holds part of the truth: the part that includes the struggles between sons and their parents — especially their fathers, who fought in World War II — and between young Americans and their country.

II

The total number of individuals receiving deferments from the draft as conscientious objectors during the Vietnam War was approximately 170,000.* As many as 300,000 other applicants were denied CO deferments. Nearly 600,000 illegally evaded the draft; about 200,000 were formally accused of draft offenses. Many of these lawbreakers were men who had been denied CO deferments or who refused to cooperate with the draft on grounds of conscience. Between 30,000 and 50,000 fled to Canada. Another 20,000 fled to other countries or lived underground in America.

Until 1967, most successful CO applicants were from the traditional peace churches — Mennonite, Quaker, and Brethren. Under the law in force through 1966, CO deferments were available only to individuals who were opposed to all wars based upon belief in a Supreme Being. Beginning in 1967, the law became slightly broader, requiring that conscientious objection be based upon "religious training and belief," rather than specific faith in a Supreme Being. Still, applications that were fundamentally political, or that objected only to the Vietnam War, were denied.

Two Supreme Court decisions during the war were landmarks for COs. In the 1965 Seeger decision, the court expanded the definition of religious training and belief to include philosophical and moral beliefs that occupy a place in one's life "parallel to that filled by orthodox belief in God." In 1970, the Supreme Court ruled in *Welsh* v. *U.S.* that the central requirement for CO deferments was a deeply held conviction that participation in the military violated one's "religious or moral" beliefs. Thus, after 1970, COs no longer had to call themselves "religious" at all, although religious ap-

---

* Sources for statistics about draft resisters include Lawrence Baskir and William A. Strauss, *Chance and Circumstance* (New York: Alfred A. Knopf, 1978); John Whiteclay Chambers, *To Raise an Army* (New York: Free Press, 1987); D. Michael Shafer, ed., *The Legacy* (Boston: Beacon, 1990); David S. Surrey, *Choice of Conscience* (New York: Praeger, 1982).

plicants, especially those affiliated with recognized Christian churches, still had a much easier time gaining CO deferments.

As the war dragged on and the legal definition of conscientious objection broadened, the number of COs increased dramatically, from 18,000 in 1964 to 61,000 in 1971. But as the number of men claiming conscientious objection rose, so did the prosecution of those whose claims were rejected. Between 1965 and 1972, the number of federal prosecutions for draft evasion rose from 340 to nearly 5,000 annually. During the height of the prosecutions, draft cases accounted for a tenth of all cases in the federal courts. During the war, the average prison sentence for convicted evaders increased as well, from twenty-one months in 1965 to thirty-seven months in 1968, then dropping to twenty-nine months in 1971. The decrease in the later years of the war reflected the growing influence of antiwar sentiment after the 1968 Tet Offensive, when North Vietnamese and National Liberation Front forces won a major psychological victory by simultaneously attacking towns and cities throughout South Vietnam.

Yet, overall, the 170,000 individuals who received CO deferments were only a small fraction of the total number of individuals facing the draft. Throughout the period of heaviest American involvement in Vietnam, from the Gulf of Tonkin Resolution in August 1964 until the cease-fire on January 27, 1973, more than 26 million men were draft-eligible. Approximately 11 million Americans served in the military during this period, about 2.6 million in Vietnam.

Not all CO applications were from men seeking to avoid military service. About 17,000 were from individuals already in the military. These applicants faced special difficulties, as the military review of conscientious objection applications was especially intense, involving interviews with psychiatrists and chaplains, and months of waiting. Before 1971, most of these applications were turned down. In addition, applicants during the early war years often received orders to report for Vietnam before their applications were processed, and unsuccessful applicants had substantially increased chances of being ordered into combat. But in 1971, federal courts ruled that the military had to follow the same rules as civilian draft boards when reviewing CO applications. In particular, that meant that the criteria from the Seeger case had to be followed. In addition, the military was unprepared to deal with the huge increase in CO applications, and so approved many in order to avoid being overwhelmed with paperwork and lawsuits. The result was that the majority of CO applications from within the military were approved from 1971 until the end of the war.

Individuals applied for conscientious objector status by filling out Selective Service Form 150. The form required applicants to state whether they were requesting I-A-O status, which meant that they were willing to serve in the military in a noncombatant role, or I-O status, which meant that they were not willing to serve in the military in any capacity. Form 150 also required applicants to write essays answering questions about their reasons for requesting I-A-O or I-O status; the religious nature of their beliefs; the development of their beliefs from early childhood; and any public or private expressions of their pacifism. In reviewing the application, the draft board was supposed to be concerned primarily with the applicant's sincerity, though in fact there was wide variation across the country in the draft boards' handling of CO applications.

If the local draft board rejected the written application, the applicant could request a personal appearance before the board. These interviews, conducted without attorneys, often placed COs in direct confrontation with hostile draft board members. If the personal appearance did not result in a CO deferment, a written appeal to an Appeal Board (one for each judicial district) was the next step. Beyond that, applicants could appeal to their state directors or to the national director of the Selective Service System.

COs classified I-A-O were inducted into the military and underwent regular basic training. Many served as combat medics in Vietnam. I-O deferments required civilian ("alternative") service, often as orderlies in hospitals.

If the CO applications were denied, individuals were classified I-A and subject to being drafted. Those who were ordered for induction were required to report to a military induction center for a physical examination. Those who passed were instructed to take one step forward to signify their acceptance of induction. Anyone who failed to do so was informed of the consequences and the procedure was repeated. Inductees who refused a second time to step forward were subject to prosecution. Conviction for a draft law violation meant imprisonment for up to five years and a fine of up to $10,000.

A crucial Selective Service rule was that draft boards could not process CO applications from individuals with student (II-S) deferments. This meant that many young men voluntarily gave up their student deferments in order to force the draft board to consider their CO applications. The risk was enormous: if their CO applications were turned down, they would be classified I-A and they could be drafted.

Service in the Peace Corps and VISTA did not exempt individuals from the draft. Upon completion of service in one of these organizations, men were then placed into the pool of individuals most likely to be drafted.

III

Those were the rules and regulations. But what did it really mean to be a conscientious objector? One of the important political, legal, and moral struggles of the Vietnam era was over the question of what constituted true pacifism. From the beginning of this project, I decided not to limit interviews only to individuals who fit the strict Selective Service System criteria for conscientious objection. I interviewed some men who never even applied for a CO deferment. Some had refused to cooperate with the draft at all and were prosecuted for failing to register or report for physical exams. Others were poor or working-class men who were opposed to the war, but believed the CO deferment was meant for others — for rich kids and college kids. Some joined the National Guard or sought noncombatant assignments in the military. All of these stories are included here because they are essential for understanding the struggle over what it meant to be a conscientious objector during the Vietnam War.

Like the war in Vietnam, the war at home did not go on forever. COs finished civilian service, returned from Canada, were released from prison, and surfaced from underground. Many families sought reconciliation, made their peace, and went on with their lives. Others have not yet found that peace. Some never will. These stories, the lingering consequences of America's longest war, are documented here as well.

What about women who opposed the war on grounds of conscience? Like the men, they faced fundamental moral and political choices. Don't their stories belong here, too? Originally, I planned to interview women. But it soon became clear that the story of the

COs was fundamentally the story of "the draft, the draft, the god-damned draft." Many women opposed the war, but none faced military induction. And so there are no women in this book, except when they appear in the COs' stories.

A word about the format of this book. I set out to document the collective experience of those who expressed principled opposition to the war in Vietnam. My goal was not to glorify individuals, but to convey the struggle of ordinary people with their families, with their country, and with their own conscience. For that reason, I did not include a series of separate, individual stories. Instead, the book is organized around the major experiences of the COs. Also, in some cases, names and places have been changed to protect individuals' anonymity. When I told the COs about this plan, most understood and agreed immediately. They opposed the war not for individual fame or recognition, but because they felt they had no choice. Few want to be praised. All would like to be understood.

More than a little fear and courage pervade this book. The men whom I interviewed have often heard the official line that they hid in alternative service or in Canada while others fought and died in their place. They know that many of their fellow Americans consider them to be cowards, and partly to blame for America's first wartime defeat. Perhaps this book will reveal the depth of their cowardice, or of their courage.

Chapter 1

Deciding Not to Fight

A yellowed envelope stuffed with carbons and handwritten notes from a time before photocopy machines and word processors is retrieved from the top shelf of a storeroom in the garage. Selective Service System forms, a parental letter of support — and one of condemnation — two copies of the essay describing family history, religious belief, and conviction, all are laid out on the kitchen table for viewing.

He begins cautiously with stories of the days spent typing and retyping these forms. Now, after twenty years unread, the words on these pages seem to him too adolescent. Surprised at how young he seemed then, the forty-year-old hesitates and apologizes as he reads the philosophy of a college dropout — his philosophy. "I'd never write this way now."

Yet the innocence of pacifist youth is not all those pages convey. There is also bold, in-your-face self-assurance, the certainty that THIS WAR IS WRONG.

"No system will make me participate in this evil war. I will willingly go to prison before I kill another human being."

As his wife takes the children upstairs to bed, our talk moves from the dinner table to his basement workshop. In the pale light of the windowless room, events he summarized earlier in a few words are recalled again, this time with the full memory of sound and vision. *His description of his first night in the county jail brings the first tears. Anger shows in his face as he recalls a trial that lasted less than four hours, for him an eternity of fear and frustration. My question about his two years in Leavenworth Federal Penitentiary leads him to a box that contains an unframed painting of a seated figure posed in meditation, a gift from a fellow inmate. Our admiration of the painting yields gradually to his harsher memories: furious family arguments, the grilling before a hostile judge, the euphoria of mass protest, and lonely months in a prison cell. And, coloring it all, like bloodstains, memory of the violent images of Vietnam.*

"This is the first time in twenty years that I've told the entire story — my trial, what it felt like the day I was released. Not even my wife knows everything."

Reliving now the strength of his convictions, he forgets his concern that I may judge his beliefs. True, today he would use different words, the language of the adult who knows well the powerful forces that make war. But faced with the reminder that he had the strength not to fight, he proclaims: "Take it back? No way. Being a CO was one of the benchmarks of my life. I was only a kid. But I was right. We were right."

Although many people opposed the war in Vietnam, only a few considered themselves to be conscientious objectors. Why did some young men openly refuse to be drafted? What led them to take a stand that meant alienation from family and friends, exile in Canada, or imprisonment? In this chapter, conscientious objectors tell how they came to their decision to refuse to fight in Vietnam.

▬▬▬

There was a part of me, frankly, that wanted to go to war. It was a manly thing to do, a way to get out of the house, a way to grow up, and a way to see the world. A lot of it had to do with machoism.

▬▬▬

I was in junior college in the LA area. I played electric bass in a folk-rock group. We played on a TV show called the "All-American College Show," hosted by Arthur Godfrey. Three acts competing with each other. An Irish tenor won, but as a result of our appearance, we landed a contract to do a USO tour in Asia. I knew if I left for the tour, I'd risk losing my student deferment, but I fantasized that my draft board would accept the work as supporting the troops and grant me a continuation of my II-S deferment when I came back from the tour. So I went.

We left in September 1969. Four of us, two guys, two girls. Our first stop was Japan. A week on the hospital circuit. Mostly casualties from Vietnam. We'd play acoustically and sing and visit and talk with the patients. All men, all my age, eighteen or nineteen. Ward after ward of men my age who had pieces of themselves missing. Eyes and ears and arms and legs. Day after day, orderlies would roll people into auditoriums on gurneys and in wheelchairs. The patients would ask us about our draft status. The more severely injured they were, the more extravagant the action they'd tell us to take to make sure we didn't end up in their situation. I remember one man — it's hard to call him a man. He was my age. I wasn't a man — I remember one guy who said, "Shoot your foot off. Shoot a finger off. But don't let them get you."

It was like running into a brick wall. The war suddenly wasn't on TV. It was right in front of me. These were human beings who were just like the people I'd been going to school with. No matter what the outcome of the war, these guys weren't going to get better. How could they be absorbed back into the United States? Planeloads of them. I thought, "If I cooperate with the draft, I may be in this position. I'll be forgotten. I'll have my arm blown off for the rest of my life." It was very scary and very sickening.

One day, I was with one of the women in the group. Sue was her name. We turned a corner in one of the wards, and there right in front of us was someone she knew from high school. He was missing some limbs. I can't remember which ones. She spent quite a while talking with him. Afterward, she was shaking. I remember being very scared. I felt it would happen to me.

After Japan, we went to Korea. One of the first shows we did there was located far from anything else. We were told that the men we were going to see probably wouldn't talk to us. That it wouldn't be like any other audience. Our guide told us they'd been stuck there a long time and would be kept there for the rest of their lives. That's all we were told.

We were driven in a bus for several hours over awful roads to the north, way up near the DMZ [Demilitarized Zone]. It was a pretty area, full of pine trees. We arrived after dark. I could smell the trees. We walked along narrow paths to a tiny, very old, long, low barracks. Inside, it was open, with a simple wood frame and wood floors. No stage and no special lighting. About twenty or twenty-five men were sitting around, most staring off into space. They looked old to me, I guess in their forties or fifties. They were from the Korean War.

The room was uncomfortably quiet. We began the show. They didn't sit close to us. Some didn't pay any attention. Some talked to each other or to themselves. They never applauded, and they didn't seem to know that it was appropriate to applaud. I kept wondering why we were doing the show. No one came up to us afterward.

The men seemed to be stockpiled, maybe an embarrassment to the U.S. government or military. I don't know. Later in my life, I became a psychiatric nurse. When I think back about the men's behavior, it seems quite certain to me that they were probably on maintenance medication of some sort — psych meds. Their behavior certainly was very similar to a lot of behavior I've seen on psych units since then.

We did three weeks in Korea. I gradually realized that our music was incidental. We were there to provide human contact for people. After Korea, we spent a weekend in Tokyo, and then flew to the Philippines. We were there during the national elections, which were very violent, with civilian shootings, gory TV commercials.

I remember riding in a pedicab, a three-wheel tricycle. We were passing someone when another trike came toward us. The two raced toward each other and at the last possible moment swerved, barely missing each other. There was wild laughter. It wasn't funny, but it was a relief. I felt such relief there. I wasn't going to get shot. It was so beautiful there.

After the Philippines, we did Guam, and then flew home, arriving at Travis Air Force Base in northern California. As I walked off the plane, I realized that my stomach had been hurting the whole trip. My father and younger sister were there to pick me up. I remember putting my amplifier in the back of my dad's car, and the relief I felt. The trip was finally over and I was safe again.

I arrived back at home convinced that I never wanted to play music for money again in my life. I immediately sold my amplifier and hung up my electric bass. Getting rid of my amplifier was a way of rejecting the whole experience, washing my hands of it. I had been daydreaming about a bass flute since Korea. I had made a drawing of it, which I had kept in my back pocket for the last part of the tour. So I went to Sherman Clay Music Store in Vallejo and traded my bass as down payment on a bass flute. I started making payments for the first time in my life — $28.15 a month.

Within six weeks, I had made up my mind. One morning in our basement at home, I told my father that I didn't think people in the United States were worth defending. I told him I was going to refuse induction. He told me I was wrong. He was appalled and shocked. I clearly didn't have his support. I didn't tell him then about the ward after ward of crippled, shot, lost men my age.

My dad was a navy man for thirty years. He had been a prisoner of war for three and a half years in the Philippines during World War II. I was born at Bethesda Naval Hospital. We moved every three years from one base to another. When he was captain of a ship, we lived in Arlington, Virginia. When he was a commander of a reserve training center, we lived in Alabama. Then we moved to Japan, where he skippered two ships.

As a kid, I was very involved in military things. In Alabama, every Mardi Gras, I'd ride on a float in a little sailor suit. In Japan, I'd spend days at a time on cruises with my dad.

Years later, in 1969, I flunked out of community college. My lottery number was 139, so it looked like a sure thing that I'd be going to Vietnam. I wanted to avoid ending up in the infantry, so in 1970, when I was twenty, I enlisted in the army. My plan was to get trained as a neuropsychiatric technician. The day I left, my folks dropped me off. They were really sad, because they knew their son might get hurt or die in the war. But they were also proud of me.

I went to Fort Knox, Kentucky, for basic training. I enjoyed it. It was like an athletic event. Carrying a gun, shooting, walking through mud, crawling through barbed wire with live ammo being fired above you. For me, it was a competition. I thrived on it.

After basic training, I went to Fort Sam Houston in Texas for 91-Charlie — ten weeks of medics' training. That was followed by

91-F20 — neuropsychiatric specialist training "on the hili," as they said there. It was "on the hill," because it took place on a hill high above where we did basic.

When I finished training, I got assigned to Fort Ord as a psychiatric technician. There was quite a bit of smoking grass, drinking wine and beer. We discussed things. It was an emotional time. My beliefs were slowly influenced by people there and by events around me. I began to feel that maybe the government was not being honest. I was seeing and hearing every day about people getting killed, about atrocities that the United States was committing. I worked with people just back from Vietnam who had traumatic stress reactions. I talked to them about what had happened to them, about things they did and things they saw other people do.

I had never had a serious belief in my life. No feeling for God or religion. Nothing more than love for a girl. I had never taken a political stand. But I gradually thought about accepting differences and accepting all cultures. I thought about taking a stand against a culture that included war. I saw the actions of resistance that others were taking. I knew people at Ord who broke loose, who took a stand, who filed as COs, and got discharged. Those guys made all of us think. I began to separate myself psychologically from what I was doing and what was going on in the military around me. I began to ask questions, do a lot of soul searching and thinking. I made attempts at articulation of my newly found beliefs. That was the first time the word "articulation" came into my vocabulary. It was the first time I ever really had to put something into sharp focus.

I contacted an attorney in Carmel who had helped other COs at Ord. I wasn't being impulsive. I did it with a lot of feeling and emotion. It turned out to be one of the real identifiable turning points of my life.

━━━

I grew up with the forties and fifties war movies, cowboy movies, Tarzan movies, Superman movies. The list is endless about how the good guy finishes off the bad guy with force after being pushed too far. That was my model.

I remember as a kid being really interested in church, even though my parents were atheists. When we lived in Fairbanks when I was ten, I went to a Baptist church. The minister had a wonderful huge dog that wore saddlebags full of religious tracts to distribute to drunks around town. I'd ride the dog after Sunday school. The minister told me that if I prayed for forgiveness of my sins, I would be saved. I didn't know exactly what that was, but I tried it anyway. Lying there one night, praying, suddenly this tingling whoosh went through my body from my feet to the top of my head. I was astounded, and told the minister all about it next Sunday. He hugged me, jumped for joy, carried me downstairs to his wife, and cried, "Ol' Jimmy's been saved." That was probably the peak of my spiritual life.

I was raised with guns. I remember my father buying a .22 rifle for $5.25. He said that it had a spring-loaded bolt at the back for cocking it. He told me that when I was big enough to cock it, I could have the rifle. It was in his closet, never loaded. I'd go into his room and spend afternoons trying to pull back that bolt. When I was finally able to do it, he kept his word and taught me how to shoot. That experience was one of the closest things my dad and I ever did together.

I was an exchange student in Berlin during high school. I was there before the Berlin Wall. Germans admired the United States. I visited East Germany, where the East Germans were standing in lines with their ration cards. It was not yet rebuilt from World War II. It always seemed dark there, like a dungeon, such a contrast to West Berlin, with its beautiful parks and lights and cinemas and cars and people everywhere. I came back to the States feeling pride in my country, feeling that we had a mission against communism. I wanted to work for the CIA, to put my energies into overthrowing the bad guys.

In college at Stanford, I joined ROTC. I liked ROTC. Playing outdoors, playing with guns with a group of guys. It was fun, exciting, and satisfying. We went to Fort Lewis for summer training. I liked the discipline and I did really well. I was the top student from my school at summer camp.

But I had reservations about the war. I heard Arthur Goldberg, who was then the U.S. ambassador to the UN, try to defend the war in a talk at the University of Oregon. He said that the government of South Vietnam had been democratically elected. I knew that the elections were a sham. He was just another government person lying to us.

ROTC guys hung out at a bar off campus. The bar had two

17

jukeboxes. One had the song "Ballad of the Green Berets." Sometimes, someone from another table would actually play it, and then someone from our table would jump up to the other jukebox and play Bob Dylan's "Quinn the Eskimo." There would be cacophony in the bar until both songs ended. Already then I knew which side I was on.

I finished school and then was called to active duty in the spring of 1967. I was to report in July. I was married, and we lived in Haight-Ashbury in San Francisco because rent was cheap. We were there for the six months that acid was legal. I didn't use it, but I enjoyed the scene. It was a circus, a lot of fun.

In July 1967 I went to Fort Benning, Georgia, for infantry officers' basic training. What I witnessed over the next months was the collapse of our country's morality. I watched it disintegrate, piece by piece. There were a lot of people from West Point at Fort Benning who were refusing their commissions. There wasn't much about it in the press, but we knew about it. They were supposed to be the leaders, and they were quitting.

Once, we were practicing digging foxholes. I got paired with a stubby little guy from East Lansing, Michigan. On his elastic camouflage band around his helmet, he had written "Thou Shalt Not Kill." We became good friends.

The John Birch Society passed out bumper stickers that said "Win in Vietnam." An officer plastered them on all of our clipboards. We complained. We didn't think the John Birch Society had any business imposing its political will on us. We had LBJ's face on our dart board.

The most important part of our training was helicopter practice. I was in intelligence, but most of the officers there were infantry — which meant that they were about six weeks away from leading forty nineteen- and twenty-year-olds into battle. Over and over again they were going to have to put men in helicopters, co-ordinate the landing, and spread them out in the battle zone. Our helicopter training was supposed to culminate in a two-day night practice. But John Wayne was at Fort Benning to make a movie, *The Green Berets*, I think. We were told that the helicopters were unavailable because the movie needed them for shooting scenes. They gave us trucks to practice with instead.

Insurance salesmen often sat in the officers' lounge. I always wore an insignia that showed I was an intelligence officer, not infantry. The insurance salesmen would pull me aside and say they could offer me a better deal on life insurance than the guys in infantry. I could have killed them.

Each of the training companies had to make a banner with our slogan on it. Something like "Drive All the Way." We were supposed to stand and shout our slogan when the instructor walked in. My company decided that we wouldn't. Instead, when he walked in, we stayed real quiet. Then one guy way in the back of the room stood and said, "Well," and then five guys on the other side of the room said, "Here we are." And that became our motto. We finished our basic training with a banner that said, "Well, Here We Are."

In October, I was sent to Fort Hollabird, Maryland, for advanced training in intelligence. While we were there, my wife and I went to see the nation's capital. It was wonderful, a beautiful place. Late in the day, I was sitting on the Mall, looking at the Capitol steps from some distance. There were these little black shapes walking up the steps, and suddenly it dawned on me that those little black shapes held the power of life and death over me. They were the power of the nation, but they looked really small. I had a sense right then that they didn't deserve that power, and that I needed to get it back for myself. It was an autumn day, crisp and beautiful, and those little black shapes looked like beetles.

Three months later, in January '68, I was sent to Salt Lake City to work in intelligence. I liked it. I did background checks on people. I learned interviewing techniques. I investigated people who needed clearance for access to classified information.

After three or four months in Salt Lake, I got my orders to report to Vietnam. I knew the stakes by then. I talked with my parents about refusing to go, and about going to prison for up to five years. My father's reaction was very moving. He said if it were him, he would not refuse an order, but he would understand if I did. Then he paused for a long time and said he wished he could do my time for me. "I could do five years standing on my ear." My wife wanted me to go. She didn't want to be widowed, with me in prison for five years. In the end, I figured I'd probably just shuffle papers, not do anything horrible to anybody. So I climbed on a plane in San Francisco and flew to Hawaii, Tokyo, and finally Saigon.

I assumed I'd be assigned, like most intelligence officers, to a regular U.S. Army unit, where I'd keep track of the battlefield situation. But upon my arrival, I learned I was to work as an adviser with the Vietnamese. I had been assigned to the Phoenix Program.

I had never heard of the Phoenix Program. But at a bar on one of my first days in Saigon, I mentioned it to a guy who was just finishing his tour of duty. He told me all about it. He said I would be assigned to one of the provinces, where I would work directly with the Vietnamese Army to hire spies to find out the names of people working politically for the National Liberation Front. Since most males of fighting age were in the army, that meant getting the names of kids under thirteen and women and men over sixty. We could offer money, booze, draft deferments, drugs, women, boys — anything in exchange for information. When we got the names and maybe the photographs of people, we would send them to the U.S. ambassador's office in Saigon, where the Central Intelligence Agency worked. They would dispatch a team of twelve, two Green Berets from the American side and ten South Vietnamese Rangers, out to the village where these folks lived. The team would assassinate them.

That was the last straw. I walked back to my room, sat down on my bunk for ten minutes to think, and then went to the officer in charge of personnel. I said, "Sir, I have a legal problem." He said, "Of course, Lieutenant, I'll get you a driver and a jeep," which took me to the Judge Advocate General's headquarters near General Westmoreland's office, just outside Saigon. I took a number, waited, and then went into the office of a navy lieutenant, a young guy, probably just out of law school. He said, "What can I do for you?" I said, "I want to apply for conscientious objector status." He snapped up, stared at me, and said, "Why?" I told him I had just been assigned to the Phoenix Program. He leaned across the desk, looked at me, and said, "Good for you." It turned out that he was from Harvard, and before he was drafted he had helped people get CO status back in Boston.

I got the CO application and filled it out sitting on my bottom bunk. I used a drawer upside down on my lap to write on. I had to answer all those questions like, "Why do you want to do this?" I didn't pause for a second. Everything just poured out. It was clear and just flowed. First draft, I typed it up and turned it in. My Phoenix orders were canceled and I got assigned to the personnel office while my application was considered.

The army moved me to just about the worst room in Saigon, over a generator that powered electricity for four hotels, running at maybe two thousand rpms right outside my window. I got issued my equipment. A corporal in the supply shop gave me a gun. I stuffed it in the closet in my room. There were nights in Saigon in '68 when there was firing, attacks by small groups of National Liberation Front soldiers, sometimes against U.S. military officers. I would sit there on my bunk, thinking about what to do if they came through my door. About half the time I left the pistol in the closet and just sat there on my bed. The other half of the time, I loaded the pistol and slept with it under my pillow.

A friend of mine in high school was drafted, so he enlisted because he was told that he would get better treatment. He did his basic training at Camp Pendleton. Around Christmastime, he came back for a visit. He was shaking all of the time. He told us about the part of basic training where their aggressiveness was channeled through bayonet practice. They had these dummies set up and they were taught how to lunge and thrust and parry. They had to scream at the top of their lungs, "Kill! Kill!" It was called "the creed of the bayonet."

To encourage the soldiers, local citizens had set up a huge billboard right on the outskirts of camp with a Merry Christmas message and a loudspeaker system that played Bing Crosby's "I'm Dreaming of a White Christmas" over and over again. So there they were, screaming at the top of their lungs, "Kill! Kill!" to the refrain of "I'm Dreaming of a White Christmas." They were celebrating the birth of the Prince of Peace while learning the creed of the bayonet. My friend thought it was insane.

By 1965, I was convinced that Vietnam was a civil war and that we were intervening on one side. That seemed appalling. I studied American history. I could just imagine what the North would have felt if the British or the French had intervened on the side of the South in the American Civil War. The sense of outrage they would have had.

By 1966, they were drafting about fifty thousand young men a month. They were getting minimal training and then being shipped off to Vietnam. The escalation of the war was continuing and I couldn't figure out why it was happening. Our leaders were generating public support through carefully calculated propaganda campaigns. Officers and men were going beyond their orders, conducting themselves in ways which were criminal, such as killing prisoners. A B-52 at fifty thousand feet dropping bombs on a radar grid is indiscriminate slaughter. They used chemical agents. The same kind of conduct that the special commando groups in the Soviet Union used when they killed 17 million civilians. After the Second World War, we put Nazis to death for killing civilians. We hunted them down. We blasted their cities off the face of the earth and killed their government because what they were doing was inhuman and unjust. Thirty years later, we were doing exactly the same thing. It was a crime against humanity then, and in the 1960s it was a crime against humanity too. No difference, except it was our side doing the killing.

I remember the film *Hearts and Minds*. There's a pathetic sequence when they interview a coffin maker in Saigon while he's building a coffin about three feet long. They ask him how business is and he says, "Well, it's never been better." They ask whether he makes all kinds of coffins. He says, "No, I only make coffins about this size." And then in the background you begin to realize he's got coffins stacked up to the ceiling, and they're all for children. He's making a thousand coffins a week. Business was good, he said.

I was in the sole surviving son category. My uncle, my father's brother, had been wounded four times in the Second World War. But he never had any natural children of his own, so I was the last surviving male member of the family, other than my father. I could have had a deferment on that basis, but by 1965 I'd become angry and amazed and disgusted at what the United States was doing. I figured, even if I managed to get through university and get a teaching job, I'd still be living in a state that found it a good thing to kill people by the hundreds of thousands for no reason. So I decided I would look for the opportunity to go to Canada. I would get out of a society that had gone off the deep end.

By that time, I had taken sides in the war and I wanted to see the Vietnamese win. Simple as that. I think Donald Duncan, the ex–Green Beret, put it very well. He said alienation is when your country is at war and you want the other side to win.

I grew up just outside of Newark, New Jersey, in a traditional, liberal, Democratic area. As an early alienated teen, I was a militaristic right-winger. That way, I could be the only Goldwater supporter in my town. It was a way to define myself as an outsider. Some of this also came out of reading science fiction, which I think subliminally impressed me with its high-tech, militaristic, wham-bam shoot-'em-up literature. When I was fourteen or fifteen, which would have been 1964 or '65, the Vietnam War was still a bad science fiction novel. It was far away, and our people were doing glamorous things with high technology, conquering the evil planet. If I gave Vietnam any thought at all, I was in favor of whipping the Commies and finally standing up for ourselves.

My family is Jewish, but it was never really religious. For several years as kids we went to Hebrew classes after school, which I hated. Really, we were ethnically Jewish rather than religiously Jewish.

My father was a World War II vet and had served in the Normandy landing. He had enlisted rather than be drafted, partly so he could choose his service. He has always been politically conservative, and yet politically alienated. He feels like politicians are corrupt, that there's no one representing him, and that there's nobody honest in the system. He believes he votes to throw the bums out, but he just keeps trading bums. I certainly never felt that he wanted his children to enlist, but we never really talked about it. My dad and I have never talked about emotions and important things. We only talk about how our cars are holding up and the weather and where we have gone, but we don't talk about things that matter.

I think that he was embarrassed by my being an antiwar protester. At one point, I stopped in on my way hitchhiking back from the May Day, 1971, demonstrations. As long as I was far away, he didn't know about what I was doing, but here I was hitchhiking back from an antiwar demonstration where I had been arrested. What he'd seen on TV were shots of dirty-looking demonstrators starting fires in garbage cans. That just didn't seem to him like a way for anyone to behave in public. He couldn't understand how I could associate myself with people like that. It wasn't a question of being opposed to the war or being in favor of the war. This just wasn't a way to behave. Correct social behavior was very important to him.

The red sheep in my family were an uncle and aunt I love dearly. They had been fringe members of the Communist party. The rest of the family thought of them as the crackpot loony Commies. They thought what was missing from the antiwar movement was some organization to play the role that the Communist party tried to play in the thirties, where you might be working in the trade union movement, but through that work you made connections with the antiracist movement, and eventually saw a broader need for change. In some ways, they provided me with role models at a time I really needed them. They questioned me about how I felt about the draft and whether I knew the words to Phil Ochs's "Draft Dodger Rag." They were trying to plant a seed in my head. As I gradually found my own politics, I realized the similarities I had with theirs.

I grew up in a segregated community. In my first three years of high school, there were no black students; in the last year I was there, there were four. There were just no black people in this town right on the Newark city line. Our Thanksgiving football classic was with a high school in Newark. The rivalry had gone on for fifty years, but the year I graduated it was canceled for fear of race riots at the game. Having this white suburban team with white suburban fans playing this black inner-city team with black fans was just too volatile in the fall of '68. They never reestablished the game, but instead invented a new classic with some other white team in the 'burbs.

I think there were a couple of contradictory forces in the historic Jewish experience that affected me. One was the thousands of years of not being part of any country, and so not being patriotic. My grandfather and most of his generation fled Russia at the end of the nineteenth century because of the draft. That was something that was never really said explicitly — "You come from a family of draft dodgers." But that's why people came from Russia. They were facing a twenty-five-year draft by the Russian empire in its effort to wipe out the Jewish communities. At the same time, it was in 1967 that Jewish people for the first time in history walloped somebody else and felt, hey, we got some respect! People supported Israel's military prowess.

There was another contradiction. During the sixties, the Jewish community was very active in the civil rights movement. Some of this was a remnant of 1930s radicalism. Some of it was a sense, which died out later, that Jews as a minority needed to fight oppression nationally, because having an American culture that didn't oppress minorities was the only way that the Jewish community could be safe in the United States.

Yet a lot of people in my town had grown up in Newark and moved out, though they still owned small shops and apartment buildings there. So on the one hand, we had this Jewish idealism about fighting racism, while on the other hand, we were racist scum landlords. They didn't see themselves as racist scum landlords. They just felt that this black subclass was trying to chisel them on the rent and not taking good care of the buildings.

By mid-1967, I found that I was in opposition to the war. Some of the change was due to being exposed to the early hippie subculture during the summer of '67 in New Orleans. There was federal funding that summer to send bright high school students to universities so they could learn science as part of the keep-up-with-the-Russians program. I looked at it as a wonderful scam. I applied and picked neat places. Honolulu, Seattle, and New Orleans were my choices. I ended up in New Orleans, attending science classes at Loyola University.

People there looked on me with great amazement, as this Jew they'd never seen. Women kept trying to take me to church with them. I wasn't a Zionist, partly because the community I came from was so Jewish that until I went to New Orleans, I wasn't even aware that there was anything odd in being Jewish. Suddenly, in New Orleans, being the only Jew for miles around, almost a creature from another planet, I was an outsider. It was fun sexually.

I ended up spending a lot of that summer hanging out in the park with hippies. When the summer ended, I was back in high school in New Jersey, and all my peers concluded I was a hippie. To a large extent, we are what people perceive us to be, so that year I led a group that walked out of school one day in opposition to the war. To be perfectly honest, we did it partly to skip school and have a fun day off. We spread the rumor that if our high school administration dared challenge us, we would go public that this was an anti-Vietnam walkout and create a controversy. So they left us alone. We went into New York City and had a good time.

In my last year there, Newark burned. First in the summer of '67 and again in the spring of '68 following Martin Luther King's assassination. My school was about a mile and a half from the riot boundaries. I remember one news report that the police were lined up with submachine guns on the street that separated us from Newark.

Because my birthday was at the end of the year, by the time

I turned eighteen, I would already have graduated from high school. I planned to apply to Columbia and Yale and all sorts of high status, expensive American places. My mother suggested that I consider McGill University in Montreal. McGill intrigued me as an exotic, romantic place to go. We discovered that the cost of an elite university in Canada was about equal to the cost of a state university in the United States. So McGill became more and more attractive.

Then, in the spring of '68, I dropped in at a draft counseling office on the campus of Columbia University to talk about filing for conscientious objector status. They discovered that I was going to be in Montreal in September and that when I turned eighteen I would actually be filing in Canada. The draft counselor's eyes lit up, because he remembered an obscure subsection of the Selective Service Act that he'd never had the opportunity to test out on anyone. There was this thing called "Local Board 100."

Local Board 100 was a draft board in Washington, D.C., for American citizens around the world who claimed they had no address in the United States. Local Board 100 had never drafted anyone, even though at that time boards had quotas to fill. Their quota seemed to be zero. Rumors varied as to why this was true. One rumor was that they processed all the army brats living in Germany, and so many of them enlisted that Local Board 100 never had to draft anyone to fill its quota. So I decided that would be my plan. I'd go to McGill and register in Canada with Local Board 100.

━━━

I can remember the first time I really started to think about Vietnam. It was the fall of 1964. I was a freshman at Harvard. Vietnam was just cranking up then. According to a straw poll, most college students were supporting Barry Goldwater in the presidential campaign. I was coming out of a lecture hall and was handed a leaflet by some of the SDS [Students for a Democratic Society] students on campus. This leaflet said, "Did you know that General Ky's personal hero is Adolf Hitler?" Ky was then the air force general of Vietnam. That started to shake my marbles.

By the time I was a junior, I was pretty clear about Vietnam. I staked out the first half of my senior year to do independent research into the Selective Service law. I spent a semester looking at CO law and the history of conscientious objection in the First and Second World Wars.

My dad was a frontline surgeon in the Second World War, patching up soldiers right after they hit the beaches in the reconquest of the Pacific. He spent two and a half years in combat and lost a brother in the South Pacific. I think it was extremely painful for him, having come back from a patriotic war, to see what was happening in this country in '68 and '69 — the campuses erupting, the enormous antiwar movement, and the divisiveness of the war. He was very upset by the stance that I was taking. But I always had a sense that I had his permission to do what I felt was right. I always appreciated and loved him for that.

Partly as a consequence of the havoc I was raising with my beliefs, he ended up volunteering to be a surgeon in Vietnam for two months in '69. I was amazed. It was an astounding thing for somebody to do, to pick up in the middle of an active surgical practice and take off for two months to do volunteer war duty.

He did triage emergency surgery for civilian and military casualties in South Vietnam, and was just appalled that the South Vietnamese medical staff would come in at nine in the morning, go out for a two-hour siesta from noon to two, and quit at five, even with stacks of bleeding bodies left there. He came away with a sense that they just didn't care, that it wasn't their war.

I applied for CO status and turned in my draft card. I was well aware that that was an offense for which I could be arrested. I considered the alternatives and decided that I'd stay in the United States and go to jail rather than flee to Canada.

Why? I think because I didn't want to be what my grandfather called a "slacker." He had organized the first volunteer medical unit out of the state of Washington in World War I. I grew up with him in the house in back. He was alive until he was ninety-seven. He was a rabid right-wing Republican, but a dear old man and somebody who never had any truck with "slackers" and "draft dodgers," as he called them. I was willing to be a soldier, but for a different cause from the one for which my dad and my granddad had fought.

▬

As a kid, I loved guns. Texas, where I grew up, is a sportman's paradise. My dad and I often went hunting. Duck hunting was my favorite. You go out before it's light. You're freezing. If your feet stay dry, you're lucky. Otherwise, you're in for hours of misery.

27

The Strength Not to Fight

You get set up in a blind. It's real silent. You swat the spiders away. You got your hot coffee or cocoa. Then you hear the birds, birds of all kinds. The light comes up and the birds explode into this unbelievable cacophony of nature calls. Pretty soon you can see the trees over by the horizon, and the water. You've got your decoys out. Once it's light, the ducks start coming. My dad would call them on the duck caller. I'd try to shoot ducks a hundred yards away with a shotgun. My dad would say, "The shotgun won't go that far. Here's what you should do."

So I was brought up with guns. I thought guns were invincible. It was the killing of civilians that gradually convinced me the war was wrong.

I went to college in 1964. In '66, there was a rash of "We Won't Go" statements. I was one of the signers of the original statement. Our first action to get attention was in 1966, when Secretary of Defense Robert McNamara came to Cambridge to give a talk at the Harvard Kennedy School of Government. We had the building surrounded, but he didn't want to talk to us. They sent a decoy car and hoped to sneak him out back, but we caught him and filled the street around his car with people. So he had to get out and talk with us. We detained him for five or ten minutes. The headlines and editorials the next day said what we did was uncivilized and barbaric, that all the photos should be analyzed to see who was there, and that Harvard should kick us out. For those of us who were there, it was hard to recognize our event in the media coverage. Back home, my dad was mad because I was attending what he called the Kremlin on the Charles.

In '68, back home near Killeen, Texas, I stopped in at a GI coffeehouse. I ended up working there for six months. I met GIs fresh back from Nam. The antiwar activists and the GIs supported each other. Some of the guys running the coffeehouse were veterans. We had a very rigid rule against dope, because you could get sent to jail for years for just a microscopic amount. Texas is not a very tolerant state.

Locals didn't like us. And they didn't like the GIs either, whom they called "dopers." The people in the town were for the war, but the GIs were stigmatized. Especially the nonwhite GIs, who'd get their asses kicked if they went in the wrong place. The townspeople were, however, willing to take their money. There were pawnshops, movie theaters, used car lots, liquor stores.

Those of us who worked at the coffeehouse lived a couple of miles out of town in a poor black and Mexican neighborhood, which was our way of protecting ourselves against what we called the "goat ropers." Those were people who would have liked to set fire to our house or our cars if they felt they could get at us.

During the time I was there, we got word that some of the GIs from Fort Hood were going to be sent to Berkeley for riot control during People's Park demonstrations. So we made up leaflets encouraging troops not to shoot people in the streets. I went one night with a friend to distribute the leaflets on base. It was hot. The base was crawling with cops because of the tension over sending troops for riot control. We parked in the lot and started leafletting cars, when a jeep full of MPs suddenly pulled up. My buddy hid under a car, while I stuffed the leaflets in a mailbox. But the MPs found both the leaflets and my buddy. They arrested me within minutes. We spent the night in jail. It was a good thing it wasn't Brazil. The MPs were really hostile. Some couldn't understand why they weren't allowed to beat us up. It was a real education. It just made me madder at America.

Near the end of the fateful year of 1968, I told my folks I was going for CO.

▄▄▄▄▄

It was shortly after I decided to go for a CO deferment that my mother approached me — it was when my dad wasn't around — to tell me she supported my decision. It didn't surprise me. It was just like her to go for peace.

My father had fought in World War II. He was going to be drafted, so he joined the navy. He always joked that he did it because he knew he could always get a shower in the navy.

When I was young, his war stories were part of the family mythology. He made a little plastic model of the troop transport ship he was on. He was a photographer and had a yearbook that he put together for the men on the ship. One of his main stories was about proving some corruption involving the Coke machine on board. Coke was a very busy concession, and apparently there was some graft in the upper echelon of the ship's command. My father was asked to work in the concession and keep records about the money changing hands in order to document the graft. He was told there was some risk if he got caught. But he did it. One of the last nights before the ship got into port, there was some scuttlebutt that the men who were taking the money had found out about the records being kept, and were going to chuck my dad over the side. There was a locker inspection and Dad's coworkers took his record book and passed it among themselves to hide it from the inspection. But then the watch assignments got changed and my dad was assigned to the fantail in the middle of the night, which was very odd. Dad said it was apparent he was going to be offed. So another man offered to stand watch for him. And he survived. When the ship got into port, federal authorities came on board and took the men who had been stealing the money. Dad said he wondered for a long time whether they would ever come after him.

I don't think he ever knew how powerful that story was for me. I saw him as doing something right, something moral and ethical, despite the risk. I felt like I was taking a moral stand by choosing not to participate in the war. But he couldn't accept my choice. He could never see that I was trying to live up to his example. He never understood that he had inspired me.

———

I decided that I would be a CO when I was fifteen. I had just become an Eagle Scout. One morning at my school — South Pasadena High School — people were chatting in the hallways before class about their older brothers going through military training. There was a lot of sexual talk and talk about the brutality. It just occurred to me standing there that I was going to be a CO. It had to do with my perception of the nature of military training, especially its psychological abuse and denial of human rights. I decided I would have no part of it.

From that point on, I billed myself publicly as a person who would eventually apply for CO status. Being a CO was a job to be done. Like joining the Marine Corps. Someone had to do it. That was 1962.

My first year in college began in September of 1964, at the University of California at San Diego. The place was built on a former military camp, kind of a posh training center from World War II. There were vestiges of the training apparatus around — long lines of toilets with no partitions and miserable living quarters. The Greyhound bus from my home to the university would often stop at Camp Pendleton. You could hear the people marching, and the profanity and the debasing of human character. A free nation ought not to behave toward people that way.

The idea of forgiveness was essential to my pacifism. It came to me in a curious way. I knew a divorced woman who had a child. She was a rather nasty person, antimale, but paradoxically she decided that her thirteen-year-old daughter ought to have some sort of male figure in her life. So she hired me one summer to spend a day a week with her daughter. The daughter was seductive, profoundly disturbed, and probably had been sexually abused. I had been reading some work by Fritz Perls about forgiveness and letting go. I was thinking a lot about forgiving one's family, not carrying grudges, and how you could help heal other people through forgiveness. The first day I spent with the girl, we talked about her father, who was an alcoholic English professor in the eastern part of the state who had obviously been an absolute bastard. We talked about how she needed to learn to forgive her father. That got me thinking about the idea of radical forgiveness of people as a political maneuver. Take the Lord's Prayer, the statement, "Forgive us our sins as we forgive the sins of others." The most radical part of me took that as meaning the will of God is that no one gets forgiven unless they are capable of acting out complete forgiveness of others. Jesus was trying to tip people off: if you could learn to live this way, then you could create an entirely new kind of world.

As I followed up this idea, it suddenly occurred to me that I was no longer nominally interested in Christianity, but I had had some kind of threshold experience. I was over into the other side. I hate to call it a born-again experience. Some people would. It was the beginning of my understanding that dominance and violence, the failure to forgive, can only lead away from God.

———

I was raised in a very tight, conservative Lithuanian-Catholic ethnic community in Grand Rapids, Michigan. The roots of that environment were the church and the military. My father had fought in World War II. He flew thirty-three missions over Germany with the Eighth Air Force. So my dad was a war hero, although he almost never talked about it. While a lot of kids above the age of twelve started chasing girls, my interest in military matters continued and grew deeper. I went from building models and playing with little tanks to buying World War II history books.

31

The Strength Not to Fight

In 1959, at the age of fourteen, I entered the seminary to become a Catholic priest. In the seminary, I became a skilled player of war games. The Civil War, World War II, any war. During the Cuban missile crisis, I phoned my parents to say, "Be sure to keep your gas tank full and have lots of canned food on the shelves." I even insisted that we have some rendezvous point where we would all meet after World War III. I think it was in Arizona somewhere. I was always the strategic thinker.

My consciousness was very firmly rooted in my childhood, which meant I had that virulent anticommunism typical of American Catholicism at that time. I was the sort of person who actually read Eisenhower's book *Crusade in Europe*. The only war on the planet was the war against ruthless, atheistic, godless communism.

My views about war began to change because of my fascination with the topic. My interests took me beyond literature that glorified war to literature that revealed the horror of it. One book that was absolutely critical to my formation was *The Fortunes of War*, by Andrew Rooney, who still comments for CBS. It's about four great battles in World War II. Its introduction states that one of the reasons a lot of writing glorifies war is that the people for whom war was a bad experience aren't around to tell any stories about it. It goes on to say that the truism is right: war is hell. The first battle it covers is the absolutely, unbelievably horrible battle for Tarawa in the South Pacific, during which five thousand people died for one square mile of Coral Island, in just a merciless, vicious, brutal, hand-to-hand struggle. I also read General S.L.A. Marshall's study of combat infantrymen during World War II, which revealed that when push came to shove, over 50 percent of the troops admitted they never fired their weapons. Another high percentage admitted that if they did, they intentionally aimed high or closed their eyes. Taking another life seems to be deeply antithetical to human beings.

And I read poetry. I memorized one poem by Randall Jarrell, who, like my father, had been in the Eighth Air Force. It was called "The Death of the Ball Turret Gunner." I especially remember the ending, when the dead gunner's corpse is washed out of the turret with a hose. I still have my written analysis of that poem, so I have early documentary evidence of my beliefs.

I was ignorant of American military involvement in the war in Vietnam until the summer of '63, when those pictures of the Buddhist monks who immolated themselves were splashed on the front pages and on television. Those were such startling, shocking images that all of a sudden I realized something was going on in this faraway place called Vietnam.

My first critical analysis of the war took place in the fall of 1966. We had a great deal of speech training in the seminary. One day, the speech and preaching professor said, "This week, we are going to debate the war in Vietnam." He asked, "Who wants to take the antiwar side?" Not one of us did, since from our perspective there was no debate. We knew that the war was wonderful. Finally, out of an old-school notion of gallantry, I volunteered to take the antiwar side. And in my usual thorough fashion, I started reading all those "Commies" who were writing against the war. What I read shook me. It shook me up badly.

One of the main points of the critics was that Vietnam was a civil war. It wasn't evil Communists directed from Moscow and Peking invading a wonderful, peaceful, democratic people. I read solid evidence of the number of civilian casualties. This was not World War II. Tarawa, as horrible as it was, was only American and Japanese soldiers, not families caught in the middle.

Gradually, I began to agitate for more discussion of the war. Our classes in moral theology and ethics focused on questions like: Is it okay to remove an ectopic pregnancy? Is it okay to snip the fallopian tubes? I finally led a student rebellion in 1968. We threatened to have a strike unless a number of things occurred, among them more access to television news and newspapers and open discussions of the war in our classrooms. Cardinal McIntyre came to the seminary and clearly stated his position: "If you strike, we will dismiss you. There are plenty of young men in Ireland who would love to come to this seminary."

Unfortunately, his threat worked. I said, "Follow me," and all I heard was my own echo. I was a revolutionary with no party. I was disgusted and angry and bitter. I concluded that the church was hopeless on the matter of the war. So, in what for me was an absolutely gut-wrenching move, I left the seminary. I had been in it for nine years.

My family had always thought about taking a vacation in Europe. My father decided now was the time for it. So in April 1968, my sister, mother, father, and I left for Europe. The high point was a visit to Attlebridge Air Force Base near Norwich, England. My father had been stationed there in World War II. It was still largely intact, because it had been turned into the largest turkey farm in all of Great Britain. With no small irony, we drove out on the runway in my Volkswagen to see where he used to take off. It was like the opening scene in *Twelve O'Clock High*, where the wind is blowing across the tarmac. It was one of the few times my father talked about his experiences in the war. For me, it was my last pro-military moment.

I eventually went to Paris in May 1968, just in time for the student uprising. That is where my first on-the-street, committed antiwar activities occurred. I got a crash course in New Left politics, as I sat in smoke-filled rooms with Sartre and others. I was there when the Communist party and all of the labor unions pulled out, leaving the student movement completely exposed. The French government viciously cracked down. There was gunfire and beatings and hurled cobblestones. People were killed. It scared me off radical, violent street protest. I am lucky I didn't get killed.

When I came back from that vacation in the third week of May, I plunged myself into the campaign for Bobby Kennedy in California. Here was a way I believed I could work against the war that would really make a difference. I became an intense volunteer in the campaign. I was about ninety feet away from him, in the Ambassador Hotel, on my birthday, June 5, when he was assassinated.

I was devastated, but I felt I had to continue working against the war. I hooked on with the McCarthy campaign and went to Chicago for the convention to work as a McCarthy volunteer. I was in the street when the police rioted. They used barbed wire, jeeps with machine guns. They pushed a bunch of people through a plate-glass window. We carried the injured up to the McCarthy campaign office and made phone calls for medical assistance. I was later swept up on the street and arrested, and put in Cook County jail. There I observed a young woman protester have her guitar stomped on before she was raped by a Chicago policeman with his nightstick.

I talk on military matters today, and people say, "Were you ever in the military?" And I say, "No, but I have been in combat." And I mean Chicago.

In Chicago, I concluded that everything I had been taught about the American political system was false. There was no democracy when it came to the war. I saw the McCarthy campaign locked out of the convention. I saw Hubert Humphrey cast as the peace candidate. I realized the political system was geared to produce two war candidates. It was not going to represent the antiwar movement in the '68 elections. And dissent was going to be met with state violence. It was horribly disillusioning. It became clear that there was little point in working at American presidential politics. Any candidate who really stood for change would be shot.

Of everything that happened in 1968, I think the Tet Offensive was the final straw. It demonstrated that our government had been lying. I knew enough to understand that the Tet Offensive didn't accomplish much militarily. But for the National Liberation Front to wage that kind of assault, there had to be tremendous support right in Saigon. You don't get a commando squad into the U.S. embassy without a lot of people helping you. So despite what our government had been saying, it was clear that there were lots of people in the south supporting the other side.

I decided to go back to the seminary. A number of my former classmates who had been in my little rebel group had gone up to a progressive seminary in the San Francisco Bay Area, St. Patrick's Seminary in Menlo Park, near Stanford. So I did the same.

Although the Stanford area was hardly Berkeley, still, in the fall of '68, the antiwar movement was very active there. A turning point for me was a lecture at the Stanford Memorial Church by Father Daniel Berrigan. In May of 1968, Daniel Berrigan and his brother, Philip, and seven others had poured homemade napalm on draft records at a draft board in Catonsville, Maryland. That was international front-page news. I had read about it in *Le Monde* when I was in Paris. I thought, "Boy, that's bizarre. Who are these guys, napalming draft records? What the heck, let's go see what this guy has to say."

Berrigan's talk had a dramatic, powerful effect on me. Here was this enigmatic, eloquent poet-priest. I couldn't imagine this guy napalming draft records out in some parking lot in broad daylight. He put the war and resistance to the war in the context of Christian theology. He was a pacifist *and* a Catholic priest. He said that what was needed was massive nonviolent resistance. We should pack the jails. That just blew my mind. Pacifism was something Quakers did, not Catholics.

I was so excited that I don't think I slept for a week. Suddenly, it seemed two of my life's passions had come together. Catholicism and my hatred for the war. I enrolled in a class at Stanford called

35

"Jesus and Nonviolence," a cram course in Christian pacifism. I read Thomas Merton's writings and *The Nonviolent Cross* by Jim Douglass, the famous activist. It startled me that here was a two-thousand-year tradition of nonviolence in the Church.

About that time, two Catholic pacifists, Tom Cornell and James Forest, came to the seminary to talk and to lead discussions. Tom Cornell was one of the original draft card burners in '65. Jim Forest had just come back from torching the draft records in the Milwaukee draft board. He was one of the Milwaukee Fourteen. Jim and Tom had formed the U.S. Catholic chapter of the Fellowship of Reconciliation. One night at dinner, we had corned beef and cabbage. The only thing that was remotely edible was the corned beef, but neither Jim nor Tom were eating it. I was thinking, "Who are you guys, what's the matter?" They said, "We are vegetarians because we see that nonviolence extends into this too." I was impressed. Nonviolence is not just something you read about in books. It shows up on your dinner plate.

My life continued to change. I helped organize major demonstrations. I began to be a regular speaker on the antiwar circuit. I hate to think how many times I drove from Menlo Park to San Francisco State to Berkeley to Hayward to San Jose State to Stanford and then home. Around and around the circuit, because at that point there still were not very many Catholic clergy speaking out.

My work reached an apex with the invasion of Cambodia in May 1970. Campuses began shutting down all over the country. We shut down the seminary, and within twenty-four hours the entire faculty joined us and spread out to do teach-ins. There is a statue on the lawn in front of St. Patrick's, similar to the big Jesus on top of Sugarloaf Mountain in Rio, with the hands outstretched. We put a sign saying "On Strike" in Jesus' hands. We were the only Catholic seminary in the country that closed down.

I went to work in the Black Panthers' breakfast program with the pastor from one of the churches in San Francisco. That was during all the police raids of the Panthers' offices. I like to think that one of the reasons the police didn't hit the San Francisco office was that every night for about two weeks, the two of us sat in folding chairs in front of the place in our clerical clothes.

At that time, I still had my IV-D ministerial deferment. I publicly burned my draft card and informed the Selective Service in a letter. I got a reply that they couldn't take my word for it, and they sent a new card. So I burned my new draft card, saved about a third of it, and sent that in to them, whereupon I got back another draft card with a letter saying, "We want to replace your loss." At the time, I assumed they were going to arrest me, but the Selective Service System had effectively collapsed in northern California. They had stopped going after people who refused to cooperate.

The archbishop of San Francisco was Joseph T. McGucken. In more angry moments, seminarians applied a certain adjective that rhymed with his last name. He called me on the carpet in his big mansion up on Russian Hill with its marble floors and huge desk, and told me he had friends in the FBI who had informed him that my antiwar and revolutionary activities were being funded by Communist China. I was so broke at the time, I wanted to say, "Really? Are you telling me the check is in the mail?" He said he was going to inform my bishop and expel me from the seminary.

I went back and told the rector of the seminary about the meeting. The rector was outraged. He told the archbishop that if I were canned, he would quit. I was stunned by that sort of support. The rector saved me. Archbishop McGucken desisted.

My bishop in San Diego called me there for having led the strike at the seminary. I was packing my bags, presumably to have the buttons of my cassock snapped off, when three of my fellow seminarians came in and said, "We are not going to let you take the heat alone for the strike. The rest of the students have drawn lots. The three of us were selected to tell the bishop that every one of his seminarians was involved in the strike." And that's what they did. They saved me.

Nonetheless, the bishop still had power over me. The seminary required us to serve a year in the field before being ordained. So when my bishop was assigning people to their posts, I got assigned to a tiny parish in the town of Carlsbad, California, not far from Nixon's Western White House at San Clemente and right next to Camp Pendleton and thirty thousand Marines.

I continued my antiwar activities there. The largest boys' military school on the West Coast was nearby. On Sunday mornings, all the Catholic cadets would march to church down the main street with their mock rifles. I made them stack their weapons at the door. I also helped to run an antiwar coffeehouse in Oceanside. One night

37

about two minutes after I had closed up, somebody drove by and fired several rounds from a shotgun through the door. Another time, my car was forced off the road. I often got death threats.

I was scared spitless and completely isolated. I got on the phone to the priests at the seminary and asked, "Do you have any openings as far from here as you can get me?" They said, "How would you like to teach at St. Mary's Seminary in Baltimore?" Baltimore! Phil Berrigan's home! I said, "You bet your bippy." So, as I shook the dust of Oceanside off my sandals, my first assignment following ordination as a priest in 1971 was Baltimore.

After a rather epic journey, during which my car engine blew up, I arrived in Baltimore the morning after the FBI ambushed twenty-eight Catholic Left draft board raiders in Camden, New Jersey, and J. Edgar Hoover announced, "We have broken the back of the Catholic Left." The major cause célèbre was the pending Harrisburg conspiracy trial of Daniel and Philip Berrigan, Elizabeth McAlister, and others who were accused of plotting to blow up heating tunnels under Washington, D.C., and kidnap Henry Kissinger. I walked into the headquarters of the Harrisburg Defense Committee and said, "Reinforcements have arrived from the West Coast." At that point, I plunged head over heels into what remained of the Catholic Left.

I remember in grade school, the good sisters, God bless them, asking what we would say when the Communists take over and put us up against the wall and ask, "Are you a Christian?" Little did I realize that years later somebody would indeed put me up against the wall, but it wouldn't be the Communists. It would be my own government.

———

I grew up under Eisenhower. I would have been Wally to Beaver Cleaver. I liked Ike. Everybody liked Ike. He was everybody's grandfather. Then there was JFK and the ideals that surrounded his early administration. The idea of questioning authority became widespread during the years with LBJ. And then of course there was Nixon.

My household came out of 1950s mainline Evangelicalism, which basically argued for very hierarchical relationships in the family and in the church. It didn't lead to an antiwar stance at all.

Although it was a stable home, it was nonpolitical, not particularly in touch with current affairs. My folks would watch the news, but there was no real sense of connection to it, even in the middle sixties. Yet sometimes my father surprised me. I can remember my jaw dropping once when Angela Davis was a fugitive, and was finally caught across the bay from us. My father said he was concerned that she might not receive a fair trial, given the political milieu surrounding her. It was not the response one would expect of the generation associated with World War II. Those kinds of surprises were a part of my family.

When I became eighteen in 1969, the year after the Tet Offensive, I was a high school student in the Bay Area and interested in marine biology. I was ready to sign on the dotted line, to sign up with the military. It wasn't because I was motivated in any kind of macho, kick-ass way, nor did I have any particular sense of patriotic duty. It was just an expedient choice. I was a good student and the navy was interested in me. I won a four-year navy scholarship at Stanford. My plan was to get into grad school with the naval connection. So that was my thinking at the time. It was not related to the purpose of the military.

In the end, though, I didn't take the naval scholarship. Again, it was not for a principled reason. It was because it didn't work out logistically. I ended up at the University of California, San Diego, at Ravelle College, which is the science/math school there. That's where my metamorphosis began. It happened quite dramatically.

One of the first events that rocked my world was when a student who was a year ahead of me at Ravelle College burned himself to death on our Free Speech Plaza. It was patterned after the Buddhist monks in Vietnam who immolated themselves. He called out something like, "My God, stop the war," and then he poured gasoline on himself and lit himself on fire. The teaching assistant in my physics course tackled him with a blanket and put him out. He died shortly after in the hospital. It was an unbelievably distressing, overwhelming time for the campus.

The Kent State and Jackson State shootings were also marker events. Kent State caused campuses across the nation, including my own, to erupt. The racism of our country was demonstrated, because it was the Kent State shootings, not the Jackson State shootings on a black campus in a poor black neighborhood, that caused such a tremendous sense of outrage. Ronald Reagan was governor of California. He closed down all the UC campuses, as well as the state schools.

I was nauseated by the My Lai massacre, and the reasoning that Lieutenant Calley used — following orders. Such a loss of connection with humanity. Is there a part of me who could have done the same thing? I may not have shot at peasants and dumped them in a ditch. But I kept wondering about my own dark side.

Another major event was the night that Richard Nixon announced we were in Cambodia, after saying for so long that we were not. I was on campus that night and joined hundreds of other students in a room where there was a television. You should have heard the descriptions of that man, the profanities, and the gestures that were hurled at the television set when he finally made his confession. All along, we had talked about not trusting the leadership. Here was an explicit example of direct lying and duplicity.

I would go to the airport periodically, to pick up a friend or to fly to northern California to see my family. Sometimes, there'd be a bunch of new draftees there. I'd watch these civilian young men my age, scared, pale, lined up in a variety of clothes with a DI [drill instructor] out of Camp Pendleton screaming in their faces, right there on the sidewalk in the airport. They hadn't even got on the bus yet. Oh, Jesus. That image helped me remember who the soldiers were, eighteen- or nineteen-year-olds like me, scared to death. I tried very hard and very consciously to stay away from expressing the babykiller image when they returned from Vietnam. They shouldn't have been there. I was convinced of that, and dramatically so. But I refused not to be thankful for their sacrifice. They were there, their life was on the line. For whatever reason, I wasn't and they were. I wanted to be thankful for those lives and those people.

Chronology is fluid, not linear, and another element in this swirl was the movie *Hearts and Minds*, an exposé of Vietnam. I remember vividly a scene in which two U.S. soldiers were in a whorehouse having sex with two Vietnamese prostitutes. There was a blanket between the two beds, and the soldiers were talking to each other while they were having sex. One was saying that, if his girlfriend could see him now, she'd flip out, and the other one was saying that he was frustrated because the prostitute would not remove her blouse. The first guy responded, "You paid for it." The comments went back and forth. You could almost smell the sourness of it. It was so absolutely objectifying, so absolutely lacking in any human value. It was a noncombat, violent experience.

That image expressed the violation of an entire people that was so much a part of my thinking. I decided that if I was drafted, I could only serve as a noncombatant. In a year, I had moved from being ready to sign on the dotted line to deciding I could not be in combat.

I was in the first or second lottery, I can't remember which one, but I remember the setting vividly. I had just come home from work at Sea World. It was still light outside. I grabbed a sandwich and a pop and turned on the TV. I was spellbound, watching an individual with two drums, pulling dates out of one drum and draft numbers out of another, and putting them on a board. It was mind-boggling. I was astounded. I couldn't believe that this was my life and death being determined by random number. I was committed in my Christianity and I believed in an all-powerful God. But that didn't make any difference. The reality was that a random number table was being used to determine my life and death.

I ended up having a reasonably high number — 267, I think. It was a year in which the draft wasn't supposed to get higher than 200. I thought, "Well, I have no idea what's going to happen two years from now when I graduate and lose my student deferment." So I decided to gamble. I wrote my draft board and said I'm dropping my II-S student deferment. The choice-making was just blowing me away, the sense of intensity in choice-making.

I got a I-A just like that, and then I spent the rest of the year with that I-A in my back pocket, wondering what I had done. They got to the low 200s that year, and so I survived the gamble and I was out of jeopardy.

It was only then I began to think about CO. It had no expedience at all. It was strictly a private decision based on how I viewed my world as a human being on this planet, as a follower of Jesus of Nazareth. I would never be asked to serve my country in the military. Nevertheless, near the end of my undergraduate career, I contacted my draft board and said I wanted to drop my exempt status and apply for CO. For me, it was an individual, private act. It was myself, by myself, at a desk writing to my draft board. And so I set in motion the wheels for CO classification.

41

I was aware early in life that I was different because I was born in Bridgeport, Connecticut. In the farming community of Mennonites in the Freeman-Marion area of South Dakota, people asked questions. Why was I born in Bridgeport, Connecticut, and not in the local Freeman Community Hospital?

The answer is that my father had taken part in I-W alternative service for conscientious objectors during the Korean War. He was part of a contingent of Mennonites, including fifty or sixty couples, who worked in a large mental hospital in Bridgeport. I was the first I-W baby born there.

Our family had a farm about twenty miles north of Freeman, in a rural area. I went to a one-room country school with anywhere from nine to twelve kids in all eight grades and one teacher. I tell people we had a kerosene TV.

The Mennonites in Freeman had come from Russia in the late 1800s, after having traipsed around Europe, from Switzerland to France to Austria. Some went eastward into Prussia and then into Russia, invited by Catherine the Great to farm the Ukraine. They left when Czar Alexander Nicholas ended their privileges, including military exemption. They migrated to the United States, where they bought land from the railroad in godforsaken places like Kansas, Nebraska, South Dakota, and Manitoba. You can find Mennonite communities all along Highway 81, which runs from Manitoba to Texas. The Mennonites took over land that had been the Indians'. Some Lutherans and later a few Catholics did, too.

The railroad gave Freeman its name by mistake. While building depots, they were going to put up a "Menno" sign where the Mennonites lived. Down the road was going to be a "Freeman" sign. But somebody got them turned around, so you have a colony of Mennonites living in Freeman, and down the road is the town of Menno with no Mennonites. The Mennonite high school, which I attended, is in Freeman. When we played Menno High, you'd hear everybody yell, "Big Menno, Big Menno, Kill Menno."

In the Mennonite community, it was fine if you wanted to be a CO. Nobody in Freeman went to prison for nonregistration. No one went to Canada. Everyone knew, if you were a Mennonite in Hutchinson or Turner County, the draft board would give you a CO deferment and you'd do alternate service. Most people felt, just don't make us shoot anybody and we'll do anything you say.

For some of us, though, the question was whether you should cooperate with the Selective Service System at all. I began to question alternative service, and I gradually came to the conclusion that the government was cutting itself a deal with the Mennonites, just like the rulers in Russia, Prussia, and elsewhere.

I was in the first lottery. As it was held, I listened to the radio with other students at Freeman Junior College. I remember one lucky guy getting over 300. My number was 45, which impressed me as the only lottery I ever won. If I had gotten a high lottery number, I would have just gone on with my life. But now I knew something important was going to happen.

In January 1970 I turned eighteen. Instead of registering for the draft as I was supposed to do, I wrote a letter to my draft board. This is what it said:

Today, I am eighteen years old. On this day, I am required by the law of this country to register with the Selective Service System. But my obedience to a higher law compels me to refuse to do so. This has not been an easily or hastily arrived at position. It comes as the result of much thought and introspection. I realize that in doing what I am doing, I am breaking the law, but I am ready to accept whatever consequences my action may bring upon me. I have watched with growing horror the actions my country has taken in Vietnam. Under the guise of defending freedom, we have destroyed a country and its people. However, my stand is even more than this. It comes from a deep personal belief that all war is wrong. The people of the world are my brothers and I cannot participate in or support the killing of my brothers. My purpose in living must be to affirm life, not to be an instrument of destroying it. As a member of a so-called "Peace Church," I could easily apply for and receive a classification as a conscientious objector. But this would be, in effect, an acceptance of the system of conscription and the militarism for which it exists, and would also be a way of effectively silencing my conscience. To accept a classification from the Selective Service would be to recognize the legitimacy of the

System, a legitimacy that does not exist. The action I am taking shows my own refusal to participate in war, but even more, my belief that no man should be forced into war. So, today, instead of bowing to a god of war and destruction, I am affirming a God of peace and love. By saying "no" to death, I am saying "yes" to life.

———

My parents had a house on the South Side of Chicago. I was quite close to one uncle, my mother's brother. My mother had gotten sick with multiple sclerosis when I was twelve or thirteen. My father became very involved in caring for my mother. So my uncle stepped in and took up some of the slack. He always made sure Christmas was organized, that we'd have Easter dinner, and so on. So I felt quite close to him.

I entered seminary in the Chicago area. Our deferment put us in a special category. We were divinity students — IV-D — which put us with the homosexuals and the disabled. So we were pretty safe. Still, the war was all around us.

In 1966, a ceremony was held at Navy Pier in Chicago — Cardinal Cody blessing tanks being loaded on ships for Vietnam. Sixty of us from the seminary went there in our robes and our collars, unmistakably Roman Catholic seminarians protesting the war.

The cardinal arrived in a black limousine. He was dressed in his finest, with his monsignors and the bishop surrounding him. He used some holy water on tanks that hadn't yet been loaded onto the ships. We were orderly, but we had signs that said, "End the War," and "Stop Blessing Death." Clichés, perhaps, but we were pretty excited. He never said a word to us. He just looked at us once, blessed the ships and the tanks, and then drove away. We followed up by picketing at his residence.

Within three weeks, all of us were called in to be interviewed at the seminary by various staff and by psychologists. Several people had to take tests. Others were counseled to leave the seminary. Of the original sixty in our group, only four actually became priests. The rest left or were pressured to leave. I was able to hold on longer than a number of others.

My decision to leave came at a time when I had a pretty intense relationship with a girl in downtown Chicago. I was sneaking out at night and coming back in the morning for morning prayers, and was less and less able to reconcile myself to a celibate life. So I saw the writing on the wall.

After I left the seminary, my deferment was lifted. My parents encouraged me to go into the navy and another uncle, who was a former Marine, encouraged me to go in the air force. There was no problem about my leaving the seminary. Everyone said, "You gave it a good shot. We're proud of you. Now your country is calling. We heeded the call. We expect you to heed the call."

I decided that I wasn't going to kill anyone, even though my family was set on it. So I confided to my parents that I wasn't going to go in the military. They couldn't accept it. They called my uncles, who didn't want to believe it, either. I was just a punk, right? I was the oldest of twenty-eight grandchildren. Everyone had high expectations for me. Everybody was watching what I was going to do. I was eighteen.

I got a job for the Chicago transit system and took some classes. And I spoke out publicly against the war. At Loyola University and the University of Chicago, some professors invited me to their classes to talk about options people had, about Sweden, about Canada, what prison would be like, and legal defenses for anyone refusing induction. One session at the University of Chicago was in December of '67. There were about four hundred students in the lecture hall. Eight of us spoke. We answered questions, gave statistics about the war, and talked about what it cost us socially. We addressed people who were afraid or who were going into the military because they felt pressure from family or friends. There were so many who went to the war without reason, without really thinking about it.

We learned later that the FBI was there tape-recording our speeches. The tapes were later used in charges against me — treason, sedition, they had a whole bunch of nasty names for it. The government claimed we were counseling people to commit a felony, and they had it on tape.

I realized I was going to be drafted. So I went down to Sixty-third and Kedzie Avenue, to my draft board. I went into the office and tore up my draft card in front of one of the clerks. I left it and walked out. It was very quiet and nonconfrontational. I didn't pour blood on files. I simply had decided that I wasn't going to go into the military.

I requested the forms for conscientious objector status. Months later, the forms arrived on November 11. But they were due in the draft board on November 1. They had sent them to be sure I'd be too late. I filled them out anyway, although I never expected to receive CO status.

I had become the black sheep of the family. I was shunned by everyone. Yet I still felt that I could trust my uncle — the one who had helped our family so much. So I told him that I planned to go to Canada. That turned out to be a mistake. He said, "The FBI will be interested in this. It is my duty as a citizen. If I find out someone is going to rob a bank or commit some other felony, I should call the police and tell them I know a felony is going to be committed. And that's just what I'm going to do."

And that's just what he did.

Early in my life, I equated Christianity with the idea that we are meant to *serve*. I believed that faith isn't what we say, it's the way we live.

I loved going to church. At a church youth conference in Monterey, California, I heard Joan Baez talk about pacifism and sing songs of peace. Most of us didn't agree with her, and I'm sure Joan left the meeting thinking, "God, what a waste of my time." I didn't know then what to do with the information I heard from her that night, but she planted a seed in me that grew as time went on. By the time I reached college, I had begun to actively oppose the war.

During college, I participated in many marches and vigils and demonstrations against the war. I volunteered as a medic during antiwar demonstrations in northern California. By the time my student deferment ran out in 1969, I had come to feel that the Selective Service System did not have the right to judge whether my conscience met their standards.

In October 1969 I tore my draft card in half and mailed it back to my draft board. I wrote, "I do not recognize your authority to judge my conscience." Yet returning the draft card was not enough. The war didn't stop. The killing and maiming continued. What else could I do? I felt I needed to be a moral witness against the war. I wanted to say "no" to the war, to resist the system that sent men to their deaths. I couldn't live with myself unless I acted on my faith. Finally I began to think about burning draft files.

I knew it would be like jumping off a high dive. Once you're in the air, there's nowhere to go but down. But I felt no real fear.

———

I read a book by Daniel Berrigan, who was later to become a good friend, about the resistance action he and his brother had carried out in Catonsville, Maryland, where they burned Selective Service files. In the book, he asked why more people weren't following their example. For me, it was like a Zen experience, a flash of light going through me. That's it! That's what I should be doing! It was scary, but it was also clear, that's what I should do. It was the summer of 1970.

With the help of a nurse, I began to gather blood from friends, intending to pour it on files in the San Jose Selective Service office. In October 1970, the day before I planned to do it, I went to my mother's house to tell her that the next day I'd be in jail. I found her there dead. She had had rheumatic fever as a child, and had a weak heart.

I disposed of the blood, but my calling remained. In December 1970, on Christmas Eve, two months after I had found my mother, I carried homemade napalm, made from Ivory Soap flakes and gasoline, into the Selective Service office in San Jose.

———

I come out of a Catholic family from a pleasant surburban neighborhood in New Jersey, about eight miles from New York City. We were middle class, maybe a touch upper-middle. I was raised fairly devoutly. I attended Mass and received communion regularly, I went to Wednesday CYO [Catholic Youth Organization] classes, and I went to confession at least once a month. I walked three miles through four-foot snow drifts to attend church on the first Fridays and first Saturdays of every month. I did extra penances and Stations of the Cross. Mine was a Roman Catholic family, and that's what you're supposed to do.

I was the oldest of five children. Only my brother actually turned out the way we were programmed to be. He ended up marrying a woman who had a priest and an FBI agent in her family.

As a kid, I became almost phobic about going into New York City because I read so many science fiction stories in which the city was Ground Zero for a thermonuclear World War III. I worried about terrible weapons of destruction ending all life on earth. Late at night, when I would hear fire sirens, I'd worry, "Is it the Big One being dropped on New York?" During the Cuban missile crisis, when cars driving by my school flashed sunlight into the classroom from a piece of chrome or a windshield, I'd tuck and roll out of my desk, thinking, "This is it. They're dropping it." I had this fear of being trapped in New York. Too much concrete and steel. A crush for exits. No way out. Later, I would relive that nightmare in my prison cell.

I went to Cornell University for one year before I flunked out. At Cornell, I saw my first antiwar demonstration. I had a friend in ROTC who complained about those "goddamn beatnik protesters." At one of his drills, I saw shaggy-haired peaceniks, some of them with old "Ban the Bomb" signs. They were protesting Vietnam. I thought it was very unpatriotic of them. They were probably Communist agitators. That was the first time I saw the peace sign. It was October 1964.

When I flunked out of Cornell in June of '65, I was mortified at losing face. I decided the only way I was going to make an identity for myself, the only way I was going to establish my manhood and experience my right of passage, was to go into the service. It was also a way of saying "fuck you" to my family.

I told my parents I planned to enlist, but as I was driving out the driveway, they literally blocked my car with their bodies, begging me to reconsider. It wasn't that they didn't want me to go into the service. They wanted me to go to another college, enroll in ROTC, and attend officer candidate school. My father had been a lieutenant in the navy. In my family, being a grunt or a petty officer was just not what you do. So I pulled the car back into the driveway and said, "Okay, I'll go to college. I'll work my way into the service in a different way. But something around here has got to change." That was 1965.

By the summer of '67, something had changed. I was in Bellingham, at Western Washington University, studying to be a teacher. I associated with counterculture people involved in everything from communal living to drugs. I lasted two quarters at Western before I dropped out to hitchhike to Mexico, take drugs, and cruise into San Francisco. After a few months of that, I decided to drop back into school to study sociology. It was at that point that I really started looking hard at where our country was going, what role we were playing internationally, and what the hell was going on in Vietnam.

I read as much as I could — especially Thomas K. Merton, Martin Luther King, and Gandhi. I quit watching TV. I didn't start again until the mid-seventies. I didn't watch the nightly news with the body bags and the war coverage. The sensory stimulus of the war on TV was too horrible. I saw it only a few times in houses with TVs, and it horrified me.

I remember a pivotal event around that time. I was riding in a car in Ferndale, in Whatcom County, through beautiful dairyland and pastureland. I was tripping on acid, watching some high-flying military jets go by, and admiring the contrails. Below them was a farmer in the fields with his dairy cattle. It was spring and the land was partially flooded.

Suddenly it wasn't Ferndale. It was Southeast Asia. Those were rice paddies. That wasn't a cow, it was a water buffalo. The farmer was Vietnamese. The planes were B-52s and they were carpet bombing, and the farmer was leading the water buffalo around giant craters blasted in the rice paddies. He was no threat to the people in the B-52s. He was just trying to go on with his life. I felt an identity with the farmer. I felt his powerlessness against something that was technologically superior. Oh, my God, it seemed so wrong.

As time passed, school didn't seem real to me compared to what was happening in the world. I benefited from being in school, because I was safe from the war, but I had enough of a sense of caste and social status that, goddamn it, it was unfair that white, middle-class people could get deferments because they could afford school. It was not just that my folks could help me pay for school. I could walk in anywhere, even as a bearded longhair, and get a job as a shoe salesman, a dishwasher in a cafeteria, or other odd jobs. I could stay in school and be protected from the draft because I wasn't poor, I wasn't black, and I wasn't from the inner city.

I started to attend demonstrations, listening to speeches and watching people burn draft cards. I felt a kinship with them, but because of my Christianity and my background, I thought draft cards were government property and I didn't have the right to destroy them.

Finally, I thought, "This is bullshit. I'm dropping out of school. I'm going to apply for CO status. I'm not going to get it, but I'll see how long I stand up to the system before it gobbles me up. Do I have the moral integrity to resist to the point of being arrested?" My God, being arrested was inconceivable, completely alien to my upbringing and my social background.

I wrote a letter to the student newspaper, saying that I was not going to destroy my "peace card" because it was government property, but I also didn't want to carry it anymore, and I formally renounced its existence. Today, that's called "creating your own reality." I didn't have that phrase back then, but I wanted to create a world where the Selective Service System did not exist.

So I stamped a peace sign on my draft card, mailed it back to Washington, D.C., and dropped out of school. I traveled, hitchhiked, and waited for the machinery to churn. I agonized over the CO application, saw that it was an exercise in futility, and finally just said the hell with it. I decided I was not even going to respond to the draft board, and I would see what happened.

Well, what happened was I got drafted. They gave me notice to report to New Jersey. I said, "Hey, guys, change my venue to Bellingham." So that took some time, stalling, dragging my feet, delaying the inevitable. I hoped that the bureaucracy would lose me — which it did, but that is further along in the story.

Bellingham is near the Canadian border. I became involved in the underground railroad, helping deserters and draft evaders get to Canada. Once, I went to Canada to visit two AWOL soldiers I had helped. They were opposed to my returning to the United States and risking going to prison. "You don't deserve jail," they told me. "We think you're a foolish martyr to go back. For your own good, we are keeping you here." They tried to make me stay in Canada. All three of us ended up fighting, punching and wrestling in a pigsty full of shit and mud. It was a bizarre scene. Three peaceniks, rolling around in pig shit, fighting over the issues of freedom and autonomy and choice. I won. They said, "All right, be stupid, go back down to the States."

I had a friend whose boyfriend in the service went AWOL and headed to Bellingham on the train. The FBI found out about it, and he literally jumped off the train with her in Mt. Vernon. They went along back roads to Bellingham, and ended up in my apartment, hiding out for the night. He had his knapsack of belongings and his ID. The next morning, a group got him across the border, but there was so much heat on him, they had him in disguise, with fake papers. He left all his true ID and his belongings in my apartment for safekeeping. We were going to smuggle them up in a week or so in another vehicle.

Unfortunately, that afternoon I was busted for marijuana I had received in the mail. My apartment was surrounded by narcotics agents and the police, who came in with guns drawn and proceeded to tear apart my apartment in a three-hour search, literally leafing through books and magazines and going through the contents of my refrigerator. All this time, in the middle of my living room, was the knapsack with military ID for a guy wanted by the feds. All I could think was, "Boy, I'm beyond busted. I'm never going to see the light of day again."

For a while, I was freaked out, in shock and immobilized, but gradually I relaxed and had breakfast while they searched. I started getting a little sarcastic. I had them look through my box of Wheaties to make sure I wasn't ingesting illicit substances. I started finding other places they hadn't searched, saying things like, "You better pull out that Bible. There might be a section cut out in the middle with drugs in it." There was a lot of junk in my place, and a lot of drugs, which they put in a pile. But there were a lot of places where they were finding nothing, and they were getting fatigued going through the search. I had been scrupulously honest with them about what was going on. I essentially admitted to everything — until they got to the knapsack. They wanted to search it, and I said, "Look, that belongs to a friend who is on a camping trip. He's a fastidious packer. If you tear that knapsack apart, I expect you to fold it and repack it exactly the way he did it. That is not my property. I swear to you there are no drugs in that knapsack. None of my belongings." They said okay, and didn't open it. So even as I was taken downtown in handcuffs with boxes of drugs and drug paraphernalia to be booked in the Whatcom County jail, part of me was smiling, because I had crossed the first hurdle right on the cusp and landed on my feet.

Chapter 2

Trial
and
Imprisonment

It had been a remarkable week. On Monday, November 24, three Apollo 12 astronauts completed a ten-day trip to the moon, the second lunar expedition in history. On that same day, the bitter trial of the Chicago Seven, charged with conspiracy to incite a riot at the Democratic Convention in August 1968 continued in Chicago. On Thursday, November 27, Thanksgiving Day, only eight GIs out of 141 soldiers in the Seventy-first Medical Detachment at Pleiku, South Vietnam, showed up for the traditional dinner of turkey, cornbread dressing, cranberry sauce, sweet potatoes, and pumpkin pie. Declaring that there was no reason to be thankful as long as the war continued, the rest of the soldiers fasted in a silent protest against U.S. involvement in Vietnam. On Saturday, November 29, a Defense Department investigative panel reported that racial unrest in the U.S. military in Vietnam was pervasive throughout all branches of the service. Most gut-wrenching of all was the continuing news of the massacre at My Lai, in which American soldiers slaughtered scores of Vietnamese civilians. Everywhere the boyish face of Lieutenant William Calley, Jr., accused of murdering 109 Vietnamese, stared out from the front pages of newspapers and the covers of magazines. In Saigon, officials announced the body count for the week: American soldiers dead —

130. *South Vietnamese — 567. North Vietnamese and Vietcong —
3,201. U.S. troop strength in Vietnam stood at 479,500.*

*It was Monday, December 1, 1969. Like a million other men
between the ages of nineteen and twenty-six, I was anxious to
watch the first Selective Service lottery, the televised drawing to
determine who would be drafted during the coming year to fight
in Vietnam.*

*The Jesuit priest who taught my late-afternoon eighteenth-
century literature class talked right through the bell. When class
finally ended, I hurried through the drizzle across campus to meet
four friends at Campion Tower, the Seattle University dormitory
where I had lived the previous year.*

*I joined my friends on the floor of the already crowded lobby
of the dorm. We sat just in front of the TV, which had been placed
on top of two tables stacked high so everyone could see. My friends
knew I had decided to apply for conscientious objection. Although
I did not know whether my draft board would grant me a CO
deferment, I was determined not to go in the military. The television announcer explained that the first third of the numbers
drawn would certainly be drafted, while the last third probably
would not. The risk for those in the middle third would depend
on the troop levels in Vietnam in the coming year. I held out hope
that a high lottery number would set me free from the war.*

*The first number would be drawn by Representative Alex-
ander Pirnie of New York, and all other numbers by members of
the Selective Service System's Youth Advisory Committee. Loud
boos swept the dormitory lobby at the mention of the committee —
people our age who were cooperating with the draft. We cheered
wildly when someone yelled from the back of the room that two
members of the committee had refused to participate — David Par-
ker of Alaska and Mike Hudson of Michigan.*

*Just after 5:00 P.M., Representative Pirnie stepped forward to
draw the first date. Having memorized my friends' birthdays, I
said a silent prayer for all of us. Reaching into the mammoth glass
bowl, Representative Pirnie withdrew a tiny blue plastic capsule
and handed it to Colonel Daniel Omar, who opened it and read
the first date: September 14. From the back of the dorm room came
a sharp "No! No!" Then the next birthdate was read: April 24. The
numbers continued in easy rhythm: December 30. February 14.*

October 18. September 6. Within minutes, I heard my birthday: February 19 — number 25.

Of the five in our group at Campion Tower that night, I was the only one to end up in the high-risk category. Later, as we said goodbye in the dark outside, my friends tempered their personal relief with sympathy for me. I walked home alone, knowing that this night meant I must continue my journey toward conscientious objection.

Young people everywhere undergo transitions to adulthood. In some cultures, elaborate initiation ceremonies involve painted faces, special costumes, religious rituals, and tests of endurance. During the war in Vietnam, in this culture, the rite of passage for American males was the draft. Many young men were gathered up, herded onto buses at induction centers around the country, and sent off to war. Others enlisted, hoping to salvage some control over their lives by getting into programs that might increase the odds they would not end up in the infantry. Still others enlisted in order to act out their John Wayne myths of manhood that had been fed by the television fantasies of the 1950s — Davy Crockett, the Lone Ranger, Superman. Others wanted to get away from home, to see the world, to serve their country — to fulfill one of a thousand dreams that the culture offered in war.

Those who escaped the draft with high lottery numbers or deferments went on to school, to jobs, or to travel, free of their personal Vietnams. But those with low numbers could no longer hide from the war. The Vietnam-era draft forced them to decide whether they would cooperate or make a stand.

Once they made their decision to apply for conscientious objection, COs faced hearings before local draft boards, long appeals, and preinduction physicals. COs whose applications for deferment were turned down faced military induction ceremonies, criminal indictment, trial, and imprisonment. In this chapter, COs describe their confrontations with the Selective Service System, the FBI, the courts, and the federal prisons.

I've had lots of experiences when I thought I knew what I was doing, but it was only after I stepped into the shit that I realized how it stunk and how it felt. When you make a commitment to something, you can't always have foreknowledge of the consequences. They may be uglier than you fear or better than you imagine. You have to find out by doing — by committing — and that involves taking a risk. You have to have some courage and some heart.

▬▬▬

Sometimes in history, you're on the losing side. From a biblical perspective, that's not so bad. A crucifixion — some form of persecution — is to be expected.

▬▬▬

Dan Berrigan once said, "Apologies, good friends, for the fracture of good order, the burning of paper instead of lives." I got the recipe for homemade napalm from a Special Forces handbook. I wanted to save lives by using a substance that was killing people in Vietnam. I wanted to show what draft files really were — death certificates, part of the paper process that sent people to kill and be killed.

I picked Christmas Eve as a symbol of hope. It is the Christians' festival of light, when light comes into the world with the birth of Jesus. My action would be my gift to Jesus and the community, like the Magis'.

A week before burning the draft files, I went to the San Jose Selective Service Office during regular office hours to case the joint. First, I walked into the front office and saw that the files were beyond a wall that was behind the counter. Several typists sat between me and the files. It would be difficult to reach the files, especially since I wanted to make sure I wouldn't start a fight getting to them.

I left the office and went around the corner to find a bathroom. I noticed another door. I put my hand on the doorknob and turned it. It opened, and there, to my surprise, was the file room. The file cabinets were only three feet away.

When I went in that back door on Christmas Eve, several file drawers were open, so it was simply a matter of pouring the napalm onto the files and lighting it. None of the people working in the office rushed to stop me. I went to a typewriter and tried to break off the "I" and "A" keys, I-A being the classification for people to be drafted, but I could only bend them. While the staff hid in the next room, I waited until the police and the FBI showed up to arrest me. I accepted the idea that I should be accountable for my actions.

I was taken to Santa Clara County jail, where I was taunted by the deputies with remarks like, "Hey, here's the big man for peace." Finally, after more than an hour of insults, I swore at the deputy who was fingerprinting me. Instantly, I felt ashamed because it was a negation of nonviolence. It was also just what they were waiting for. The deputy immediately laid into my face with sharp blows. I went down. He picked me up, pinned my hands behind my back, and then put a choke hold around my neck. Finally, I was thrown in the drunk tank for seven hours.

I refused to let the jail nurses clean me up before I was taken to the U.S. commissioner for my arraignment. I showed up there with my mouth caked in blood. The commissioner was very disturbed by my condition. The newspapers reported that I had been roughed up. The sheriff's department responded by charging me with assault and battery. They said I had become unruly, wiped my inky hands on the deputy's shirt, lost my balance, and fell, striking my mouth. Later, a judge found me guilty of assault and battery.

After my arraignment, I was taken to a maximum security cell. As I was being led there, I passed a large cell block with a television on. Suddenly the guys started pointing to the TV and to me. Though I couldn't hear them through the security glass, it was clear they were saying they had seen me on TV. That was my first awareness that there was a hubbub about my action.

After a couple of days in the Santa Clara County jail, I was moved to San Francisco County jail. It was much rougher there, filled with poorer prisoners, and very overcrowded. The cells were filled with bunk beds, and mats filled the floor between the beds. There was a lot of tension and arguments, like, "Hey, don't put your hand on my towel. Don't put your hand on my blanket." The food was out of Dickens's *Bleak House*, watery, pasty gruel. Oatmeal gruel in the morning, hot water with a few things floating in it for lunch and dinner. In shame, one sheriff bought us oranges out of his own pocket.

We had an absolute lack of privacy, even for bodily functions. The lights were always on. The noise was incessant. I had no pattern of sleep. I couldn't ask, "Could I have some quiet, please?" So I just summoned up my inner resources and endured. After three months, about ten days before my trial, I was finally able to make bail — $50,000. My parish priest had raised it for me.

My trial began in late March 1971 and lasted four days. I came into it physically and emotionally exhausted from being in jail, deprived of sleep and food. I was incredibly nervous about speaking in front of the court but I felt I had a mission, a vision. I wanted to be accountable for my actions.

My defense was to admit that I had burned the files, but to argue that I had done it to stop a greater harm. I said that I broke into the draft office in order to stop the crimes of the war, the killing and the destruction. The judge said there was no evidence that the Selective Service System was committing a crime. He told the jury that it didn't matter why I burned the files. So the jury decided in only three hours that I was guilty of destruction of government property and interference with the Selective Service System — felonies. "We the jury find the defendant guilty as charged in the first indictment. We the jury find the defendant guilty as charged in the second indictment. We the jury find the defendant guilty as charged in the third indictment."

I asked that the jurors be polled individually. Several cried, one saying, "Sorrowfully, this is my verdict." I was sentenced to six years. The judge also ruled that I should be taken into custody immediately because I was a threat to society.

The image of my trial that has stuck most in my heart: as I was surrounded outside the courthouse by U.S. marshals taking me through the dark evening back to jail, one of the sobbing jurors stretched her hand out to me and said, "I'm sorry."

On the hundredth day of my imprisonment, I was transferred along with three other prisoners from Santa Clara County jail to Lompoc Federal Prison. We were quite a sight during the transfer. Our handcuffs were attached to a chain around our waists, with another chain running to leg irons that kept our feet from being more than a foot apart. It was difficult to move. I remember riding through the Valley of the Flowers, very conscious that it was the last time I'd see it for a long time. At the prison, I glanced up at gun towers as we drove through a fence with barbed wire on top. We stopped at an ugly, long, gray cement building. That was to be my home for the next two and a half years.

On my first night in jail, a cop walked back and forth outside my cell, saying, "It looks like it's just about time for a haircut." I kept thinking that if they tried to cut my hair, I would fight back, and then they'd probably beat me up. I wasn't going to just sit there and let them do it to me. I was going to stand up for myself.

I lived in Cambridge, near Harvard, and was involved with the Unitarian Church. The Selective Service System was much too sly to let people apply for CO status where they were going to school. Can you imagine the scene at draft boards near universities? So everyone had to apply in their hometowns. For me, that meant Killeen, Texas.

I didn't want to be half-baked about my application. I talked to people at the Central Committee for Conscientious Objectors and to a lawyer. I knew that I couldn't just naively tell the truth. I didn't plan to lie, but I had to make sure I said things in a way that didn't antagonize the draft board.

My first appearance before my local draft board was in Houston in February 1969. The hearing was on the eighth floor of a building downtown. The board members wore cowboy hats, cowboy boots, and little string ties. They were insurance agents and car dealers, all volunteers. After I was sworn in, they asked me if I would fight if the country was attacked. I told them I wouldn't. One guy said, "Wouldn't you go over there to Vietnam as a medic to help soldiers who get their arm or leg blowed off?" I had read the army field manual, and I knew a medic's job was to support war by getting wounded soldiers back into battle. So I said, "No."

The hearing lasted only a few minutes. When it was over, I waited outside the office, trying hard not to gulp and sweat and fidget. The board talked behind a door with frosted glass. When the door opened, nobody looked at me or spoke to me as they left. I could tell they had turned me down. Two weeks later, back home in Killeen, I got the letter saying they had denied my application.

The next step was to appeal to the same board. I waited as long as the law allowed before I filed the appeal. Like being on death row, one of the things you do is stall. In April of '69, I had my second hearing. The same guys, the same discussion. Again, I was rejected.

Meanwhile, I had to take the preinduction physical in San Antonio. I told them I had asthma, which was true, but they passed me anyway. They passed everyone — "You're fine. You're fine. You're fine, boy." Only a dope fiend with fresh tracks would have gotten turned down. So there I was, physically fit and I-A.

They say that if you go to the afterlife and there's a crossroads with one sign that says "To heaven" and another sign that says "To lectures about heaven," Unitarians will take "To lectures about heaven." I was like that. I had the education and the class background to be good with words. So in May of '69, I wrote a fifteen-page essay appealing my case to the state board.

I had already decided I would refuse induction if my appeal was rejected. But I didn't want to do it in Texas, because I knew I'd be found guilty and get the maximum prison sentence.

———

I was in my senior year of high school in Kansas City in April 1966, when I applied for CO status. Later that year, the FBI investigation took place, while I was enrolled at the University of Missouri at Kansas City. The FBI interviewed my mother, my father, my professors, the priests at the three churches I had attended in the cities where we had lived, and many of my friends. Not everyone knew why they were being interviewed. My calculus professor thought the FBI was investigating him.

My application was turned down and I was classified I-A. I appealed, and in July 1967 I was interviewed by a judge in his chambers at the courthouse. I went there alone. We talked for about twenty minutes. He asked why I wanted to be a CO. He was quite friendly. When we were finished, he shook my hand and said he would recommend that I be given CO status.

But soon I received a letter from the draft board saying I had been turned down. It turned out that I was rejected because of the FBI report. I got a summary of the report at the time, and years later a copy of the full report. One of my priests had told the FBI that the Catholic Church believed everybody should serve their country. Someone else had implied that I was afraid of the service. In her interview with the FBI, my mother had said I was willing to serve in a noncombatant role. She had meant the Peace Corps, which I wanted to join. But the FBI and the draft board used her statement as evidence that I was willing to serve in the army as a noncombatant.

So I appealed. At my appearance before my board, I faced everyone across a long table. They asked ludicrous questions, such as what I would do if I was at home with my grandmother, holding a Colt .45 in my lap, when an intruder with a machine gun broke in. I said flippantly, "I'd blow the guy away, of course." I told them their questions were ridiculous and had nothing to do with war. They seemed to think that to be a CO you had to be willing to allow a stranger to kill your grandmother.

The board turned me down, and continued to do so during all my appeals. During my fourth year of college, without explanation, the board revoked my student deferment. My lottery number was 80, so I prepared myself for jail. But then a friend asked, "Why not go to Canada?" So I wrote to a committee in Vancouver that supported Vietnam War objectors there.

After the USO tour, I returned to school, but I knew I didn't have enough credits to keep my student deferment. One day, I got an envelope from the draft board. I picked it up, put it down, picked it up, put it down. I was shaking so much I could hardly open it. Finally, I tore it open and saw I-A. I knew then I was prime meat.

I was working as a box boy at a supermarket. One of the cashiers had been in World War II. He hated war. If anybody in line at the check stand said anything about Vietnam, he'd rant against the war and against anybody who let their kids participate. When I showed him my I-A card, he challenged me, asking if I knew I was going to be in Vietnam in a few months if I didn't do something to change my status.

I filled out the forms for CO and appeared before my draft board. The hearing was in a low brick building, a very utilitarian room with a folding metal table surrounded by chairs. Four men and women from the community asked me questions. I told them about the USO tour, trying to suggest that I was doing it for God and country, while wrapping myself in the flag. Then they asked me how much I got paid for the tour. When I told them $220 a week, which was a lot of money then, there was an audible gasp. I knew immediately that my chance of getting my CO had just gone right out the window. My choice was going to be between the service and jail.

I read everything I could about prison — David Harris, the Central Committee for Conscientious Objectors, and others. I listened to speeches by Joan Baez. I was in northern California, where a lot of people transferred their cases, hoping for easy sentences, but word was out that sentences were skyrocketing to five years and $5,000 fines because Nixon had appointed a bunch of new judges.

I received my draft notice and went for my preinduction physical. At one point in the exam, the doctor suddenly said, "Get your clothes. You're out." I felt like I had been hit in the face. I dropped out of line and started slowly putting on my clothes, feeling everyone's eyes on me. After I was dressed, I asked, "Why am I out?"

"Undescended testicle, an automatic out, due to risk of cancer," the doctor told me. I had known before asking that was the reason. I had been too young to remember, but my mother had told me that I had had surgery to correct it when I was little. My testicle had been removed and there was no risk of cancer for me.

My father had never spoken about it. Somehow, for me, it had become wrapped up with manhood, with not being man enough to be in the service. So I said suddenly, "That has been taken care of." The doctor checked me, immediately realizing he had missed the scar from my incision. Without hesitating, he told me to complete the rest of the physical.

For a few minutes, I had a medical out. But I blew my cover because I wanted to be hardline true to my beliefs and because I was afraid of not being judged man enough.

I moved to Portland for school, but eventually was ordered to report for induction at the Oakland Induction Center. I took the bus there and showed up with my sleeping bag. Because the other inductees were planning to stay that night in the army barracks, they didn't have any gear. Seeing my belongings, an officer told me to move to a separate room where he asked if I planned to refuse induction. I said, "Yes."

I was separated from the main group and taken to a room with other people planning to refuse induction. There were about thirty of us, out of about a hundred and fifty people altogether.

An officer made sure I wasn't carrying any weapons or explosives. Then he took me aside and told me I could go to prison, but

61

it wasn't too late to change my mind. I was returned to the other resisters, then interviewed separately again. Three interviews altogether. Finally, they moved all of us to another room and read us our rights. We were reminded that if we did not step forward when our name was called, we were committing a felony.

Then they took us in groups of five to a small side room. The room was plush and carpeted, with huge flags at the front, walls decorated with pictures of snow-capped mountains and prairies, and the biggest picture I've ever seen of Richard Nixon.

All five in my little group were white. One was a skinny, nervous guy dressed in a dark suit and holding a Bible. Another was a rowdy building subcontractor from the coast who was boiling for a fight with the military. I don't remember the other two. A very fancy, very crisp officer came in, with posture like I've never seen anywhere else, along with an enlisted man. The officer told us again that if we stepped forward when our names were called, we would be in the service, and if we didn't, we were committing a felony, could be prosecuted, and would spend up to five years in prison.

They called our names one by one, and no one stepped forward. Standing with those guys in that plush room, keeping silent, I felt empowered, scared, and strong — like I was saying, "Stop the war right here."

Just as we breathed a sigh of relief, the officer said, this time real mean, "Okay, now we're gonna do it again." In defiance, I turned my back, stepped away from the line, and strolled around the room looking at the pictures. I was ordered back to the line, and did it. They read our names again one by one. Again, no one stepped forward. I began to wonder if they ever got takers the second time they called names. Perhaps sometimes people passed out and fell across the line into the army.

Finally, we were interviewed by a kindly old FBI agent. He said, "Relax, take it easy, it's all over." He asked if I planned to leave the country and if I would be available for prosecution. I said I was going to Portland to school and I'd be available through my parents' address. I promised to notify my draft board and the FBI of any change. He told me the courts were backed up and it would be a while before I heard from them.

They made us leave through a side door, so we couldn't talk to anyone still going through induction. I took the Muni across the bay and stayed in San Francisco with my sister and her husband, an ex-Marine who was in total support of my refusal. I was setting a real hard road for myself. I was headed for prison. I think I had a strong well of anger. And I think I also had a real martyr's complex that I got from my mother.

It was fourteen months before I went on trial.

During my draft physical, I told the psychologist that I was a Communist revolutionary and that my greatest joy would be for the government to give me a gun and teach me how to use it. I flunked. But I had to return six months later for another exam. I passed that one.

I was raised in the Church of the Brethren, one of the traditional pacifist churches. My lottery number was 330, which was too high to be drafted. The draft board said if I registered, nothing would happen to me because of my high number. But I felt there were more important issues than just keeping myself out of the war. I felt that a lottery — a raffle — to decide who would live or die, and who would become a killer, was unjust and wrong. Whether or not I "won" the lottery, as I had, the draft was a moral issue. So I refused to register, and I was charged with a felony. I was nineteen.

After I was indicted, I contacted the FBI and asked if they wanted to see me. An FBI man in Wenatchee told me that he, too, was a Christian, and he wanted to talk to me as a father talks to his son, to tell me the foolishness of my ways. When I arrived in his office, he slammed the door behind me, put handcuffs on me, and led me out the back door to jail.

I was put in a drunk tank at the county jail. There was just one drunk and me. I was afraid. Late that evening, I heard a group of supporters singing outside the bars. When I looked out, they saw me and waved. It was a wonderful feeling. It felt like family. I'll never forget it, and it confirmed my faith that this was a special time.

A big police officer, who seemed two feet taller than me, threatened me as we went to the magistrate's hearing to post bail. He said, "Listen, I have a something-caliber gun under my belt. I don't like to have cuffs on my prisoners, so I'm not going to put them on you. But if you take too many steps or if you move too quick, I want you to know my gun's right there."

I turned around, looked him in the eye, and said, "Don't you know, brother, why I was arrested? I'm not running. You don't have to be afraid of me."

The six months of waiting for the trial was a wonderful time. I wasn't working toward a degree or starting a business or doing anything that led to practical or financial gain. But in terms of character development and thought processes and formative friendships that have lasted to this day, it was an amazing time, and I wouldn't have given it up.

But I wasn't completely foolish as a nineteen-year-old. I was astute enough to know that I might not survive prison. It might be too emotionally damaging. I wanted to be sure I counted the costs before I went ahead.

On the night before my trial, my family and my supporters all got together and sang songs. I especially remember "Hobo's Lullaby." Pete Seeger once said that he sang it for Woody Guthrie on his deathbed.

We also had a foot-washing ceremony, where we reenacted the Gospel of John, the Last Supper, in which Jesus wrapped himself with a towel, knelt before Peter, and washed his feet. It's a very tactile sensation to have someone kneel and humble himself before you. The threat of persecution can lift or it can crush your spirit. Seeing Christ among us as we washed one another's feet lifted my spirit. To feel Christ in our midst was a very emotional and spiritual experience for me.

On the morning of my trial, the courtroom had all the trappings of authority. There was a reporter or two, a defense table, and a prosecutor's table. It was a very small courtroom. It seated only thirty or so. I remember a partition dividing the judge's bench into two sections, chairs that looked like they belonged in a governor's mansion, and plush draperies. I had never been in court before, so it was pretty intimidating. But I had a sense of confidence. Although the government had the power to imprison me, it did not have authority over me. I sensed I had control over my life.

I felt that if I strived to win in court, I would violate my faith. My mindset was, "Don't challenge. Don't fight over the jurors like the prosecution does." My thought at the time was, "I'm here to make a statement of faith. God's with me and I'm doing the right thing."

I felt it wasn't my place to get a high-powered attorney, so I had accepted a court-appointed lawyer. My attorney was convinced of my sincerity and quite touched by my beliefs, but I had to be the one to do a lot of the objecting. For instance, the prosecutor entered into evidence the introductory phrase of my letter to the draft board saying I refused to register. I objected, saying the jury should see the whole letter, so we could talk about the motivation for my refusal. The judge denied my objection.

Throughout the entire case, everything we tried to present was ruled irrelevant. To show the jury that I would not have been drafted, I asked an official from the draft board about the lottery number for my birthdate. The prosecutor objected to it as immaterial. When we asked about the likelihood of someone with the lottery number of 330 being drafted, the prosecutor said, "Objection, let that be stricken from the record." The judge sustained him every time.

When I tried to show that my refusal to register was protected by the principle of freedom of religion, I was not allowed to do so. We argued before the judge, without the jury present, about what would be admissible evidence. I still have the transcript:

> *Defendant*: Freedom of religion means that the government should not require one to act contrary to their beliefs and convictions. The Amish were given this freedom when their faith required that they not participate in the public school system. The prosecution contends there is only one question: whether or not I registered. My faith insists that is not the only question. My church supports me in what I'm doing. To say my religion is irrelevant is a denial of religious freedom.
>
> *Prosecutor*: The defendant seems to think it is unfair that the law is the only issue. The law was simply violated, no matter how high the motives. Whether the defendant did knowingly and willfully fail to register is the only issue of this case.
>
> *Judge*: Were we to open this case to the whole question of First Amendment freedoms of religion and speech, we

65

would be free to ignore the mandates of the law. I think we are all aware that none of our constitutional rights are absolute. We may as individuals disagree with the decisions of our government, but it is the law of the land that we need an inventory of who we have between the ages of eighteen and twenty-five, or twenty-six, or whatever it is. I think that all this case involves is the government's inventory of manpower. To open up this case and ponder whether a person's firm and honest religious convictions should supersede the direction of our duly constituted authorities is opening it up to issues that are not really in this case. The issue is did you or did you not willfully fail to register. The issue of why you did it is immaterial.

It was frustrating as the day wore on, but there was no point in kicking and screaming when the powers-that-be muzzled you. It happened in a lot of civil disobedience trials throughout the sixties and seventies.

At the end of the closing arguments, I was supposed to be able to make a statement, but the prosecutor objected and the judge stopped me. So I opened up the Bible and started reading the Beatitudes, with tears streaming down my face. "How happy are the poor in spirit; theirs is the kingdom of heaven. Happy those who mourn; they shall be comforted. Happy the gentle; they shall have the earth for their heritage. Happy those who hunger and thirst for what is right; they shall be satisfied. Happy the merciful; they shall have mercy shown them."

The prosecutor objected, but I kept reading. "Happy the pure in heart; they shall see God. Happy the peacemakers; they shall be called God's children."

When I finished, the judge said, "Does the government have any rebuttal?"

I thank God that I had the strength to read the passage. It stands on its own and I don't have to be ashamed of it.

It wasn't until the jury went out to deliberate that I was given the chance to present my case, out of hearing of the jury. I had been waiting all day to speak, so it was very emotional. I explained why I couldn't register for the draft, why war was synonymous with killing, and why killing was incongruent with Christian faith. Only at that time were my witnesses allowed to testify. One was my mother. She said:

> I have always thought of nations at war as being like little kids that get into fights because one accidental tap or gesture might start a fight with the justification "He hit me first." One blow leads to another. Nations often do that rather than talking it out. There should be a better way. I was a very small child in Chicago when our country entered World War I. We had young men who were guests in our home who had refused to be drafted and were facing prison terms. We looked up to them as heroes. It is very difficult to face the possibility of my son going to prison. But all of us are standing behind him. We are proud of him.

My neighbor, who owned a nearby apple orchard, had the last name of Apple. He always introduced himself by saying, "Apple's my name, apple's my game." While I waited for the jury's verdict, I heard his booming voice from across the room saying to someone, "Apple's my name, apple's my game." I felt very warmed by the fact that he had come to my trial. He didn't agree with my stand of resistance. But he was my dad's friend. As a little kid, I had played in his yard.

The jury took only thirty minutes to convict me. When they announced the verdict, my supporters didn't boo or make any noise. We were law-abiding and respectful of authority.

I don't remember feeling a sense of panic or despair. I expected that most people wouldn't understand my actions. There are plenty of precedents for convicting those who simply say, "I won't kill people."

"God will protect me," I thought.

In 1968, I was sixteen and living in Lancaster, Pennsylvania. Nineteen sixty-eight was such an important and formative year. First, the Tet Offensive led Lyndon Johnson to announce he wasn't going to run again for President. Then Martin Luther King was killed, and two months later, Bobby Kennedy, and two months after that the Democratic Convention took place in Chicago, with the police riot. I was in high school, but these events made me very aware of the world beyond my classes.

Just after I entered college in Harrisonburg, Virginia, in the fall of 1969, I went to Washington to attend some of the largest demonstrations in U.S. history taking place in the fall Mobilization and Moratorium.

In early 1970, I sent a letter to the Selective Service System, saying that I refused to register for the draft. At the time, I felt that if I was opposed to participating in war, I should equally be opposed to participating in the system whose sole reason for existing was to provide manpower for the war.

Soon afterward, in March 1970, two FBI agents came to interview me. Their visit was short, mainly to verify that I had indeed written the letter. I wasn't intimidated, but it was the first indication that my action was something the government took seriously. I realized this wasn't a game.

In April 1970, I was taking an exam in the college chapel when the teacher came to me and whispered that someone in the back wanted to see me. Completely unaware of what was happening, I walked back, and there were two FBI agents, who informed me I was under arrest. They took me to their car, and off we went, to Harrisonburg, where I was fingerprinted and photographed.

The Harrisonburg jail was not on the approved list of secured jails for federal prisoners, so the agents put me back in their car and drove me to Stanton, where I was jailed for a few hours, until I paid bail.

By the time of my trial in Philadelphia in March 1971, I had come to the conclusion that I would do what I could to stay out of jail. I felt there was no virtue in prison, and the point of resistance was not to become a martyr. So I pleaded no contest, which meant that I did not admit guilt, but for practical purposes it was the same as pleading guilty.

Before being sentenced, I was allowed to read a brief statement of my views. So I stood up in court and said: "At times, we will have to disobey laws set up by the government we live under. This is something we can joyfully accept as a result of following the lifestyle taught by Jesus, who said: 'This is my commandment, love one another.' We must begin to take this seriously and dedicate our lives to caring for all people. We are now faced with the choice of obeying the law of love or the manmade law of death. Will we obey murderous laws and thus be responsible for the deaths of our brothers and sisters, or will we affirm life and follow God's law? The choice is here. It must be made. I have made my choice."

━━━

My father was engaged in designing and manufacturing nuclear weapons at the Savannah River project in South Carolina. I knew very little about his work, because it was highly secret.

When I turned eighteen in 1958, I never thought about the draft, except to go to my draft board in Cincinnati, which was a very patriotic city, and fill out the forms. That fall, I entered Antioch College in Ohio, with a student deferment.

During my first year of college, my father died of cancer. He was only forty-six at the time. In my mind, his death was associated with his exposure to radiation in his work. I never talked about his death or confronted the reasons for it. I just repressed it for many years. But I think I blamed his work for his death, and that encouraged me to respond positively to radical political movements. At Antioch that first year, I joined a vigil for Hiroshima and Nagasaki at the Wright-Patterson Air Force Base.

At Antioch, I also became involved in the effort to integrate the last segregated barbershop in Yellow Springs, Ohio. The barber there refused to cut black people's hair. Our demonstrations against his shop grew bigger and bigger, until finally we blocked the state highway in town. That brought in the police, who broke up the gathering and arrested many people. Our campaign ultimately drove him out of business. He said he couldn't put up with the demonstrations. So he retired and moved to Arizona. He never did integrate his shop.

One of the oddities of that campaign was that we were arrested by the only black police chief in all of Ohio.

In the fall of 1960, I joined the Student Nonviolent Coordinating Committee, and went to Atlanta for its first national conference. I heard Martin Luther King and James Lawson speak there about the need to withdraw support from institutions that supported segregation. Somewhere in my mind, I began to make a connection between the draft and civil rights. It was a question of who got drafted. Black people were more likely to be drafted and certainly more likely to be sent into combat.

When I returned to Antioch from the SNCC conference, I decided to return my draft card to my draft board. Soon after I did, they sent me a duplicate, which I also returned along with a long letter of explanation. It never occurred to me to tear up my card or burn it. This was before draft card burning became a popular form of protest.

The draft board then sent me Form 150, the application for conscientious objection. I wrote a letter objecting to the question on the form asking whether I believed in a Supreme Being. I felt they didn't have a legal right to ask me that question.

By 1961, I was active in the Student Peace Union, which later merged into the SDS. I organized a national campaign to get five hundred people to sign a pledge to mail their draft cards to the national Selective Service headquarters. I don't think we got even fifty signatures, but we did get the attention of the FBI, which interrogated me and threatened me with arrest for sedition.

In 1962, I dropped out of college to engage in full-time antiwar activism. I helped organize the national student demonstration against nuclear weapons in Washington, D.C., that year. It turned out to be a tremendous success, with eight thousand people picketing the White House, the Russian embassy, and Congress. We got a lot of publicity, and ended up on the front page of the *New York Times*.

In 1963, I was ordered to report for induction at Fort Knox, Kentucky, but I didn't appear. In August 1964, Congress passed the Gulf of Tonkin Resolution, which was the official beginning of the Vietnam War. One week later, I was indicted by a federal grand jury in Cincinnati for failing to report for induction.

Six months after my indictment, I was tried in federal court in Cincinnati. On the recommendation of my lawyer, I waived a jury trial, because he said that most federal jurors in Cincinnati would be retired American Legion members, and very hostile to me. But the judge was even worse. There were only two witnesses. The clerk at the draft board testified that I had been ordered to report for induction, but hadn't shown up. Then I testified, to explain to the judge why I had refused to cooperate. I explained that the requirement for belief in a Supreme Being was unconstitutional. I cited Supreme Court rulings that no religious tests could be imposed under the U.S. Constitution. The judge let me talk for ten or fifteen minutes, but it was quite obvious he was hostile to me. When I finished, he looked down at me and said in an extremely condescending tone, "Young man, where did you go to law school?" I later learned that he had a son serving in Vietnam.

On the spot, he found me guilty of two counts — refusing to take the physical and refusing induction. After the trial, I had an interview with the federal probation officer, who was very sympathetic. He recommended that I not go to prison, saying there was no reason I needed to serve time. My lawyer expected me to be sentenced to probation, and that's what I expected, too. But at the sentencing a month after the trial, the judge held up the probation report, waved it dismissively, and said mine was a very serious crime. Then he sentenced me to five years on each count, to run consecutively.

Ten years in federal prison. I was stunned. My lawyer sat there like a sphinx. The prosecutor was visibly shocked, and immediately asked for a conference with the judge. He went to the bench, where they spoke for five minutes or so. Then the judge said, "At the request of the U.S. attorney, I will reduce the sentence to three years on each count, to run concurrently." So my sentence dropped from ten to three years. Which was still three years more than I had expected.

I appealed my conviction, and meanwhile returned to school and graduated from Antioch. In early December 1966, I heard from my lawyer that I had lost my appeal. I thought briefly about appealing to the Supreme Court, but I had no more money, so I decided to serve my time. Fortunately, the U.S. marshal in Cincinnati was a friend of my lawyer, so he let me wait until after Christmas to turn myself in. On New Year's Eve, 1966, I did so, and was immediately sent to the Hamilton County jail. After two weeks there, I was transferred to the federal prison at Milan, Michigan, about ten miles from Ann Arbor.

Just after I arrived at Milan, I met an Amish guy from a little farming community in Minnesota. He was a real hick, a real farm boy, who broke into his draft board and poured buckets of shit into the files. He was convicted not only of violating the draft law, but also of destroying government property. Whenever I saw that guy, I thought, "He won't take any shit." I decided that would be my motto.

After about six months at Milan, I was admitted to the University of Michigan graduate school as a special Ph.D. student. That meant that I would be able to leave the prison to attend classes and then return at night. But just before fall classes were to begin, the government ended all outside programs for draft violators. The new rule was that no one convicted of a draft offense could get out for work release, for school, or for church.

I responded by writing letters to Congress to complain about the policy. My letters were intercepted, and I was identified as a troublemaker. So suddenly, in the middle of the night, I was dragged out of my cell and transferred to the federal penitentiary in Terre Haute, Indiana.

The prison at Terre Haute was the worst place I have ever been. It was run by the Ku Klux Klan, which was very strong in southern Indiana. Many of the guards were Klansmen. I was threatened with death by the guards. I was put in a cell with a racist who continually threatened me. My family and my lawyer were not informed of my transfer, so no one knew where I was. I wrote letters to let them know, but a guard would always bring the letters in and tear them up in front of me. I even tried writing letters in Latin. It was a month before anyone found out where I was being held. And then I was transferred to Danbury, Connecticut, where I spent the next year and a half.

Danbury was better than Terre Haute. Each week, we got to see a movie in the cafeteria. It was the highlight of the week. Sometimes, we'd have semi-skinflicks. I especially remember *One Million Years B.C.*, starring Raquel Welch in a very tiny, tiger-skin bikini. That was the most popular movie they ever showed.

One weekend in 1968, we saw *The Green Berets*, starring John Wayne. The theater was segregated, with black inmates at the front, Puerto Rican inmates in the middle, and white inmates in the back. In *The Green Berets*, there's one scene where the Vietcong overrun a little village. They pull down the American flag and raise the Vietcong flag. At that point in the movie, the whole front half of the theater erupted in cheers. Five minutes later, a helicopter gunship comes in, totally decimates the village, blows up the Vietcong, and turns them into hamburger. John Wayne jumps out of the helicopter, runs over, hauls down the Vietcong flag, and runs up the American flag. At that point, the whole back half of the theater erupted into cheers. There was a lot of yelling and shouting, and then the guards stopped the movie because it was getting too tense, and they sent us back to our cells.

After I was convicted in New York, I was held in jail a month or so. On my way to my sentencing hearing, they put me in leg irons. They also put handcuffs on my wrists and a metal belt around my waist. A chain was run from my wrists through the belt down to the leg iron. Then the chain was run between my legs and hooked onto another guy behind me. I couldn't move more than about six inches. We had to shuffle, just like some Devil's Island movie. We walked two blocks like that, through the streets of Manhattan, the chains clanking loudly as we walked. I was humiliated. Manhattan was my home. I had grown up there. Until that day, I had been able to have a sense of humor. I had tried to keep a smile in my heart, and tried to understand the guards and realize they were just doing their job. But that two-block walk was so brutal and humiliating, I was angry forever after that.

I'll never forget being locked in my cell the first time. My cell was at the lower end of the double-decker tier of cells, about thirty feet from the guard station. When I went in, the guard told me to close the door behind me. He essentially wanted me to lock myself in my cell. I didn't think I belonged there, so I refused. I wasn't going to help them lock me up.

Another time, I watched four guys being chained together. They had leg cuffs and a chain around their waists. They passed the chain back and forth, stringing themselves together, like they were sewing each other up. I was shocked. I couldn't believe it. Here these tough guys in jail were chaining themselves together, like sheep. I swore I would never do that. If the guards wanted to chain me, they'd have to do it themselves. I wouldn't help them.

I remember reading the book *The Organization Man*, and not wanting to be one. I didn't want to conform to social institutions. I wanted to purely be me, even at the risk of social ostracism or punishment. Yet in a way, I was a chump, a dummy, a patsy, a dupe to let myself get into a goddamned federal penitentiary for moral and ethical beliefs.

After I got my order to report for induction, I changed my address from Bellingham to Portland, because I had read in one of the draft resistance newsletters that there was a judge there who was handing out alternative service or six months in a forestry work camp for draft resisters.

I got ordered to report for my physical, so I decided to try to fail it. I showed up a rambling wreck. I hadn't bathed for three weeks. I hadn't changed my clothes. I had been loaded and drunk for days beforehand. I figured, "Surely, they will see I am unfit for military service." It wasn't brave and it wasn't noble and it wasn't upstanding, but it's where I was at the time.

At the end of the physical, I got ordered to return for an interview a few days later. For two days before the interview, I stayed at a friend's house and took speed. I didn't sleep, and got as strange as I could. At the interview, I spun this very loose, disorganized, paranoid militaristic rap. I made up a fictitious organization called the Amalgamated Federation of Unassociated Freaks. I wouldn't swear we were dedicated to the violent overthrow of the U.S. government, but I wouldn't swear we weren't either. I said we didn't have any cards, so I couldn't say I was a card-carrying member, but on the other hand, there were a lot of us. At the end of my story, the two guys interviewing me just looked at each other, laughed, and said, "We don't buy a word of it. Get out of here." But before I left, they told me to come back a week later for one last psychiatric interview.

At that point, I was desperate. How could I be sure to blow the psychiatric interview? I decided to take a double hit of LSD. So I did, and I was peaking just as I walked into the psychiatrist's office. It was the wrong thing to do. I scared myself so badly with such a heavy hit of acid that I clamped down the lid on myself. I was so conscious of trying to remember where I was and what I was doing that I was perfectly coherent. Instead of being loose and strange, I became Joe Q. Straight Citizen. Yet, in my mind, there were times during the interview when dozens of giant fuzzy electric-blue beach balls floated through the room. I had a terrible time just maintaining eye contact with the doc, because of all the floating beach balls. Also, the acid made my mental processes very concrete. At one point in the interview, the psychiatrist said, "People in glass houses shouldn't throw stones." I literally saw stones sailing through the room and I was engulfed by flying glass. I leaped out of my chair and yelled, "Can't you hear the glass breaking! Why would anyone want to be so stupid?" Apparently, he thought I was deliberately trying to skew the interview, so he told me to sit down and shut up. So I passed. When the interview was over, I stumbled out the door, gibbering all the way back home, where I crawled into bed and hid for the next two days.

Because I didn't report for induction, I was contacted by a prosecuting attorney for the federal government. He said we were going to have a trial and I had to get an attorney. I didn't have any money, so I applied for indigence and the court appointed one.

My biggest income that quarter, ironically enough, was from a National Defense student loan. By then I was starting to be aware of how big the bureaucracy was — how the left pinky didn't know what the left thumb was doing. So, I thought, "I'll bet things are so stupid that even though I'm facing trial for refusing to submit to induction, I can apply for a National Defense student loan." The people in the student loan office knew my position exactly, and they said, "We don't care. We're not going to say anything. Let's see what the feds think." It was only a measly $250, but I thought, "Hey, this is great." I loved it.

I got my court-appointed attorney. Ironically, strangely, bizarrely, he was a draft-resisting CO himself from World War II, a Quaker who had served time in prison for refusing to submit to induction back then. He was a renowned draft attorney. "I hit the big time," I thought. "My luck is changing."

Until I met him. He was straitlaced, conservative, and religious, not prepared at all for a paisley-eyed, long-haired, tie-dyed freak. Everything from my poor hygiene to my shoddy apparel to my carefree life-style appalled him. It gradually became apparent to me that I was going to get token defense — which was okay because I wasn't sure what defense to offer anyway.

The trial was scheduled for May of '69. I had already worked the summer before at the state hospital in Clarkston, as an aide in the psych unit. I was telling everyone I knew that all citizens owe a debt to their country and that for my sentence I would work two years in a mental hospital without wages or benefits.

But it didn't quite work out that way. As word spread that the judge in Portland was giving lenient sentences, he was contacted by good old Nixon Justice Department people, who pressured him to enforce the law. The very next draft case he heard was mine.

The trial began badly. Some antidraft people brought a class of alternative education high school students to view the judicial process. "Sure," I thought, "kids ought to learn how the law works."

They stood up and cheered when I walked into the courtroom, and when the judge came in they booed.

The trial was a farce. It lasted less than an hour. I admitted that I had refused induction. I got on the stand and said, "The hell with the Selective Service System. But I've tried to be respectful every step along the way, Your Honor. Find me guilty if you must. Sentence me to two years working in a state mental hospital."

Bang, bang. He gave me two years in the federal penitentiary. I was stunned. I couldn't believe it. I thought maybe at worst I would get six months in the slammer. But *two years* in a federal prison!

That day was the first and only time in all of my peace activity that I've ever met an admitted, bona fide Communist. When the court adjourned, this guy introduced himself, saying there was nothing he could do for me now except get me stoned. So he took me to his house, got me very, very stoned on excellent dope, and sent me on my way. I thought, "Well, I've heard a lot of bad things about those Commies, but this one was all right."

I was out on appeal and heard nothing for the rest of 1969. I returned to Bellingham, where a professor of the sociology of deviant behavior made a local hero out of me for being so entrenched in my unconventional, antisocial beliefs that I would refuse to submit to induction and use drugs openly in spite of the consequences. That analysis was bullshit, but it was nice to have some recognition.

Periodically, I called my lawyer in Portland, who said appeals were backed up, so who knows when they'll get around to dealing with me. In January of '70 I got busted for having a fair amount of marijuana, so it was bust with intent to sell. That, plus waiting for the appeal of my draft case, meant I had really painted myself into a corner. My fiancée broke up with me over my bust, and her folks took her away to separate us.

I was faced with uncertainty about when I was going to go to jail, and on what charge. In the past, when I hadn't known what else to do, I had hitchhiked to Mexico. I wasn't supposed to leave the country, but I figured I was already in serious trouble, so I left. I spent a week on the beach there, and on the way back, I floated into Portland to see my attorney.

I offended him by showing up at his office looking like a hippie who had just spent two and a half weeks on the road — which I had. He said he hadn't heard a thing about the appeal, but it was time to find out. So he went into his back office to call the federal prosecutor. I sat in the waiting room, leafing through glossy magazines, when this dim bulb went on in the back of my head, "Warning! Warning! Warning!" We hadn't heard anything for a long time. No news is good news. Don't rock the boat. Hang up the phone. I jumped up and charged through his door, yelling, "Drop the phone! Drop the phone! Don't tell them who you are!"

He said, "They already know my name. They're looking for your file and they can't find it."

"What!" I said.

He ordered me, "Go back out there, sit down, and don't ever barge in my office again."

So I left, thinking, "Oh, shit, what have I done?" After about fifteen minutes, he came out and said, "It's the most amazing thing. Your file had fallen out of the back of the drawer. They had to pull the whole drawer out of the cabinet and move the cabinet to find the folder. They had lost it months ago."

"What do we do now?" I asked.

He said, "They'll process your case and I'll get in touch with you."

A month before school ended in 1970, I went on trial for the marijuana bust. By then, I had persuaded the prosecutor to reduce the charges to a misdemeanor of possession. I was already sentenced to the federal penitentiary for two years for refusing induction. What the hell else could they do to me? The judge was very lenient and gave me six months. He said he'd notify the federal judge of my drug sentence, so I could serve the sentences concurrently.

"That's real decent," I told him; "I'll just do his time, and your time will be included."

He said, "Yeah, yeah, that's enough for you." We were in and out of court in twenty minutes.

But the federal judge wrote back, "Make him do the time for the marijuana conviction. Every day of it. Then I'll make him do every day of my time."

So just before I finished school, the local judge told me to turn myself in on Monday following graduation to begin serving my six-month sentence. My mom came out for my graduation. That was the first contact we had had in years. Everyone else was talking about their jobs and graduate studies and traveling in Europe. "What are you going to do?" people asked me.

"Well, I'm going to jail next Monday for six months, and after that I'm going to the federal penitentiary for two years." My mom got pissed.

I served part of the drug sentence and then got out on probation. Almost immediately, I heard that there were people on campus asking questions about me. I assumed they were FBI, because they looked straight, they were large, and they wore shiny black shoes. I was unofficially and illegally living on college property twenty miles out of town. A few people knew it, but no one would tell them.

At some point, the FBI thought they had notified me to turn myself in on the draft sentence. One day, when I went to see my probation officer, FBI agents jumped out from behind closed doors, handcuffed me, and took me into custody with a new federal charge of being a felony fugitive from justice. My bail was set at $100,000. They were convinced I had left the country or gone underground. My guess is that they also knew I had been involved with helping war resisters go to Canada.

I had hoped to have a few farewell parties, get high one last time, kiss all the girls goodbye, and then go off in a blaze of glory. Instead, I was locked down right back in the same Whatcom County jail where I had been for the marijuana bust.

After a few days there, I was moved to King County jail for two weeks, and then to Rocky Butte jail in Multnomah County in Oregon. Rocky Butte was a hellhole, built at the turn of the century and first condemned as unfit for human habitation in 1946. It was rotting old masonry and brick, with rusty iron bars. On my first night there, I saw one guy have his eye put out and another guy have his jaw broken. I saw a rat run over a guy in the bunk next to mine. In less than two months, I saw people stabbed, I got tear-gassed, and I had a shotgun stuck in my stomach by a guard as I was trying to get away from a riot.

I got clinically depressed. I slept fourteen to sixteen hours a day. When I was awake, I would read or hold a book over my face and try to make believe I wasn't in a giant tank with sixty other prisoners. I withdrew socially, didn't have much of an appetite, lost weight, and didn't exercise. Finally, just after Thanksgiving, 1970, I was transferred to McNeil Island Federal Penitentiary.

My first day at McNeil, I went through rituals to make me

less of an individual and more of an animal. My clothes were taken away and I was given standard issue. My head was shaved, I got sprayed for body lice, and I had body-cavity searches. For me, the worst was getting sprayed with insecticide. It made me flash on a Jew in Germany being processed for the ovens. It was like I was a cow, I was a piece of meat, I was just a slab going down the conveyor belt, getting poked, prodded, and sprayed.

I was scared shitless at McNeil. I didn't want to have anything to do with those bad-ass people. They were bank robbers, father stabbers, and mother rapers. Of course, that was my own misconception, because some of them were just like me, lightweight drug offenders and hippies at the wrong place at the wrong time. A couple of bank robbers had master's degrees in literature and were really great people, enlightened damned-near Buddhists. But I didn't know that then.

Until one evening, when a group of five guys approached my bunk. One said, "We know who you are and what you're here for. You may or may not know us and what we are here for. You are trying to do time the hard way. You might as well be in a single cell for as much contact as you've had in this tank of sixty people. You can make a pretty good time out of being here if you lighten up and trust people to communicate."

"That makes sense, guys," I said, "but look around." I pointed to one guy who was just totally gone, flat-out psychotic and withering away in his bunk. There was another guy with bandages on his wrists from his most recent suicide attempt and still another guy in the bunk below me who had been so depressed and so ill it seemed like he was willing himself to death in front of me. "Maybe, guys, we'll see," I said.

Then someone said, "You probably like to get high, don't you?" At that point, all I imagined was people shooting up, which appalled me. I never liked needles, I never liked opiate addicts, and I was chagrined that here I was in a maximum security penitentiary and I could see people shooting up heroin everyday.

Surprisingly, he said, "Two hundred of us are dropping acid tomorrow. Would you like to join us?"

Well, I did.

I had taken LSD over a hundred times, but that was probably the second or third strongest, highest microgrammage, purest LSD

I've ever taken. It was god-awful, mind-melting strong. I went totally bananas. Almost immediately, I went to my bunk and started screaming. I had the good sense to put my face in my pillow so I wouldn't attract the guards. The most intense part of the trip was a vision of a biblical God with flowing beard and hair, who was holding a big book listing every interaction I had ever had in my life. As he flipped the pages, he frowned and muttered and made "tsk-tsk" sounds. After he turned the last page, he pointed thumbs down. Suddenly an execution squad of prison guards appeared with shotguns, and I was blown away and killed.

God knows how many eons had passed when I felt I was looking out a window that looked like the window that I used to look out when I used to be in prison years and years and years before. I turned to the person in the bunk next to me and said, "What year is this?"

He laughed and said, "How long do you think it has been?"

I said, "Twenty years."

He said, "It's been about seven hours. It's still the same day as when you first tripped."

I looked around and realized then that I really was in prison. I really had made a set of choices to end up sentenced to two years in a federal penitentiary. That moment was a breakthrough, an acceptance. And at that point I decided to make friends.

I never took LSD again in prison. My God, it was way too intense. But about once a month, I'd get together with other guys out in the pasture to share one tiny, thin joint. We'd be high for a whole day because we made so much of it. As I got to know more people, I learned there could be camaraderie in prison. We could play Scrabble and exchange books. We even started a religious and social-awareness discussion group that met weekly with a Lutheran minister from Tacoma named Jeff Smith, who years later became the Frugal Gourmet on TV.

Still, going to prison meant my parents wanted nothing to do with me. My mother and sister were forbidden by my father to write to me or even acknowledge that I existed. My folks had incorporated my sister's boyfriend as my replacement in the family — as the idealized other son. He was even the same age as me. He had gotten engaged to my sister, then he enlisted and went to Nam. Just two weeks before he was supposed to come home, the same week I entered prison, he was killed in action.

When I first arrived at Lompoc prison, I was put in A and O block — Admission and Orientation. In that first week, I drew a detailed picture of my cell block, including the fences and the gun towers. I was going to send it to friends to show them where I lived. But I was called in by the authorities, who thought it was part of an escape plan. I said, "Where would I escape to? I'd just go back to my family, which is the first place you'd look." They saw then how naive and innocent I was.

After I left A and O, I was assigned to a cell about six feet wide and ten feet long, with a bunk, a chair, a little locker, and a couple of shelves. A contraption folded down to make a writing surface. There was a combination sink and toilet. When you brushed your teeth or shaved, the water would go into the toilet. I guess it saved space and plumbing costs.

One of the first events after my arrival was the destruction of the prison library. Officials came in with wheelbarrows, loaded the books, and took them to the dump at nearby Vandenberg Air Force Base. I don't know why. That was my first lesson in prison. Nothing makes sense. Later, they created a Department of Education, with lots of primary colors and little partitions for the so-called instructors from outside. It looked great when visitors came, but nothing happened there. It was just PR.

My most interesting job was movie projectionist on weekends. It was quite an experience — people making wisecracks, jumping up and yelling things at the screen like, "Hey, what are you doing that for?" Movies were also a time to shank other prisoners — to stab them in the dark. I finally quit being projectionist when Vandenberg started sending films about what a great job they were doing in Vietnam. I went to the warden and said I would have no part in showing those films. "Get me a job change now or I'm in the hole," I told him.

Some guards were sad sacks, some were drunks. Once, a guard at mail call picked up a letter, saw that it was upside down, then turned it over to read the address. He went through the whole pile that way, saying, "Every goddamn one of these letters is upside down." I thought, "Turn the pile over! God, we're the inmates and they're the guards?" The guards stole food while I lost a lot of weight. The chaplain was a drunk, an ex-Marine who drove a pink Cadillac.

The Strength Not to Fight

Some guards had animosity toward me. I wore a peace cross —
a peace symbol with a cross on top. Once a guard told me to tuck
it in or he'd rip it off. Sometimes, guards would try to act buddy-
buddy. But you couldn't have an honest relationship. The question
would always be, "If I go over that fence, would you shoot me?"
The answer would be, "Yes." You can't form a friendship on that
basis.

We had three riots while I was there. The main conflicts were
between African Americans and Latinos, minorities fighting over
crumbs off the table. The prison administration knew how to play
them off against each other, because a divided prison population
was more easily controlled. One time, someone cut in chow line.
A scuffle broke out, and then another one the next day, then another
to avenge that one. Ultimately, the word was out that it would be
settled on Sunday out in the yard, when everybody was together.
Lines at the commissary were very long on Saturday as people
stocked up on food. Sure enough, on Sunday groups formed, shanks
buried earlier in the yard were dug up, a toolbox was broken open,
and the two sides rushed each other.

I climbed up the backstop of the softball field, behind home
plate. I saw one of the prison homosexuals being beaten and kicked
below me, so I climbed down and gave him first aid. Then I saw
another person stabbed. He was losing a lot of blood. I took off my
shirt, wrapped it around him, and pushed it in the wound. As I had
my hands over his wound, I saw helmeted riot troops from Vandenberg, carrying clubs, storm over the fences. They beat the hell
out of anybody still fighting. The guards trained their guns on the
yard, though no shots were fired.

Afterward, the guards had their own riot. We were in lockdown
in our individual cells for over a week. The guards went from cell
to cell, destroying personal property. They came into my cell, forced
me against the wall, and tore through my stuff, dumping my personal possessions on the floor, looking through everything. I still
have a book that they tore up — *The Complete Illustrated Book of
Yoga*. All of us were taken, one by one, down to the prison barbershop and given shaved heads as acts of humiliation. The fear and
harassment and intimidation went on for weeks. There were never
any meetings to talk things out. Meetings would have implied that
we — the prisoners — could contribute to a solution. The only me-
diation service was the riot troops from Vandenberg.

Can you be a pacifist in prison? You better be, unless you're very big. I had heard horror stories about jail. That cons were patriotic and wouldn't like what I did, and that I shouldn't bend over in the shower. I expected sexual assault and violence and political conservatism. But I didn't have that experience at all. Most prisoners were my age, young, with frustrated sexual energy. I weighed only about a hundred and twenty-five pounds, but I got a lot of respect. Upon hearing why I was there, people would say, "Right on!" Almost nobody defended the Vietnam War. The only puzzling thing to them was that I had waited around to be arrested. To some, it meant that I must be a little crazy.

There were about two dozen COs and resisters at Lompoc. We met regularly for political discussions and poetry readings. We formed the Lompoc Men's Auxiliary of the Women's Liberation Movement. We read Shulamith Firestone, Betty Friedan, and Germaine Greer.

Throughout everything, I had a clear sense that if I had kept one person from being inducted, from being killed or from killing someone else, then it was a fair trade for a couple of years in prison.

What do I remember most? I remember so many things. Like when FBI Director J. Edgar Hoover died, everyone spontaneously stood up in the chow hall and sang "Ding Dong! The Witch Is Dead."

▃▃▃▃

I was once approached by a homosexual, not in a threatening manner, and I politely declined. At the time, my job was in the prison chapel. When I told the chaplain about the conversation, he said, "If anybody bothers you, just pick up a chair and smash it over his head in the middle of the night. You'll get off. You'll never be charged for assaulting a homosexual. The prison officials hate them."

▃▃▃▃

I love ironies. I didn't want to be in the military, yet what do you wear in a federal penitentiary in 1970? Discarded, leftover, surplus army khakis. What color is the interior of prison? Institutional green, like army barracks. What do you do? You hurry up, get in line, and wait to be processed. Who are the guys telling you what to wear, what to eat, where to go, and what to do? They're all retired servicemen. I could have enlisted and had the same experience! But there was a difference: I wasn't given a gun and forced into combat training, and I wasn't killing people.

I was very young, a smooth-cheeked, white college boy. In many ways, I was prime meat. Who would pick me out as his honey and win the right to fuck me every night?

Someone asked me, "Do you carry a shank?"

I said, "What the hell is a shank?"

He said, "You better carry one for protection. It's kill or be killed."

I thought, "Wait, I'm here because I'm a pacifist. I'm supposed to find alternatives to violence. Let's chant 'om,' let's smoke a joint, let's look for some other way."

Can someone be a pacifist in prison? Yeah, and then they become a battered victim. I saw soft, gentle, and nonviolent people who would never lift a hand to protect themselves become meat, fodder for sick psychopaths who made them their pets and human slaves, who raped them and beat them daily.

So I had to make everyone realize it was going to be painful to get what they wanted from me. I was a skinny kid. How the hell could I do that? I started lifting weights. I started eating protein supplements at breakfast, lunch, and dinner. I started jogging, playing racquetball and handball, and I began a yoga class for increased range of motion. I bulked up and put on muscle. I learned how to walk the tough-guy walk, where I bounced up on the balls of my feet, had my arms tensed by my sides and my fists half-clenched. I learned to mutter "motherfucker" out of the corner of my face every bit as bad as the baddest motherfucker there. Even so, many of the prisoners chuckled and rolled their eyes, because I was posturing and it wasn't authentic. But, after a while, people who didn't know me had to stop and think, "Is it worthwhile to mess with this guy?"

The bottom line of prison dynamics was this: I wouldn't carry a knife and I didn't know how to do hand-to-hand combat or any of that shit. But I could point to five guys and say, "These are personal friends of mine. If you rip off a piece of my ass, they're going to get a piece of yours that will be a lot bigger than what you get off me."

One guy called himself my bodyguard for a while. He was a bank robber, an ex-Marine, and a part-time Brahma-bull buster nicknamed Cowboy. He wore a cowboy hat and had hair about a quarter of an inch long. He was bisexual and wouldn't have minded a sexual experience with me, but he was respectful and wouldn't force me. He didn't like the hippie life-style. Heroin was his drug of choice. He told me, "It's nice you got all those lightweight, limp-wristed peace freaks watching out for you, but if anybody really messes with you, tell them they got to answer to the Cowboy." Nobody messed with the Cowboy. It was nice to have his protection.

In prison, I became a proponent of capital punishment. It scared me and appalled me that some of those people were alive. People who killed their parents, who tortured others, who had palpable evil about them. Standing in line one day to eat dinner, I got covered with warm blood spurting from the guy behind me having his throat cut ear to ear in a dispute over heroin distribution.

One guy I remember was truly evil. Human life meant nothing to him. I was deeply relieved when he died in his cell, allegedly a suicide. I personally believe he was killed by the guards, and that is okay with me. These thoughts don't fit very well with the rest of my beliefs, but there they are.

———

I was born in Missouri and was a student at the University of Missouri in 1966. I believed everyone should do their duty. I had no feeling that there was anything wrong with being in the military. When I dropped out of school late that year, I knew I'd be drafted, so I went to the army recruiter to enlist. I told him I wanted to be an occupational therapist. He looked in his book and said that an occupational therapist was 91-A, so he gave me my written guarantee that I would be a 91-A. I enlisted in February 1967. I soon learned that 91-A was basic combat medic. That was my first lesson that something was wrong with the military.

The military concentrates on the worst macho aspects of eighteen-year-old boys. As time passed, most of us, including myself, got more and more stupid — more chauvinistic and more racist. After I did basic training, I went to medics' training at Fort Sam Houston in Texas, where a third of the guys were COs. They were in sharp contrast to the rest of us — thoughtful, introspective, and gentle. Over time, they became my friends. I learned to play the harmonica from one CO.

After leaving Fort Sam, I was stationed at Madigan General Hospital near Fort Lewis. I took care of paraplegics and quadriplegics, guys fresh back from the field who had caught a fragment in the spine or had other injuries. They were young guys, seventeen, eighteen, or nineteen years old, whose whole lives had been changed forever. They were very bitter. They'd lie there and tell me how they had been assigned to duties in Nam like guarding somebody's rubber plantation. None of them felt that they had sacrificed for a worthy cause. They hated the war.

For several months, I spent every day at work with those guys — who couldn't turn the pages of a book, who couldn't even shit by themselves, who begged me to kill them. All of us medics had discussions about whether we should kill our patients. I had been an Eagle Scout, a churchgoer, a good, clean American kid from generations of military people in small Missouri towns. But at Madigan, I became filled with a sense of betrayal, and outraged by the duplicity and ugliness underneath the grinning mask of Disneyland America.

About halfway through my year at Madigan, I decided to apply for CO status. I told my commander, who tried to argue me out of it by promising he'd never ask me to pick up a weapon. I believed him, but I persisted, and filled out the CO application in early 1968.

The army rejected my application and sent me orders to report to Vietnam. I probably would have gone to Nam, but then something happened that enraged me: I got orders to report to the rifle range. I reminded my commander that he had promised man-to-man that he would never make me pick up a gun. But he just grinned and said *he* wasn't giving me the order — the colonel was.

Out on the range, a major ordered me to pick up the rifle. I refused. He warned that I could get five years in prison, but I still refused. Instead of prison, they confined me to base, gave me an Article 15 — a nonjudicial punishment — and took away my stripes. I felt betrayed.

I had a forty-five-day leave before going to Vietnam. I spent the time in Berkeley. It was the summer of 1968, and the country was on fire. I remember sitting around the kitchen table in our little apartment, listening to the radio reports from Chicago during the Democratic Convention. It was like a picture from behind the Iron Curtain, everybody huddled in the twilight as the announcer described kids being beaten and gassed by the police. Then suddenly the announcer began coughing, yelling, "Oh! Oh! You pig!" as the police attacked him.

At Bay Area antiwar demonstrations, where I served as a medic, I saw that the cops were very brutal. Once, I watched cops go for a pregnant woman and poke her in the belly. This was not the America I had grown up believing in. I felt I was getting cheated out of my America the Beautiful.

I thought about refusing to get on the plane to Vietnam, but the army's practice was to throw resisters on the plane, and then no lawyer in the world could help you. So on the advice of my lawyer, I went AWOL. It was a legal tactic to keep me in the United States long enough to appeal my CO application. I'd be dropped from my unit and my case would be delayed while new orders were cut. And I would be punished for the relatively light crime of being AWOL rather than the heavy charge of five years in jail if I refused an order to go to Vietnam.

After being AWOL for forty-five days, I turned myself in at a demonstration in San Francisco called GIs and Veterans March for Peace. I was one of four AWOL GIs who gave speeches and then stepped across the line at the Presidio military base. I remember it was my father's birthday, Saturday, October 12, 1968.

In the Presidio stockade, I linked up with a guy named Darrel, the leader of a group of nine AWOL GIs who had been in jail after they chained themselves to clergymen until MPs used bolt cutters to arrest them. We met with other guys and decided we'd have a sit-down strike on the following Monday.

On Monday morning, about a hundred prisoners were in the yard in formation. At the planned moment, at a certain point in the roll call, twenty-seven of us walked to a corner, sat down, and began singing "We Shall Overcome."

The guards shit bricks. They ordered us to return to formation, but we sang louder. Then the commander read us the articles of mutiny, a capital crime with no maximum sentence. One guy stood up and read our demands, which included an end to the war, opposition to racism, and better treatment in the stockade. A fire truck arrived, but the firemen refused to squirt us. Then a company of MPs in full riot gear and gas masks arrived. I thought, "Oh, boy, they're really going to fuck us up now." Using various amounts of impoliteness along the way, they carried us bodily back to the stockade and threw us in a common cell.

Two days later, we were charged with mutiny. Our case was called the Presidio 27. It got a lot of publicity. Nearly every issue of *Playboy* magazine in late '68 and all of '69, in the section on civil liberties, mentioned our case.

The first trial took place in early 1969. I was supposed to be in that group, but I got hepatitis and so the judge sent me to the hospital, delaying my trial. Darrel had escaped, and in the hospital I considered doing it, too, with a friend. At night, we sawed the bars, then put soap and dirt in the marks. It was right out of *The Great Escape*. But then a Catholic priest visited me. He said that I was the only ringleader left, and it wasn't right that we who had organized the protest would leave everyone else behind to do time in prison. He was right, and so I chose to stay — though I helped finish the sawing and eventually waved goodbye to my friend.

One of the lowest points in my life was when the convictions in those first trials resulted in sentences of sixteen to eighteen years in prison. Because I was a ringleader, I expected to be treated even more harshly. When I heard about the sentences, suicide entered my mind for a nanosecond. I thought about setting myself on fire like the Buddhist monks in Vietnam, hoping to get attention so the other guys would get off. But I wasn't so sure it would help, and anyway, I didn't really want to commit suicide.

I finally went to trial along with thirteen other guys at Fort Ord near Monterey. By then, there had been a lot of publicity and so the military backed off harsh sentences. I got fifteen months in Leavenworth Federal Penitentiary.

Prisons are worse than most people think. When I tell people about my experience, they tend not to believe me, or they think I'm exaggerating. I went to a play once about a guy who was arrested and brutalized by the police. For me, the play was very real. Standing in the street afterward, still covered with sweat from the intense experience, I overheard people say the play was overdone and not believable. I realized then that people don't believe the real shit about prison. I personally witnessed guards break people's fingers. One night, all the prisoners in solitary confinement had their legs broken by the guards. People got raped by other prisoners. People committed suicide. I saw people do horrible self-mutilation. There are plenty of horror stories. It's a joke that prison is supposed to teach prisoners how to live in society by treating them in a sub-human way. It's a joke.

One thing I learned, though, is that it's not that hard to be a pacifist in prison. I found I could take a beating with the best of them. It's not any worse to be beaten up in prison than it is to be beaten up in high school. In fact, for pacifists, in some ways it's easier, because at least your head is clear.

Prisoners understand if you refuse to be complicit with society's bullshit. Prisoners know better than anybody how ugly America is. If you're in jail saying, "I ripped the mask off of America," everybody goes, "Right on!" You get more respect in prison than you do on the streets.

If you know what you're standing for and you're consistent, you can create a kind of moral authority in prison that people will respect. For example, one day, this naked gay prisoner about to get raped came screaming to me and climbed up on my bunk. All these ruffians surrounded us. I thought, "Oh, fuck, should I help him or just stay out of it?" I decided to get into my lotus position and I started chanting and chanting to beat the band. All the guys just stood there, caught off guard, looking at each other and shaking their heads. One guy finally said, "Man, we almost did a bad thing." Then most of them shuffled off. Two guys sat down and chanted along with me. It was a bizarre scene in the sixties, even in prison.

I learned that there are a hell of a lot of good people in jail, especially among nonwhite prisoners. In a country with few opportunities within the system for nonwhites, people who have anything on the ball sometimes find ways to advance themselves outside the system. Unfortunately, they may get caught and end up in jail. In a way, they're the cream of the crop, not the dregs.

I remember one amazing African-American guy who was there for having killed his commander in Vietnam. He had memorized Chairman Mao's Little Red Book. He would chant it in the style of African signifying. Another guy had been a student in junior college in Sacramento when he became fascinated with the cables sent by the U.S. embassy in Moscow during the Russian Revolution. He fell in love with the revolution and became an intellectual Communist. He didn't know any other Communists or any organizations. Eventually, he quit school and was drafted. When he got orders to go to Vietnam, he refused because he said he couldn't fight against his comrades. Of course, they threw the book at him.

One of the hardest times was in solitary. You want human interaction so badly. You want to be treated like a human being. Sometimes, a guard would slip you a cigarette. You'd think, "Wow, a human kindness!" But a short time later, that same guard, with a few others, would come in and beat you up. Then a few days later, he'd say he's sorry, he was only following orders, and he'd offer you another cigarette. If you take that cigarette, you're setting yourself up for a very painful experience. When an asshole treats you like a dog and doesn't pretend to like you, you can harden your heart to him, but when you feel connected to someone, there's a deep human pain when he hurts you.

———

Starting in 1971, I served eighteen months in prison for refusing to carry my draft card. When I was sentenced, I was taken first to the Baltimore city jail, to a special wing for federal prisoners. There were two tiers of cells there, about two dozen cells total.

Some of the guys had been there for two years, and were upset about various things — food and various policies. They wanted to talk to somebody in the prison administration, and so refused to go in the cells one night. There were only about a dozen guys speaking out. Most of us just stood back, next to our cell doors. I could think of six different ways the guards could have co-opted the situation, but instead they just brought in the goon squad — what they called the riot squad. Everyone tried to arm themselves against the goon squad, but we didn't have anything to arm ourselves with — except cafeteria trays, a mop bucket, things like that. It was pitiful.

The goon squad fired tear gas into the cell block. When you're locked in, and you don't have anywhere to go, it's pretty frightening. Pretty soon, everyone was coughing and choking and crying out. I got wet cloths and gave one to my cellmate. The gas was everywhere and the thought came to me, "Am I going to live through this?" Not being able to breathe is a fundamental fear. In time, they dragged us out two by two.

Even though half of the guards were black, the riot squad was all white. I was taken out with the other guy in my cell. He was black, and I'm white. The riot squad poked him with their sticks, but they didn't poke me.

Afterward, the jail was locked down and the associate warden came around to each cell ostensibly to hear people's grievances. One of his assistants took notes and wrote down names. Since the prison authorities had said there was no money for better facilities, one of my friends asked whether a list of senators and representatives could be posted on the bulletin board so everyone could write to Congress to tell them to give more money for prisons. The next day, they hauled off to the hole everybody who had spoken up, including my friend.

I was sent to a prison in Virginia, to a big place with several hundred acres of farmland. My case worker thought I was one of the hippies, so he assigned me to work on farm duty. I thought it was great, a city boy farming. It sounded like fun. When I got to the farm building, an old geezer handed me a hook. I thought it was strange. How do you farm with a hook? He pointed to a line of cows and said, "The killing's over there." I realized then it was a slaughterhouse and I was supposed to kill the cows. No way I was going to be chest deep in blood, so I refused. The guard immediately got on the phone and within minutes a little disciplinary truck arrived to take me back to my case worker, who told me it was a serious offense to refuse to work. Eventually, they gave me solitary confinement.

I went into solitary confinement in July 1970. The room was about four by six feet. Standing in one place, I could touch the sides and the ceiling. My bed was just a metal slat sticking out from the wall about two feet off the ground. I had no blankets, no covers, and no light.

My biggest worry was whether I would go crazy. I tried to keep mentally active. I thought about my life, day by day, and reviewed events in minute detail. For some reason, I remembered being washed as a child, and thought about it for hours. I tried to think of every song I could remember and I ran through the lyrics of every one.

The guards passed my food on a tray through a slot in the door. I was fed once in the morning and once in the evening. The morning meal was a kind of oatmeal with tea. At night, I had soup and a glass of water. That was the only way I could tell the time of day. Sometimes I would be awake all night and think that two days had passed and they had decided not to feed me. Other times, I imagined that they were delaying my meals to screw up my mind. I lived a lifetime in that little room.

I was finally released from solitary after four months. It was November. Thanksgiving. My first meal was turkey. Not canned and processed. But real turkey. I had tried to be a vegetarian in prison, but I ate that turkey. Every bite.

Chicano families put pictures of their men in the military on the mantelpiece and on top of the TV set. Something like one in ten of the winners of the Congressional Medal of Honor in World War II were Chicano. There has always been a feeling that we have to prove we're men and that we're true Americans. We always pay the price in blood far out of proportion to our percentage of the population.

I dropped out of college in Vermont in 1967. In January 1968, I was in Philadelphia when I read about the federal indictment against Dr. Benjamin Spock for counseling young people not to participate in the draft. I got mad and sent my draft card to the Selective Service office in my hometown of Denver. Then in March 1968 I filed for CO status. My friends wondered why I wouldn't go in the army. Was I a Communist or a coward? I said, "Hey, listen, how many of us from the East Side are already in Vietnam? How many have been shot or killed? How many of us are locked up in prison? How many of us are unemployed? We're getting shafted and it's the government that's doing it. That's why I'm not going to Vietnam."

My family was scared. My mom wanted me to talk to a psychiatrist. She thought there was something mentally wrong with me. My dad was Protestant and didn't even like the Catholic Church, yet he recommended I talk to a priest. Two of my older brothers were vets. They didn't speak to me for years because of my actions.

My main support came from the Crusade for Justice, a Chicano organization that publicly opposed the war as early as 1966. It was a nationalistic group that believed Chicanos must learn their own history and organize politically. Many of its leaders were middle-class working males. That helped me with my parents. It wasn't just me, a smart-mouthed punk kid opposing the war. It was older people of the same class and nationality as my family.

After filing my CO application, I heard nothing until I got an order in April of '68 to report for induction. I went down to the U.S. Customs House in downtown Denver, across the street from the courthouse. I was the only one to refuse induction that day. Officers took me to a separate room, told me the consequences, and called my name several times. I refused each time, then left.

In late April, I went to Resurrection City in Washington, D.C., for the Poor People's Campaign. When I returned to Denver, I found a notice to report to a magistrate's hearing in June. The Crusade organization put me in touch with lawyers from the National Lawyers' Guild, who represented me at the hearing. After some discussion there, the prosecutor dropped charges, because the draft board had not followed proper procedures. It had never processed my CO application. That's why I hadn't heard from them.

So I was back at square one. I applied for a CO deferment again, they turned down my application, and I appealed. My hearing was at the Customs House. I was interviewed by a three-member committee. Two were middle-aged white men, probably in their fifties. They seemed like real old farts to me then. The third member was a black man in his late forties.

As soon as I walked in, I could see they didn't like me. The guy who seemed to be in charge just slid back in his chair, tipped it up against the wall, and crossed his arms and legs. A piece of gum was lying on the desk in front of him. For him, it was all over. But they still had to go through the rigmarole. So the black guy kicked in his Uncle Tom routine, shuffling around, asking about my religion. When I told them I was Catholic, they said that the Catholic Church did not have pacifist teachings and therefore I would not qualify for a CO.

But I didn't let it end there. I said there were deeper, more profound issues than religious teachings. I said the war was wrong, the Constitution was being violated, the public was being deceived, people were dying in a senseless and criminal war, and we were killing people who had never done anything to us. I said no system could make me participate in the war. They didn't want to hear it. Soon after, in October 1968, I got my second notice to report for induction.

Some friends developed a plan to help me. They arranged with the owner of a jewelry shop for me to break a window and get arrested for burglary. My friends promised the store owner that they would stand guard to make sure no one else broke in the store after I was arrested, and they said they would replace the window. Our hope was that I would be tied up in court and couldn't be inducted. The plan was for the owner to drop charges just before my trial.

At the last minute, though, the store owner backed out. So we devised Plan B. I would pass out literature from the Communist party, the Black Panthers, and the SDS, right there in the induction center. They'd think I was a crazy anarchist and wouldn't take me.

The night before my induction, I went drinking with my buddies and ended up falling asleep in some guy's Volkswagen. I woke up at 11:00 the next day. I was supposed to have shown up at the induction center by 7:00.

I arrived there with a friend, and we spontaneously decided to innovate on Plan B. Those were the hippie days, the summer of love, the psychedelic days of '68. So I entered the induction center smoking a joint. I walked up to a sergeant and stood right in front of him, figuring I'd get kicked out or arrested. But he just said, "You were supposed to be here at seven o'clock. You should be prompt." He was scolding me because I was late! He was such a square that he apparently didn't know what I was smoking.

My friend and I began passing out the literature, when a sergeant told us it was against the law. We said we had constitutional rights — although we weren't quite sure which ones. He got perturbed, left the office, and returned with a great big guy in uniform who was a guard with the General Services Administration. He demanded our material, but I told him, "We have a right to petition for redress of grievances." He said yes, but not on federal property. We argued our taxes paid for the building. He left, and we started talking to the minority guys waiting for induction, asking, "How come it's always the poor who have to go to war?"

A procession of about fifteen men in uniform arrived, led by two guys in suits and ties. The guys in suits were U.S. marshals who said they had been called because we were creating a disturbance. Then they arrested us. We said we would not resist arrest. In the back of my mind, I was thinking, "Good, this is going to throw a monkey wrench in the machine."

We started walking down the hall, followed by a contingent of officers, when suddenly a guy pushed his way to the front and asked our names. When we told him, he pointed to me and said to the marshals, "This one's here for induction. Just take the other one." I was immediately de-arrested.

My friend had stopped, the marshals had stopped, everybody was just standing there, when the GSA guard suddenly grabbed my friend by the neck and said, "Come on, we're taking you across the street." The guard was six feet one inch, and my friend was five feet four, but a high school wrestler. He pushed backward, slipping out of the guard's hold. Once he did that, the scuffle was on. My friend was gang-tackled by six or seven guys, one pulling his hair, another shoving an arm underneath his throat. I put my arms around the shoulders of one of the marshals on the pile and pulled him backward. Then all the other guys in uniform gang-tackled me. In short order, we were handcuffed, marched across the street to jail, and charged with a felony assault on a U.S. marshal, which carried about the same prison sentence and fine as refusing induction. We made our one phone call to the Crusade for Justice, and were out on bond within eight hours.

I went to trial in March 1969, represented by two attorneys from the Lawyers' Guild. The jury was all white except one Latino woman from the suburbs, one of our Uncle Toms, our Aunt Jemimahs. My friend's arrest was ruled illegal because U.S. marshals were not allowed to arrest anyone for a misdemeanor. So he went free. One of the marshals testified that I was not under arrest when the scuffle broke out. I think he honestly remembered it that way. The technical point was that I was not under arrest, and so I was interfering in my friend's arrest, which I did not have the right to do. That meant that I had unlawfully laid hands on the marshal. My attorney tried to introduce the issue of the war, but the judge wouldn't allow it. The jury found me guilty.

Before sentencing me, the judge asked if I'd like to say anything. My knees were shaking and I knew he held my future in his hands. I said, "Yes, Your Honor." I had to swallow hard to say "Your Honor." Then I said, "I know I've been found guilty, but I'm not here to address that. Both sides have had their say. Whether I agree with the verdict is not material now. I want to say, as my attorneys tried to during the trial, that there is a question as to whether this war is legal. I'm not a scholar, but I know Congress has not declared this war. People in Vietnam are dying, but they've never done anything to me. They have a right to make their own decisions. How they govern their nation is up to them. History may decide someday that this war was illegal and immoral and unconstitutional, but I doubt that men like President Johnson or General Westmoreland will have to stand trial before a man like you. And I doubt that they will ever be found guilty for their crimes. I have been found guilty in a court of law, but I have not been found guilty in a court of justice."

When I said that, you could see the veins on the judge's face pop out. It was a pretty good speech.

The judge sentenced me, but I remained out on appeal for two years, as my case went all the way to the Supreme Court. Finally, in March 1971 I was incarcerated at the minimum security prison in Colorado.

I was sentenced as a youth offender, which meant I'd go to prison for two or three months of observation, and then the prison counselor would recommend what my sentence should be. I think the judge wanted to come down hard on me, but he didn't want to catch the heat from the antiwar movement, which was pretty strong by 1971. He probably figured I was so resentful of authority that I was bound to get in hot water in jail and then the counselor would recommend a long sentence.

My counselor in prison was a graduate of the University of Kansas, just three years older than me. In my initial interview, he said, "It says here in your file that you're here for assault. Tell me about it." I figured I was dealing with another asshole, so I took a deep breath and told him the story. I was almost through the whole chronology when he suddenly sat up in his chair and said, "Do you mean this was some sort of protest?" I think he didn't quite believe me then, but he checked into my story, and the next time we talked, he told me he was sorry I was in prison.

I gradually learned more about him — that he had social worker tendencies, that this was his first job, and that he considered Vietnam to be a moral stain on the country. He often sent little slips of paper telling me to report to his office. He'd close the door and give me radical books against the war, saying that the regular reading material in prison sucked. On one visit, he told me that my case was getting a lot of attention because the Crusade for Justice was organizing protests against my incarceration. My name was spray-painted under bridges, on walls, and along highways around Denver. He said that the staff had extra training to prepare for possible protests at the prison. He warned me that there was someone on the staff who was supposed to get evidence to keep me locked up. I needed to be on my guard at all times.

If I had told anyone what he was doing, he would have gotten in trouble. He trusted me.

━━━━

After arriving in Baltimore and linking up with the remnants of the Catholic Left, I worked on the Harrisburg Defense Committee and helped organize a series of demonstrations against the war. I was arrested a couple of times in Washington, D.C., in demonstrations at the White House over continuing aid for the South Vietnamese. The last time was just as the North Vietnamese Army was approaching Saigon in the spring of 1975 and the Ford administration had asked for another $250 million. It was surely one of the last, if not the very last, major demonstration against American support of the war in Vietnam.

I was put in a jail cell with Dan Berrigan and Dick Gregory. Dan read poetry to us. Dick Gregory started banging on the bars, saying, "Hey, I want my phone call. I've seen all those Jimmy Cagney movies. I get to make one phone call." So the guards came over and said, "All right, Mr. Bigshot, call your fancy-pants lawyer." They gave him his dime and the phone was right there in the hallway, so we could hear everything he said. He put in his dime, he dialed and said, "Hello, it's your dad. I'm in jail again, suffering for peace and justice, and when I get home this time I want a little respect." He brought down the house. Even the guards had to crack up at that one.

I spent one week in the D.C. jail on that occasion, which was long enough. One guy committed suicide by sticking his head down the toilet. Somebody else started a fire in one of the mattresses. The D.C. jail is like Cook County jail in Chicago — pretty nasty.

Being imprisoned several times for nonviolent resistance to the war confirmed my belief in nonviolence. I was never physically attacked by other prisoners. The only people who ever beat up on me were police. I realized that much of the violence in jails and prisons is a result of people having few resources to cope with what's going on around them. I learned that a middle-class person is especially well prepared to be nonviolent. Middle-class people are trained to talk their way into good things and out of bad things. They deal with boredom by reading. They bring resources into jail that can be shared with the jail population, such as helping people

97

get legal assistance, helping with paperwork, or just listening to people's stories. Pretty soon, people spread the word, "Don't mess with him. He's helping." You end up being protected.

For me, the essence of the responsible, nonviolent person is someone who holds in tension two ideals: the ideal of remaining true to your values no matter what the consequences, and the realization that your actions have consequences that play a role in any moral consideration. Neither ideal in isolation constitutes an adequate moral response. You must try to hold them in tension, and that tension is very circumstance-specific.

The question of whether to continue to resist once the prison door is shut on you is also very circumstance-specific. I felt a great kinship with the POWs — although their circumstances were far, far worse than mine — because they faced the same issue. At what point does resistance become meaningless and destructive for you and your cause?

That can be hard to answer. For example, when I was at the minimum security prison at Lompoc, California, my early attempts to talk to the black prisoners about the nuclear arms race were met with nothing but derision. I was this stupid honky who actually volunteered to get in there.

Then one day, I was given a work assignment in a factory that, it was rumored, had something to do with the military. I showed up for my assignment, and on the way in, I saw a big crate on the loading dock with a label that said its destination was the naval submarine base in Washington. The crate was full of furniture.

Some people might say that I was just being asked to make desks, but I figured those were the desks on which World War III was being planned. So I sat down on the floor and refused to work. I happened to have with me Hans Küng's *On Being a Christian*, which made good reading, but I was soon hauled away by guards in riot masks.

When they took me to the warden's office, my knees were knocking and the truth of the matter is I wet my pants. The first thing the warden said to me was, "You aren't going to start a prisonwide work strike, are you? That could cost me my job." I explained that my work assignment required me to violate the principle that got me in prison in the first place: "I came here protesting weapons, and you're asking me to help build the submarine base."

The warden threatened me with the hole, with transfer to a high-security, meaner, tougher prison, and with a worse work assignment, at the Vandenberg Air Force Base. But I persisted.

That night, as I was sitting in my bunk, the head of the Black Muslim Brotherhood came over to me and said, "The brothers were wondering whether you would talk to us about this nuclear arms race." Because of my work strike, they had realized that I was not some airhead white pansy. I could say "no" to the Man on the Man's own turf. After that, guys would see the head of the Black Muslims with his hand around my shoulders. Needless to say, I didn't have any trouble in that prison.

So nonviolent resistance turned out to be the most effective thing I did in prison. It opened up a whole new audience to the issue that had brought me there. And it was an audience that had originally considered me to be merely a curiosity.

———

You get shitty food in prison. On Thanksgiving, 1971, we got chopped, processed turkey roll that dogs wouldn't eat. The mess-hall staff pushed it out of cans and sliced it, like jelly. Each of us got what looked like a hockey puck on our plate.

Without planning in advance, we began to yell. "We're not eating this shit. We're human beings. You can give us one sliver of decency on holidays and not treat us like vermin." We started throwing the pucks and rolling them up and down the aisles. It got to the edge of a riot, so extra guards were called and we got locked down.

I had one of the few necessary work details and so I got out of my cell. I took some hockey pucks with me. When I saw the associate warden, who was a halfway decent human being who had come back from his holiday to deal with the lockdown, I gave him one of the turkey pucks and said, "What would you do if you were given this shit to eat?" The next day, they brought in real turkeys and we got a real Thanksgiving dinner.

I had a job where I worked the boats between McNeil Island and the mainland. I was the forward line guy. I learned how to take a big, heavy hawser, swing it like a lasso, rope a piling, tie it off, and pull in the rear line. I even learned how to operate the vessel. Being outside and working every day on Puget Sound was a blessing. Even though I was locked up every night, on the boat I could fantasize about being free. I had fresh air. I touched the mainland. I could see and smell and hear women, so I knew they existed.

On some days, I'd shovel silage with another peace freak. That was when I first got into composting. It was hard manual labor, but there was something basic and organic about it. And it was a great job for smoking dope. We got covered with stinky silage, so the guards couldn't smell the dope on us. One day, we got stoned, and said, "This ain't too bad. It's a spring day. It's warm. The birds are singing. The bees are buzzing. We are buzzed. We're working together. We've got camaraderie. There's enlightenment going on in the country. Maybe even the war will end."

But then we heard artillery practice rolling over the water from nearby Fort Lewis, and we watched a C-5A coming into McChord Air Force Base. Filled with coffins, we figured. After watching another plane take off with fresh troops, we wondered, "Are we kidding ourselves? Are we having the slightest impact? Is it worth it to be in prison for our beliefs?"

———

In 1967, I was classified I-A. Near the end of that year, I refused induction in the army and was indicted. My trial lasted about forty-five minutes. I was convicted and sentenced to three years on probation.

Soon after my trial, I received a new draft card with a new classification. IV-F. Because I was a felon, convicted of refusing to fight, my draft board had classified me as "morally unfit for military service."

Chapter 3

Serving
My
Country

In a letter to my draft board after I was assigned number 25 in the lottery, I asked that my student deferment be canceled and I be classified I-A — eligible for the draft. Taking this step was the only way to force the draft board to consider my CO application. The risk was great: if my request was denied, I would be drafted.

My application was eleven pages long, like a college term paper, and filled with religious references. I optimistically argued that imitating Christ's pacifism would make humans divine. Believing in the transformative power of sacrifice, I quoted the Gospel of Mark: "For he who would save his life will lose it; but he who loses his life for my sake and for the gospel's sake will save it." I wanted my board to know I was willing to go to prison. I refused noncombatant military service by quoting the army field manual: "The primary duty of medical troops, as of all other troops, is to contribute their utmost to the success of the command." I supported my application with letters from my mother; my supervisor at the cafeteria where I worked; my brother-in-law, who was a Vietnam veteran; an English professor; and my history professor, who had been an infantryman in the Third Army in Europe during the Second World War. He ended his letter with the plea: "One of the reasons I wanted to go into the service was to protect in some *small way the right of all honest men to make an open judgment on such matters as that of personal service in the military."*

For many weeks following my application, I imagined receiving my CO deferment and sharing it with friends in a triumphant celebration for our generation. Instead, the envelope from my draft board arrived during a quarter break, when university classes were not in session, and all my friends were gone. I was classified I-O, conscientious objector. But my victory was quiet and lonely, an individual, private end to what I had considered a community's struggle.

I telephoned my friends to tell them the good news. As they spoke to me from their parents' homes, they were subdued and cautious. We did not expect the older generation to share in our joy. Rather than a party filled with the sounds of Jimi Hendrix and the Doors, my CO deferment brought only long-distance, conspiratorial whispers.

I never considered calling my own parents. Like many in the World War II generation, they were angered and embarrassed by conscientious objectors. My mother's letter to my draft board hinted at the conflict they felt between family ties and loyalty to country: "We, his parents, don't agree with his being a conscientious objector, but we are not surprised. Sometimes it's difficult to see our son for what he truly is and not what we would have him to be."

This chapter includes stories of COs who performed various kinds of service. For most who received CO deferments, that meant alternative service in hospitals and mental health centers. Some served as medics in Vietnam. Others who did not receive CO deferments joined the National Guard or arranged placement in military units that would not require combat. All of the men in this chapter found ways to serve their country without firing the weapons of war.

▬▬▬

You either went in the army, you stayed in school, you left the country, or you did what I did — you became a CO and did alternative service. Vietnam changed everybody's life. I feel real fortunate that it worked out the way it did for me.

My parents were involved in the political Left in the 1930s and 1940s. They would have been involved in the fifties, too, if there had been anything to be a part of then.

I went through conventional Jewish religious training, and gradually came to think of myself as a socialist. I remember in the eighth grade getting into an argument with a teacher when I defended socialism. He asked me what it meant, and I didn't know. But I certainly did know by the time I was eighteen.

I was touched by the civil rights movement and became involved in the struggle in Ohio to desegregate the last businesses that were still Jim Crow. I continued that activism later, at Antioch College in the Ban the Bomb movement, and then in the Fair Play for Cuba campaign. I was inspired by the revolution against Batista in Cuba, which I saw as an attempt by the Cuban people to establish a new and more just society. I was very perturbed that my own government was attacking that effort.

In 1961 and '62, I lived with my parents in Paris. That was the last year of the Algerian civil war, when the French Algerian fascists finally managed to bring the war home with an extensive bombing campaign in France.

I learned a French song about draft resistance, called "The Deserter." It was a very moving song about a guy who had been drafted but wouldn't go to war. In the song, he recalls the suffering of World War II and then says he doesn't want to kill any more of the enemy — meaning Algerians. One day in Paris, I was walking down the street with my sister, who had been living there for some time, when I began to sing the song. She quickly shut me up. Because at that time you could be arrested for singing it.

Every day, headlines in the paper told of the killing in Algeria and the random bloodletting by both the Algerian National Liberation Front and those who wanted to keep Algeria as a French colony. I remember news stories of forty, fifty, sixty, eighty people being killed each day. One day, I was on a bus with my father riding through the Place de la Concorde the morning after a machine-gun attack against an Algerian antiwar demonstration. Blood was still on the street. The ugliness of a war of empire, even on the home front, made a deep impression on me.

After Paris, I spent a marvelous summer in 1962 with my parents on a kibbutz in Israel. That was in the innocent age, before the occupation of 1967. The kibbutz was just under the Golan Heights, which was still part of Syria. Most of the people on the kibbutz were refugees from fascism — from Hungary, Czechoslovakia, Romania, and Holland. One day I was working in the cotton fields, when suddenly I heard "boom, rat-a-tat." It was the Syrian Army coming up the hill. Practicing. We lived in fear, in the shadow of violence. Many nights we slept in underground bunkers.

I remember the trial and execution of Adolf Eichmann in Israel that summer. I had long talks about it with my folks. We felt if there was ever anyone who deserved to be put to death, it was Adolf Eichmann. Yet his conviction was a wonderful opportunity for Israel to say, "No. We will not take a life." It was not a matter of forgiveness. I didn't believe in forgiveness. As the Jewish partisans who fought the Nazis said, "Never to forget. Never to forgive." But I felt, even with Eichmann, we could find another way to achieve justice besides his death.

By the time I was eighteen, I had come to think of all U.S. wars as wars of empire. Meaning wars in which the ruling elite in this country seeks to pursue its own wealth and power by coming to the aid of client elites in other countries seeking to preserve their wealth and power against a popular insurgency. I struggled with the idea of pacifism, because while I abhorred violence, I felt people had the right to defend themselves when attacked. Israel, for example. So when I applied for CO status in 1963, I admitted the repugnant but necessary use of force for self-defense.

In the fall of 1964, I enrolled at Harvard and got a student deferment. At the beginning of 1965, I asked the draft board to process my CO application, but it refused to do so as long as I was a student.

Then, in December 1965, one of my cousins was killed in Vietnam. His name was Bruce. He had enlisted and was a lieutenant.

Over the next four years, I became deeply involved in working to end the war, mainly with the Students for a Democratic Society [SDS]. I worked at infiltrating groups undergoing preinduction physicals in Boston. Kids were brought in on buses from outlying areas, up to a forty-mile radius, for their physicals. I would go out to the pickup points, mingle with the guys, and find every opportunity to talk about refusing induction and resisting the draft. At first, in '65 and '66, the mood was pretty tense. I had to try to keep a low enough profile not to get thrown off the bus, and then, after the bus arrived at the physical, I had to sneak away. By 1968, everything had changed, and I got a sympathetic response from most guys on the bus.

I remember the first time I knew I had helped someone. I gave him the name of the Boston Draft Resistance Group. Later, he came to tell me he had gotten out of the draft. That was a great feeling. But I knew that the majority of those on the buses were going off to war.

By 1968, I had made a full-time commitment to antiwar work. In 1969, I was elected regional traveler for SDS in New England. Pacifism was not common in SDS. In fact, some people from SDS enlisted in the army so they could join GI resistance and sabotage the war from within. SDS had begun to self-destruct at its national convention in Chicago in 1968. The organization was unable to embrace broader opposition to the war and instead went off on a tangent as a self-styled revolutionary vanguard.

The terrible irony is that vanguard elements can earn the right to lead only by building broad coalitions that encompass conflicting interests and ideas. It makes me sad to remember how many people in SDS got chewed up, burned down, and driven underground. They might have made a more worthy contribution toward ending the suffering and violence in Southeast Asia.

Che Guevara said that love is the most important motivation for revolution. Love of humankind, not hatred of the old order. Revolutionary movements will be ineffective if they are not guided by a belief in the sanctity of life and a longing for peaceful and nonviolent relations among people. I was a committed socialist, wanting a revolution to transform this country. Yet I felt revolution was compatible with my own personal orientation toward nonviolence. I struggled to maintain my own personal values and beliefs about the sanctity of life, even as the antiwar movement was becoming more revolutionary and more bitterly opposed to everything around it.

During World War II, my father had worked on the Manhattan Project, developing the atomic bomb. He felt betrayed by the bombs dropped on Hiroshima and Nagasaki. He had thought the bomb would be used to stop Hitler. Instead, it was used on the Japanese. He never got over his feeling of betrayal.

My parents were very proud of me for applying to be a CO. My father wrote a powerful letter to the draft board recalling when, at the end of World War II, he and my mother had looked down on me in the cradle, born as I was just before the end of the war, with victory over fascism seemingly assured. He described their high hopes for a better world, and their belief that with the alliance between the United States and the Soviet Union, I would never have to be in military uniform. His letter expressed their bitter disappointment at what I had to face.

I finally got my CO deferment in 1970. But I was burned out from years of antiwar work in the Boston area, and so I procrastinated setting up my alternative service. As my draft board hassled me for delaying, I decided arbitrarily to move to the West Coast, where I arrived in the middle of the recession of the early 1970s. It took me three months to get a job working in the laundry at a local hospital, at $2.17 an hour. It was a relief to get a full-time job, even a low-paying one. I was happy to start alternative service and glad to resolve my dispute with my draft board.

There was one other CO at the hospital, who did six months' alternative service, then disappeared.

I stocked and distributed the clean linen. It was hard labor. Most of the other laundry workers were foreign-born — Eastern Europeans, Filipinos, Koreans, and one woman from Africa. I was elected by the laundry workers to represent them on an employees' advisory council.

I had a difficult relationship with one of my supervisors, a Lithuanian guy who had volunteered to join the Nazi military when it occupied Lithuania. I guess he thought he'd take the opportunity to be on the winning side. He was quite anti-Semitic, a hard-nosed bastard. Being a conscientious objector and a Jew were two strikes against me with him. He made it obvious he didn't like me.

In 1972, I lost my job at the hospital. Eventually, I got a job in the VA hospital. The war was still going on. While working there, I got to know military people as human beings. I learned that veterans were quickly forgotten by the government. Many were quite bitter about promises not kept. It was an eye-opener to see their disillusionment.

By the time I finished my two years of alternative service, almost ten years had passed since I had first applied for my CO deferment. I had forgotten the fellowship in American history waiting for me at the University of Wisconsin and the scholarships at Berkeley and Harvard. I never even contacted them. If I had, I suppose I would now be a professor of American history. Probably with a couple of books to my name. Much of my life would be different. I wouldn't have the wife I have. I wouldn't have the children I have. I wouldn't have the life I do now.

I still agonize over the fact that alternative service kept me from being a teacher. It's not that I would change anything. But now I'm forty-five, with serious obstacles to going back to school — like earning a living.

Yet, when I think about the sacrifices others made — Americans who went to war and the Vietnamese people — I consider myself to be blessed.

▬

Some people remember COs as skinny little cowards who urinated in their pants when the sergeant threatened them.

There were plenty of people who weren't conscientious objectors when they went to Vietnam, but they became COs when they saw the reality of war.

▬

I have a strong belief in spirit. I don't think I would be alive today without that spirit. I think that's what got me through.

Being a CO in the army brought me down to a suicidal crisis, right down into the darkness. I really had to walk the valleys, those dark valleys. There were moments I thought, "God, I don't know if I can do this. It's just too hard." But it made me the person I am.

Vietnam was the one place in my life I really felt a sense of belonging. It was more than the teamwork. There was something about being among guys you really know. You may not agree and you may not like each other, but it's like a family. You know who you can count on and who you can't count on. When the bullets and mortars are flying, you *know* — you absolutely know — if you can count on someone. It's a test by fire. Remembering it still brings tears to my eyes. Unfortunately, we also supported each other in doing too many drugs and in lashing out at people who weren't part of our group.

After my CO application was turned down, I enlisted in the army as a medic. That was in June 1968. Within two weeks, I knew I had made a mistake. I hadn't realized that medics went through regular basic training, including combat training. About a week into basic, they handed out rifles, and I refused to take one. The chaplain gave me your basic army speech: "You're fighting for the USA. It's okay in God's eyes." Even at eighteen, I didn't buy that. So I was charged with disobeying an order and scheduled to be court-martialed.

I got great legal advice at the army Judge Advocate General's office. Lawyers were getting drafted then, and fortunately they were just as pissed off as I was about being in the service. They told me to stand my ground, and I did. After five weeks, the army gave me my CO status.

So I did basic training again, this time as a CO. It was tough. The platoon sergeants were especially hard on COs. They weren't real sergeants. They were going through basic, too. It was like in concentration camps, where some inmates get special rank in order to keep order. The platoon sergeants took away my visiting privileges and my weekend passes. I was engaged at the time, and so I lost contact with my fiancée, who was my only emotional support.

After basic, I went to Fort Sam Houston in Texas for medics' training. It wasn't bad, because there were so many COs there. Mostly, we learned how to make hospital corners on beds, give shots, and do IVs. Real minor stuff. Not much battlefield training. After only ten weeks, I got my orders for Vietnam. I remember the night before I left, sitting with an old friend, telling him how scared I was. He said, "Have another beer." Those were the days when a six-pack could cure anything.

In December 1968, I went to Vietnam with the First Air Cavalry. On the plane, I was excited. I knew it would be an adventure, though I didn't know what kind of adventure. I was very proud, even arrogant about going to Vietnam. It seemed unique to be a CO, yet go to war. I don't think I showed any fear. I knew I had to act strong. I felt I was walking on the edge.

Two days after I got to Vietnam, I was in my first firefight. The first guy I worked on had a bullet through his chest. When I got to him, he didn't lie still. It wasn't like you see in the movies. With a bullet through him, he wasn't going to sit there. I could see daylight through his chest.

I knew I had to act fast. My lieutenant screamed at me, "Hey, we don't have time for this." Other guys tried to pull the injured guy out of the line of fire. But I kept yelling, "I've got to work on him right here. I've got to work on him now." I was crying as I worked on him.

My lieutenant smacked me on the head, screaming, "No, we don't have time for this. Get back." Then I just lost it. I cried and screamed at him to let me work.

For a long time after that, I was very hard on myself for losing it like that. Now, I realize I was eighteen years old. I had just gone through hospital training. I was two days out of the States. Suddenly I was supposed to be totally cool and collected under very hazardous conditions. I think I had pretty high expectations for myself. I think all of us did who went to Vietnam.

During my first few weeks in Vietnam, most of the other guys didn't want to get to know me. I didn't understand it then, but later I realized that they didn't want to get too friendly with a new guy. Because it was usually the new ones who got killed. As I stayed there longer, I was careful too not to get emotionally attached to new guys.

It's my guess that if you look at statistics, most guys got killed in the first three months. That's where our highest casualties were. It was because new guys didn't have a sixth sense. They didn't have the coolness. They'd do stupid things. If you made it through your first four months in Vietnam, you were probably going to live. I'm thankful I made it. A lot of guys didn't.

As a medic, I was like a mother hen. I was really protective of guys in my platoon. If they were wronged, I felt I was wronged. I used to get in huge fights with the battalion commander, because I saw first sergeants purposely send guys on patrol who had no business being out — just because the sergeants didn't like them.

I remember one guy who had a shoulder wound. I sent him to the field hospital. But three days later, his sergeant sent him back out. I was outraged. I planned to send him back to the hospital the next day. But he got hit again that night, this time much more seriously.

I was steamed. I knew if I went through the quote "normal" chain of command and put in a complaint, nothing would happen. So I got on the helicopter back to the field hospital. When I got off, the first sergeant was walking up the dirt road toward me. I walked up to him and, without saying a word, punched him square in the face. We ended up fighting and rolling around on the ground.

109

I'm amazed I was so stupid. But I was livid, and I'm glad I hit him. Even though I was a CO, I had a temper.

I gave a lot of talks to guys about what to do if they were hit or if someone around them was hit. The main thing I said was, "Don't let the fear get ahold of you." I believed that if guys were still alive after being hit — still alive when I got to them — the chances were good they'd make it out, if they stayed cool. I felt confident in myself.

But I never talked about what to do with your sadness and what to do with your grief.

My being a CO would come up once in a while in passing. Other guys' reaction would be, "Criminee! This guy's out here and he's being shot at with the rest of us. It doesn't matter whether he's a CO or not."

Some medics carried weapons. I never did. I was tempted a few times, especially the first few months. There's something about being shot at. But in a firefight, I had more than enough to do, and others protected me.

Actually, being mortared is much scarier than being shot at. It shakes you. It really shakes you.

One time, we got surrounded by the North Vietnamese Army. We pulled farther and farther back, leaving a few rifles here and a dead body there, until we were set up in a U shape. The North Vietnamese were all around us. We had a lot of cover from a double canopy of trees, but our helicopters couldn't get in to get the wounded or to give us cover fire. They just couldn't get in.

We sat there for eight days.

At first, it was only light mortars at night. After a while, we got used to it. When we'd hear a couple of mortars, I'd think, "Am I going to get in my hole for this? No, I'm not going to bother getting up."

But it got worse. On the sixth night, I was lying there hearing "thump, thump," and I thought, "Am I going to get up? Nah, I'm not going to get up." And then suddenly I heard this "tsu-tsu-tsu-tsu-tsu-tsu-tsu." One of their guys had come up to our perimeter to get a read on our location. And, boy, they just started walking the mortars in on us. We jumped into our foxholes, but they had us. They dropped their mortars right in our holes.

It was eerie, working in the pitch-dark on guys who were severely wounded. When you're surrounded, you can't turn on your flashlight. So you have to feel around for their wounds. I could help a few who had minor wounds, but for most guys there was not a hell of a lot I could do, except comfort them in death. That's all I could do.

I had never experienced death on that level before.

The next morning, we had a lot of wounded, and we still didn't know how we were going to get out of there. We had a West Point guy as lieutenant who had been in-country only three weeks. I didn't know him very well, though I had talked to him a little about his family.

West Point guys often got into dangerous situations because of what they had been taught. He said, "I'm going to take five of you guys and go further up and scout the area." I had been in-country nine months. I had friends there who had been in-country even longer. We said, "You're going alone, because we aren't going with you."

But he managed to convince five of the new guys to go with him. They got only about two hundred yards before the snipers in the trees just nailed them. We could hear them crying out for help. We got up there, and all were dead, except the lieutenant. He was shot in the stomach.

We began to pull him back, and he kept saying, "I can't breathe. I can't breathe."

I said, "We've got to put this guy down. I've got to work on him now."

But bullets were hitting all around us, following us as we worked our way back down the hill. The other guys said, "We can't put him down."

By the time we got back, the lieutenant was dead.

Even though I didn't agree with him and I didn't like him, I knew he had a family. I knew he had a couple of kids. He's one I'll always remember.

Most of us in Vietnam believed that stateside duty was really bad. Not because of the civilians, but because all the lifers were there. All the guys signing up for thirty years in the military. There was a lot of make-work, a lot of heavy-duty military "do it right, do it my way." I felt Vietnam was better than that. In Vietnam, you didn't have to do it their way. You'd just do it. There was a lot of room to be a maverick. I knew how to get my way in Vietnam. The idea of going to the States scared me to death.

111

The Strength Not to Fight

So when I finished my tour of duty, I signed up for a second year in Vietnam. I chose not to go back to the States in between. I went to Bangkok instead. That's when I fell in love with Bangkok.

My second year in Vietnam — 1970 — was with Medevac. It was all volunteer, like family. We didn't think about rank. It was a breeze. It was *fun*. I hate to use that word, but it was fun. I was a sergeant. I had enough time in-country to know how to use the system.

I had twenty-four hours on, then forty-eight hours off. Most of the time, I looked forward to the twenty-four hours on. I was an adrenaline junkie. I liked the feeling of risk, of being in situations where I had to think really fast. I would get on helicopters and we'd fly into hot zones and pick up the wounded. I'd work on guys right there in the helicopter. It was exciting. I felt I was doing something important that had meaning to me. It was the first job I ever had that I loved. And I got to walk my edges.

Being a medic was all-consuming. It was my whole life. It was who I was as a person. Then, in the ninth month of my second year in Vietnam, I got hit, and they said I had to leave. God, the grief I felt. I was scared to death to go back to the States. I had no idea what to do with my life. I didn't want to leave Vietnam.

I was twenty years old.

If I could have lasted just another month in Vietnam, I would have had an early out. Instead, I had eight months left to serve, and they sent me to Germany. God, I was pissed. I was flabbergasted. It just blew me away. Nobody got sent to Germany after Vietnam. I believed it was because they looked at my record and saw I was a CO.

I had a Silver Star, two Bronze Stars, and two Army Commendation Medals. When I got to Germany, they thought they had themselves a real Vietnam vet on their hands. And they did.

They also had a guy who had never worked with regular army before and who was very angry. I was angry at leaving Vietnam and angry at going to Germany. I didn't know what to do with myself. I felt like my whole support system had been wiped out. I didn't fit in too well, to say the least.

When I got there, they assigned me to the motor pool. I said, "Work on vehicles? You aren't going to put me there."

They said, "That's what you're going to do."

112

I said, "We'll see about that." But they had me. I had served my country in Vietnam as a medic, and there I was in the motor pool.

I know the army is just interested in your body. But in Vietnam, I experienced part of my soul. I was able to see others more deeply, the deeper parts of relationships. Love, the bottom, underneath stuff, the things that really matter. That experience joins you together with others.

In Germany, I never felt I belonged. I did my time and in 1971, when my enlistment was up, I left.

Our culture supports going to war. Everybody supports it — men and women. The army is an extension of the family, where the family gets its honor. It's the one place you can test yourself. So even though my mother supported my being a CO, when I came home with a Silver Star and Bronze Medals, she was very proud to show them off.

My first year back in the States was the hardest year I've ever had. Going to Germany had hurt a lot, because I lost the sense of camaraderie. I felt angry, not just toward the military and the government, but toward the United States in general. I hated the sense of apathy I saw everywhere when I returned, the sense of every man for himself. Everyone seemed to feel, "The government can do whatever it damn well pleases. Just don't interrupt my Monday night football."

I felt good about my time in Vietnam, about who I was there, and what I had experienced. I didn't feel I came back from Vietnam as damaged goods. But I remember talking with my brother when I got back. He said, "Let's go out for a beer and talk about the babes." I kept talking about Vietnam. He asked why I was always talking about Vietnam.

Eventually, I put that on myself, feeling he was right. Yeah, I shouldn't be talking about Vietnam. It is hard to explain Vietnam to someone who has not experienced it. Not just the place, but the feelings. If I try, I get a blank look.

I tried to talk to my grandfather. He had always been one of the few positive male role models in my life. I went to his house one day to see him. I went in, with tears coming out of my eyes. I was feeling really sad about my life, and I needed to talk. But he was real uncomfortable, and I remember him turning around with his back to me, and then walking out of the room. I really loved him, and I wish he could have been there for me. I needed someone I could touch.

Then, during my first year back, I lost most of my family. My two brothers died in drowning accidents, within a few months of each other. Both had been in Vietnam, one very early in 1966, the other in 1970. But we had never talked about the war. I never even learned what they did there.

Then, in that same year, my dad died of liver disease.

I had been counting on my brothers and my father to give me some sense of connection, some sense of belonging. Instead, I lost them all.

Robert Bly says that if you're not willing to deal with your grief, then you have depression. That's what happened to me. I felt like I was one of the walking wounded. I wondered how I was going to save my life. So I decided to move to Bangkok. That was in 1972. Before I left, I said goodbye to my mother. That was the last time I talked with her for the next eighteen years.

At first, I just hung out in Bangkok, mostly getting high. There were a lot of vets there, most of them estranged from their families, some from the government. Some were AWOL. I felt I belonged there. I felt at home. I could be with guys from Vietnam. The culture was similar. It was inexpensive. I especially liked the climate. During the monsoon, the rain came down in buckets. Other times, it was humid, so wet you could cut the air with a knife. I liked the feeling that I could taste the culture in the air. I could smell it, the spices, the urine, the dust. It was just like Vietnam.

After being in Bangkok for a while, I went to a Buddhist retreat, where I met a vet from Nam who invited me to a refugee camp where he worked.

There were three or four thousand refugees in the camp. Orphans were everywhere. I spent my time with them. I ate with them, I hung out with them, I slept in tents with them. Because I was a medic, I started treating lice, working on people with malnutrition, and setting up latrines. I didn't make much money. Just enough to get along. But I loved it.

Most of the refugees had lost several family members — children, a wife or a husband, cousins, uncles. Some had lost everyone. I don't know, maybe it's a stereotype, but I felt because they had seen war, they were able to stay in the here-and-now. They were able to grieve about the ones they had lost. They were able to live in the joy or the sadness of the moment.

It's always the civilians who suffer most. Yes, we lost sixty thousand. But the Vietnamese lost hundreds and hundreds of thousands. Many were civilians, children and old folks. Their homes were destroyed, their fields were ruined, the economic basis of their whole lives was shattered. The effects will last for generations.

When I finally returned to the United States, I felt very lonely. I enrolled in a community college to try to figure out what to do with my life. I remember the instructor in my philosophy course telling us what he would have done if he had been in Vietnam. He said soldiers were killers because they shot people. I got angry, and finally told him he had nothing to say unless he had gone through it himself. You can say you won't shoot if someone's pointing a gun at you. But until you've been there, your judgment about what you would do has no validity. You never truly know until you are there.

Without Vietnam, I probably would have spent thirty years working a job, going for the whole nine yards — the house and the car and the kids. Part of me wishes I could have done that.

But to be a CO, to have gone to Vietnam and to have really looked inside myself, even if it was painful, was worth it. Vietnam opened my eyes.

Maybe I wish my life could have been different. But I've already crossed the bridge. I can't go back.

———

When I was bar mitzvahed at the age of fifteen, there were ten of us in the class. We did a service based on the Ten Commandments. It fell to me to do "Thou shalt not kill." In my little sermonette, I quoted a passage from the Jerusalem Talmud that goes: "One man alone was brought forth at the time of creation to teach us that he who destroys one human soul is regarded as though he destroyed a whole world, while he who preserves one soul is regarded as though he preserved the whole world."

———

My philosophy is that the opposite of war is fishing. George Orwell said that.

I was an outcast among other soldiers in Saigon. Because I was a CO applicant, I got transferred out of the Phoenix Program to an office where my major gave me little jobs with no responsibility. I spent my lunch hours meditating in the chapel. Those were the only sane moments of my last days in Vietnam.

I was interviewed by a psychiatrist in Saigon, who looked over my application, nodded, and said, "You sure have moved around a lot."

I said, "Yes, I have."

He said four or five more times, "You sure have moved around a lot."

I said, "Yes, I have." Finally, I said, "You don't have to agree with me. You just have to figure out whether I'm sane."

He said, "You're not crazy."

I said, "Sir, that's all you need to put in the report."

I also had to see the chaplain to discuss my religious beliefs. He read my application and said that my understanding of ethics was not very developed. He also said he couldn't quarrel with my position. We talked a bit. He recommended some books to read. Then I left.

I hadn't been a member of any organized church, but just then, Dan Seeger's Supreme Court case was being applied, which meant that deeply held moral conviction was equivalent to membership in an institutional church. So my application became legally plausible. Meanwhile, friends in the States wrote to me that the FBI was interviewing them.

I was concerned about what would happen to me, so I wrote to Senator Henry Jackson. So did my mother. One day, the colonel who was head of personnel where I worked called me in and said, "Lieutenant, how are we treating you?" As we talked, I saw on his desk a three-by-five pink sheet with Senator Jackson's letterhead at the top. Some Jackson aide had taken thirty seconds to respond to my letter. The colonel ordered one of his captains to help me compose a letter to Senator Jackson describing my good treatment. Jackson, that old hawk who damn near invented the Vietnam War, was one of the reasons I was treated well in Vietnam.

The Tet Offensive had just ended. There were still bullet holes in the windows at the officers' mess where I worked. We were getting shot at going back and forth to work on the buses. Just then, my major told me to do a survey of all the U.S. advisers in South Vietnam. That meant I'd have to go to fire bases all over the country, right into areas where there was heavy fighting.

As I prepared for the trip, the major asked several times how I felt about it, always reminding me there would be fighting. I'd say, "Yes, sir, I understand, sir." He'd say, "It's not like Saigon." Finally, I said, "It's not *where* I am that bothers me. It's what I'm doing." Two days later, he ordered me to remain in Saigon. I think he was testing to see if I was applying for CO status just because I was afraid of combat.

One day, in November 1968, the major asked me to empty his wastebasket. I wasn't supposed to do that work, but I went over anyway and picked it up. As I did, he said, "There's something in there that might interest you." Lying on top of the pile was a letter to me from the Pentagon saying that my conscientious objection application had been approved.

After that, I waited in Saigon for orders to leave Vietnam for the States. That was the hardest time. I knew I would be discharged, but I didn't know when.

During that time, my colonel told me he was disturbed by the war. He said, "This isn't the way war is supposed to be fought. This isn't the way the military is supposed to be run." I worked in headquarters and talked to colonels regularly. I never met anybody who thought things were going right in Vietnam. Nobody.

At Christmas, 1968, I finally got my orders to leave Saigon. I was flown first to San Francisco. Once a week for the next month I had to report for duty, but there was nothing for me to do. I expected to be assigned to alternative service. But one day, when I showed up for duty, I was asked to sign a form for an honorable discharge.

No alternative service. Nothing. I just walked away. Later, I went to graduate school on the GI Bill.

━━━

I came from a privileged background, a small, rural Mennonite community. You'd think that a Mennonite congregation would have talked about the war, but I never faced any of the questions about pacifism at church. Yet the war bothered me a lot and I knew I would have to face it if I decided not to stay in college.

When I got out of high school, I went to Freeman Junior College

117

in South Dakota. I soon got tired of school, but I knew I'd be drafted if I stopped going. I was nineteen, and not opposed to the idea of serving my country in some way, so I began looking for a possible alternative service placement. I had especially enjoyed a psychology class, so I was attracted to the possibility of working in mental health.

In the fall of 1967 I applied for my CO deferment and I was soon granted CO status. No hearing. I got approval from my draft board to work as a psychiatric aide at a well-respected mental health center, an in-patient psychiatric hospital in a small town in Kansas. In September 1967, I moved there to begin my training at the hospital. I was treated like other employees, except I got more of the lousy shifts, like Saturday nights and Sunday mornings. The administrators rotated night duty among the COs. Other than that, we didn't receive any different treatment.

My job was to get people up in the morning, make sure they got their meals, and help them take care of basic hygiene. A lot of the patients were very psychotic. I fed them and scooped them up in my arms to move them from place to place.

We had many super-depressed housewives, who just sat and looked at the wall, day in and day out. I took them into a tile shower and made them scrub the grout with a toothbrush for hours on end, until they became furious. When they got mad, their anger energized them enough so that we could work on what was going on in their lives. Treating people like that was totally foreign to what I believed. But I saw it work.

Some patients were violent. When they were upset, we could usually talk them down, but sometimes there was no choice and we had to subdue them. We never tackled violent people one-on-one. We always had at least three or four to overpower them. Agitated people can be extremely strong, so sometimes it was touch and go. I hated that part of it, but I never felt any contradiction with my pacifism, because we'd overpower people only when they intended to harm themselves or someone else. We never hurt anyone.

Near the end of my time there, we began to get kids with drug problems. What a gruesome population to work with! Their pain, the problems they were experiencing, were very, very difficult. By that time, I was glad to leave.

When I finished my alternative service, I went to Wichita State

University to get a B.A. in social work. I soon made friends there with some Vietnam vets. In a strange way, I felt real close to them, even though we had none of the same experiences.

Here were guys with pain oozing out of every pore, desperately trying to put their lives back together. But to many students, they were dirt because they'd been to Vietnam. I tried to comprehend the pain these guys had built up from pulling triggers and bombing villages filled with innocent people. It's one thing to shoot at another soldier through rifle sights, but to attack villages, that's different altogether.

Do I understand vets? I don't know. I've had a few traumas in my life, and I know something about pain, but that's nothing like living with having murdered people, even under orders.

━━━

In my CO application, I said I wouldn't go in the army as a medic. In truth, I would have done it if the only other choice would have been to go to jail. But I didn't say that to my draft board in Houston.

I was working in Canada at the time, at a place for emotionally disturbed, schizophrenic kids. Kids who hallucinated and who scratched themselves constantly. Hard-core kids.

The place was beautiful. It had a one-to-one kid-to-staff ratio. Kids were set up in familylike units, with one male and one female staff member and three or four kids plus support staff. The theory was psychoanalytical. The kids were free to regress to whatever level they felt comfortable in, and then to start rebuilding themselves. I had a fabulous time in a demanding job.

I wanted to continue that job as a career, but I couldn't because of the draft. My draft board wouldn't approve that work for my alternative service. I had to return to the United States or become a fugitive. So even though I didn't get shot in Vietnam, the war changed my life.

I told my folks I was applying to be a CO just at the time the North Koreans captured the ship, the *Pueblo*. My parents were appalled, and wrote to me that they couldn't believe I would do such a terrible thing to my country. They wrote about my ancestors and the freedom we hold dear, and they asked me to write to my draft board saying I had changed my mind because of the *Pueblo* incident. I told them I loved them, but I wasn't going to change my mind for anything or anybody.

In 1968, I left Texas to visit friends in Chicago while the SDS was having its national conference there. That was the convention at which a decisive break occurred in the SDS. One faction was a dogmatic organization called the Progressive Labor party, which had split from the Communist party years before. Other factions were the Revolutionary Union, which later became the Revolutionary Communist party, and the group that eventually became the Weathermen. My friends' place was the Weathermen crash pad, where they composed the Weathermen Manifesto. It wasn't a bad statement. It didn't sound as crazy as the group later became.

The convention was held in an armory in Chicago, where I heard Bob Avakian give fiery speeches. Everybody was giving fiery speeches. Some people argued that we should go to the smokestack towns in the Midwest to do proletarian worker organizing. Others supported illegal actions against the war. Everybody felt the need to escalate their commitment. It was apparent we were dealing with something a whole lot bigger than we'd anticipated, and a lot uglier, more violent and dangerous. We had to toughen up. The Weathermen turned that idea into a religion.

I had always paid lip service to the idea that you have to defend your beliefs, go out and fight for them. But what did that mean? In Chicago, I started thinking seriously about what would be effective. Screw the symbolic stuff. If I was going to fight, I might as well try to win.

Still, I was never tempted to plant bombs or shoot people. I was skeptical about whether that could produce any results. So while I got more militant, I wasn't interested in producing injuries.

Then, right during the SDS conference, I heard that my CO application had been approved. It seemed pretty ironic that I got my CO deferment at the Weathermen convention that was planning the destruction of "Amerikkka."

For my alternative service, I got a job in a hippie free clinic called the Open Door Clinic. The people at the clinic were very supportive of anyone who opposed the war. They gave jobs to COs even when there wasn't much work to do.

I didn't put myself into an objectified, abstract religious box. I considered my CO work to be political. So while I didn't do forty hours a week of alternative service, I did sixty hours a week of political work against the war. Sometimes, I didn't show up at the clinic for weeks on end. My life was centered on trying to save America from itself. I figured America was getting its money's worth out of me. In retrospect, I still feel the same way.

My parents didn't like my being a CO. I didn't make a secret of my opinions. I'd lock horns with my dad, and I felt I could knock him down. When he threw me curve balls, I didn't hit a home run every time up to the plate, but it was a fair fight. I was pleased with myself for competing with him intellectually. My memory is that I fought intense, pitched battles with my father and blasted big holes in his defenses.

My mom tried hard to make peace in the family. That's what mothers always did.

I continued for a while to visit home to go hunting with my dad back in Texas, but we kept having memorable blowups about the war. In 1973, I stopped going home for the summers. Eventually, I stopped going altogether.

Growing up in rural Indiana, I was pretty far away from political activism. Because I was a member of the Church of the Brethren, I applied to be a CO when I turned eighteen in 1968. But I had a student deferment to attend the General Motors Institute in Flint, Michigan. During my first year there, I realized that neither the factory nor the office was where I wanted to spend my life, so I dropped out of school and entered the Brethren Voluntary Service in Baltimore in October 1969. I worked at the Joseph House, a social service center in the inner city. I interviewed people who came for help, I put together boxes of food to give away, I gathered donations, and I did a lot of other odd jobs. I quickly received my CO deferment, and my work at Joseph House was approved for my alternative service.

During late '69 and early '70, I gradually came to see my draft card as a membership card in the war machine. The Moratorium and the Vietnam Mobilization marches in October and November of '69 had a big influence on my thinking. Finally, in June 1970, I returned my draft card. My letter to my draft board in Pennsylvania was a little sarcastic. I addressed it to my "Local Death Board":

Enclosed you will find two cards, one of which declares me to be a part of the Selective Service System. The other states that I am doing alternative service through an approved civilian work agency. I will not keep either of these cards any longer. I reject the first because I refuse to be part of the most destructive war machine in the history of the world, the second because though I will continue to work through the same agency, I do not consider and never have considered this work to be "my duty to my government." I do not feel it necessary to give a part of my life in the service of my country, but that I give as much of my life as possible for the good of my neighbor. Because the Vietnamese and Cambodians and the people of every other land threatened by the American military are my neighbors, I must remove myself from the system that is trying to destroy them.

The clerk at the draft board immediately returned the cards, with a letter saying, "I would like to remind you that you are required by law to carry them. Your prompt cooperation is always appreciated." So I sent the cards back with a letter patterned on theirs: "I would like the enclosed materials to be included in my file in your office. I would like to remind you that you are required by federal law to include in my file all items which I've sent you for that purpose. Your prompt cooperation is always appreciated."

Eventually, I got a letter saying that my case had been forwarded for prosecution. Then, in December 1970, the Maryland Selective Service, which had taken over my case, changed my alternative service assignment to the Goodwill Industries in Baltimore. I think they knew I would refuse to change work, so that gave them a second count in the indictment — refusing an alternative service assignment, in addition to refusing to carry my draft card.

I didn't hear anything until September 1971, when I stopped at my parents' house in Indiana on the way to Chicago for the draft trial of a friend. I found in my mail there two letters from the Baltimore federal court saying that I had been indicted and that my arraignment was scheduled for August. I had missed my court date.

I decided to go to Chicago anyway to meet with my friend's support group. I figured I could get some advice from them, and then later decide what to do about missing my court date. On my way, I was hitchhiking near Kankakee, Illinois, when I got stopped by a state trooper. In all my years of hitchhiking, that was only the second time I was ever stopped. The trooper checked my ID and let me go, but about five minutes later, he came roaring back with his sirens on and lights flashing, and arrested me right there.

In the county jail, I was fitted with a coverall uniform that read "KKK County Jail" on the back. Maybe that's one way to abbreviate Kankakee, but I was suspicious of the Klan's role there. And the cells were racially segregated.

After two days there, federal marshals transferred me to a federal facility in Danville. I couldn't afford the $5,000 bail, so a friend contacted a local Brethren Church couple, who put up the deed to their house for my bail. The magistrate processed the papers, and as we were leaving the jail, the couple introduced themselves to me. The magistrate was flabbergasted that these people didn't even know me, yet risked their house for me. Their action was a real Christian witness of people coming to each other's aid.

Back in federal court in Baltimore, I pleaded guilty. In January 1972 the sentencing hearing took place. My probation officer seemed impressed by my personal views and my conscience, and tried to keep me out of jail by recommending probation. But the judge rejected his report and gave me three years in prison instead. I was taken immediately to the Baltimore city jail, and then transferred to the federal prison in Ashland, Kentucky.

So even though I was officially a CO already doing alternative service, I served eighteen months in prison for refusing to carry my draft card and for refusing to change alternative service assignments. I was released in July 1973.

After I was released from prison, I gave a talk at my local church. One of the people there happened to be an FBI agent, who didn't believe my story that I had done two years of alternative service but still got sentenced to prison just for refusing to carry my draft card. He did some checking into my files and later told my pastor that I was suspected of serious crimes, including urging high school students to raid draft boards and being involved in the break-in at the FBI office in Media, Pennsylvania. He said that was the reason I got a long jail sentence.

None of those allegations were even close to the truth, but they had been made in front of the judge, though not in front of my lawyer or me. That stuff could never stand up in court, but it was part of the weight on which I was sentenced.

My father was not a very verbal man. He was almost deaf by the time I was born. But I distinctly remember him talking about the Japanese internment camps in the forties as one of the most horrible things this country had ever done. He couldn't believe that we would be so hypocritical to fight for freedom but then intern Japanese Americans. My father was a quiet man who didn't show his feelings, but I remember he spoke with deep feeling about that.

After I was convicted for failing to register, I was awaiting sentencing, when a reporter from the *Wenatchee World* came to our orchard to interview me. Suddenly, the reporter turned to my dad and said, "How do you feel about your son, about what's happening to him?" Tears came to my father's eyes as he said, "We're behind him. My wife and I love him. The only bad thing we feel is that we worry about his safety." That was the first time I ever saw my dad cry.

The army says it builds character. Waiting six months for sentencing really builds character, too. For my conviction on refusing to register, I was sentenced to three years' probation, with two years of work in the national interest for no pay.

I struggled with whether or not I should accept the sentence. I had fought against a system that was still drafting people for the war. The carpet bombing was continuing and Nixon was "Vietnamizing" the war — which was his term for getting American soldiers out of harm's way while doing more aerial bombing from two miles up, oblivious to the deaths of innocent people. I had to decide whether my noncooperation with the draft would also mean refusal to do alternative service.

I finally concluded that I hadn't participated in the Selective Service System. I was a federal convict, and by doing service, I would be cooperating only with the federal probation office. I was ready to make my accommodations and rationalizations.

But I did refuse to sign the probation agreement until I added a little disclaimer. I wrote I would fulfill my probation "only insofar as my conscience will allow."

I wanted to join Brethren Voluntary Service, which had people working in day-care centers, federal Head Start programs, and health care — exactly the kinds of service jobs I was supposed to do. But the judge told the probation officer not to accept it, probably out of his hostility toward the Brethren Church. In my trial, I had attempted to use church statements to show that my church had encouraged my commitment to nonviolence. The judge probably thought that if I went into Brethren Voluntary Service, I would never be rehabilitated. I guess he wanted me to learn my lesson. It was comical.

Eventually, I got approval to work at an alternative school in York, Pennsylvania, that emphasized peace studies. I bought a motorcycle and had a wonderful adventure, driving across the country. My motorcycle broke down, I hopped freight trains, and I hitchhiked, finally arriving in Harrisburg, where I reported to my probation officer.

During my stay in Pennsylvania, the Watergate hearings were being held in Washington. It was history in the making, and I wanted to be there. I wasn't supposed to travel across state lines, but I broke probation to go to the hearings. I had a sense that something earthshattering was happening. I had to see it.

I waited in line at the Senate, and I got in to see Nixon's secretary, Rose Mary Woods. Everything the antiwar movement had been saying about Nixon — the lying, immoral bombing, sabotaging the peace movement, wire-tapping, government spying on its people — all that was being verified by the hearings. Suddenly, on national television, from the Senate of the United States of America, there was the evidence. It was shocking, yet validating and vindicating to think that perhaps the country wouldn't tolerate the lies and the deception any longer.

Ironically, the job in Pennsylvania was awful for me. It was a real counterculture group, with unstable marriages and relationships, people breaking up, exchanging partners, and no structure. I had just experienced a powerful spiritual uplifting during my trial, a sense of power and God's presence. Suddenly, there I was in a commune, a real downer, a miserable place for a young person still developing a sense of what's right and wrong. It was not the kind of Christian voluntary service I wanted.

After three months, I told the Harrisburg probation officer I needed to find another job. It was no problem. He didn't give a hoot about me anyway. Compared to the violent people he handled, I was low risk. So I got his permission to go to the Church of the

Brethren National Conference in California, where the director of the Brethren Volunteer Service found me a job as a teacher's aide in a day-care center in a Head Start program in Fresno.

While working in Fresno, I did counterrecruitment against the military in inner-city high schools. I talked to high school kids about draft resistance and why people should not kill each other. I was a white country bumpkin having my first interracial experience. It was emotionally and spiritually nourishing, and I developed friendships that lasted for years.

At the end of my first year in Fresno, my father had a heart attack. His forty-acre apple orchard was in full bloom, and my mom couldn't handle it. So on my twenty-first birthday, I flew home. I ran the apple orchard all the way through harvest, while my dad was recovering from heart surgery. At the end of the harvest, I appealed to the probation office, saying that I wasn't a threat to the community, so why not just take me off the books. They said, "Sure." And that was it. My sentence was over.

■

After I refused induction and was indicted, two friends tried to talk me out of going to prison. One of them had been in the naval reserves, where he was a dental technician with a luxury assignment — a year and a half of active duty on a tiny island in the middle of Honolulu Bay. He convinced me to go to a couple of his reserve meetings. Meanwhile, I read about people in prison, talked to everyone I could, and gradually became afraid of prison. Most of my family and friends supported my CO stand, but they agreed I should avoid prison.

I was interested in dentistry and had taken some predental courses in college. I believed that a felony record would mean I could never pursue dentistry. So all sorts of things were swirling around in my head, and I decided to contact a navy recruiter.

The first recruiter told me, "Sorry, kid, you've been indicted. You're going to prison. That's it." In San Francisco, I saw another recruiter, who took my name and said he'd see what he could do. Soon after, he contacted me to say that the Justice Department had offered me a deal. They wouldn't prosecute me if I joined the navy within a month.

I was adamant with the recruiter that I wanted a guaranteed spot in dental school. He agreed, and we made the deal, which required me to sign a four-year commitment to the navy. So I did it. I felt I was selling out, like I was being manipulated by the system, and doing exactly what the system wanted me to do. But at least I had stayed out of prison.

I had to fly from San Francisco to San Diego for boot camp. Before departing, I put on ceremonial clothes — some jeans I liked, my best running shoes, and a Pendleton shirt my father had given me for my first bicycle ride down the coast.

On my first day at boot camp, besides losing all the hair on my head, I had to wrap my civilian clothes in a box and mail them home. I wanted civilian clothes close by in case I decided not to go through with boot camp. So I sent them to my parents in Los Angeles. When they received the package in the mail, that was the first they knew about my enlistment. Until then, they had no idea I was going to join the military.

On my first night at camp, the sergeants came in about three o'clock in the morning, flashing lights and kicking over garbage cans. For the next two months, they deprived us of sleep and moved us to different barracks time and time again. We were always disoriented, really bamboozled.

I constantly thought about running away. The entire naval base was surrounded by a Marine base. There were lots of terrorizing stories about what happened to people who tried to get away by land. We heard that the Marines would catch you, beat you up, and throw you in their brig until the navy extracted you and then threw you in the naval brig.

We were on an island in San Diego Bay connected to the mainland by an arched bridge. Each morning, we marched over the bridge to the mainland. I figured the only way for me to escape was off that bridge. I planned to swim across the bay and work my way to my grandmother's house, not far away. I didn't know if she even knew I was in the navy, but I suspected she'd help me, give me some clothes, and get me a ride north to Canada.

Looking back, I think the patrol boats might have gotten me. But I didn't see it that way then. Anyway, I didn't run. I stayed put.

For a while, we carried around pieces of old rifles with barrels stuffed with lead to make them heavy. Finally, one day we went to the rifle range for real shooting. We had to lie down with a small rifle, about the size of a .22, and only eight shells. I don't know why, but I wanted to do my best. I had a .22 when I was a kid in

California, so I was pretty comfortable shooting. When we finished, we stood in formation until our commander announced the results. I was the best shot in the company. Pretty amusing, since I had refused induction.

That was my entire experience with firearms in the navy. Because I was a musician, they assigned me to the band. I spent the rest of the time in boot camp marching with a trumpet rather than a rifle.

At the end of boot camp, my mother and my grandmother came for the graduation ceremony, where the band marched around foolishly in what we called the Drum and Stumble Corps. It was gratifying to have made it that far. After thinking constantly about running away, all I had to do was walk out the gates, through the forbidden crossing. I went out with my papers, in my dress blues and my white stripes. As I left, I knew that nothing would be that hard in the next four years.

After boot camp, I went directly to dental tech school. On the first day I filled out what we called the Dream Sheet, where I listed my preferences for duty after graduation. I wanted to be assigned to the Whidbey Island Naval Base. I knew that only the top one or two graduates got their preferences. So I studied hard and really applied myself. I wanted to get the best marks in class. And that's exactly what I did. I got the best marks. And I got assigned to Whidbey Island.

At Whidbey, I worked at the dental clinic for over three years. When I had only a couple of months of duty left, my boss stood in front of the whole clinic and pinned a Second Class medal on me. It was a pretty medal. I felt gratified, like I had some control over my life, like I could win and not be powerless. I fit the bill.

I was twenty-three when I went in the navy, twenty-seven when I got out. I was hard on myself about cooperating with the military. I felt like I was doing the right thing personally, but the wrong thing in the bigger picture. By cooperating, I did a disservice to young people who came after me. Yet I believe it was best for me not to go to prison.

I'm not happy or settled with what I did. I don't accept my cooperation with the military. I don't accept what I did.

I've never run into anyone who did what I did, but there must be thousands who cooperated even though they believed it was wrong. I haven't talked to anybody about this. I feel isolated. I don't know who to talk to.

———

The killings at Kent State in the spring of 1970 were the decisive event for me. I was at Oberlin College, majoring in organ music and religion, just down the road from Kent State. The shootings conveyed violence in human terms and gave me first-hand experience of what violence really does to people. It had a major effect on my decision to apply for conscientious objection.

Oberlin's response to the killings was a performance of Mozart's *Requiem* in the National Cathedral in Washington, D.C., in memory of those shot at Kent State and Jackson State, and also for all the victims, both Vietnamese and American, of the Indochina war. The *Requiem* was performed with two hundred voices, full orchestra and soloists, after only three days' rehearsal. It was incredible. I cannot describe the deep impact that concert had on me.

When I left Oberlin, my draft board didn't immediately revoke my student deferment. So in 1972, I wrote to them and said, "Hey, guys, I'm not a student anymore. Take me off II-S status. I want to apply to be a CO." My lottery number was 95.

I decided I would take one of two paths — either Church Divinity School of the Pacific, which is the Episcopal seminary in Berkeley, or alternative service at Macalester College in St. Paul, Minnesota.

At that point, in late 1972, there were so many COs that draft boards couldn't find enough punitive places for alternative service. The clever thing was to write your draft board with a proposal and have all your ducks lined up. If you knew what kinds of questions they would ask and you could address them in your letter, they'd be relieved to get rid of you. In my case, I got a job offer at Macalester; the job was not replacing anyone who was currently in the position; the salary was only $1,925 per year; and the job took advantage of my skills and education. My draft board approved it.

I did two years' alternative service as a musician in the Macalester theater and music departments and at the college chapel. That was the start of seven years as a professional musician.

My supervisor at Macalester knew I was a CO and was very supportive. But the college president was not. Perhaps it was because I was hired outside the normal head count and my salary came from somebody's discretionary fund. Or perhaps it was because the major source of funding for Macalester was DeWitt Wallace, the owner of *Reader's Digest*, who was quite upset with the antiwar movement.

The worst aspect of my alternative service was the lack of money. Not only did I have to work for such an incredibly low salary, but I also had to start paying back my National Defense student loans. People serving in the military, including COs, had their payments deferred, but civilian alternative service did not. Even fifty dollars a month is a lot if you're making only $150 a month. I resented it, and it took me a long time to get out from under the financial debt.

———

At Harvard, I was a volunteer social worker. I worked with low-income, inner-city kids from the housing projects around Cambridge and Boston. I spent three years intensively involved, first as a volunteer and then as an organizer.

When I graduated in June 1968, I planned to continue at Harvard, working for a master's degree in education. But midway through my first year in that program, my draft board called me up, saying I had to do my alternative service.

At that time, I was volunteering as a counselor in the Cambridge technical high school. I figured working with low-income kids was a pretty good alternative service job, so I applied to stay there. But the director of the Selective Service in Massachusetts turned me down, saying it was insufficiently disruptive of my life. My draft board assigned me instead to a state mental hospital, where I worked for three years with felony sex offenders, guys who had done horrible things. Most of them had been severely abused as children. They were victims, who then became aggressors, in a clear cycle of violence.

I got to like a number of them. It was both sad and funny to see things through their eyes. I remember one time rolling on the floor in laughter as one guy told his story. He had been drunk with his buddies, driving on the highway, when they went around a corner in the wrong lane. An oncoming car drove in the ditch to avoid them, but they ran off the road too, and hit the car head-on. They killed one person and maimed another. At the time, the story seemed hilarious. Later, I thought, "My God, what am I doing here, laughing at that horrifying story?" I had a lot to learn about being around that kind of violence.

While doing alternative service at the hospital, I gradually came to see refusing to register as a purer form of conscientious objection. So midway through my alternative service, I returned my draft card to my draft board with a letter saying I didn't think the CO deferment was equitable. It was a rich kid's way out of the war. I was aware that returning the card was an offense for which I could be jailed.

Soon after I returned my card, an FBI agent came to see me. He claimed he had been a preacher, but had decided he could better serve God in the FBI. I suppose he believed it, but I was incensed and insulted by the notion that being an FBI agent was a way to serve God. I read him the riot act for forty-five minutes, and told him exactly what I thought. Then he left. Nothing ever happened to me.

Working in the projects in Cambridge had keyed me into working with kids. Working with sex offenders in the hospital keyed me into psychiatry. Eventually, I became a psychiatrist. I ended up working with predelinquent kids, trying to help these guys early in their development, before they did horrendous things as adults. I continue to gravitate to and tolerate such people, always trying to figure out how to face that kind of violence.

———

Within a month after my high school graduation, I found myself before my local board, appealing my I-A classification. I went by myself and I was real nervous. My whole future was riding on what those people thought about me. My parents gave me no support at all. On the day of the hearing, they acted like it was just another day. They ignored it. No one expressed any concern about the board's decision.

A few weeks later, my father told me on the phone that a letter had arrived from the draft board. I asked him to open it and read it to me. The answer was yes. I got my CO. It was a very emotional moment for me, one of the benchmarks of my life. But my father made light of it, treating it with the same insignificance he had given the whole process.

My father was very active in Democratic politics in his

congressional district. At a party one night, he mentioned to a friend that I was looking for some form of alternative service. The friend was working on the first congressional campaign for the liberal Democrat, Pete Stark, from the East Bay, near San Francisco. Stark was a banker in Walnut Creek who had slammed a huge neon peace sign on the side of his bank and lit it up at night. The friend put me in touch with Stark's administrative assistant, who suggested that I work on Stark's campaign, and, if Stark was elected, we would apply to the state to have my work considered for alternative service. Stark was elected, and the miracle was that the state accepted my proposal, even though my work was political. Even more, I was working for a self-professed, antiwar liberal.

Stark represented a very diverse district, including East Oakland, one of the poorest ghettos in the country. He ran his office in East Oakland as a service center for the people. If anyone had problems with a federal agency, they could come to the office and we would deal with it. My job was to be a case worker, unsnarling red tape in the federal system wherever I could.

Even though my parents opposed my being a CO, there was some parental pride in my alternative service: "Hey, our son's working for a congressman." It was a legitimate thing to do. They were proud of me.

I worked for Stark beyond the required two years, but by late in my third year, I had become disillusioned with the political system and with the congressman. I saw him change from being a maverick liberal Democrat who said exactly what was on his mind into somebody who melted into the system, doing the things you have to do to get along in Washington — and to get reelected. So I quit.

▬

One day, I went to the mailbox and there was my CO deferment. I had expected it. I say that with some cynicism, because my board in Los Angeles covered extremely wealthy areas, including the almost entirely white community of South Pasadena, where I was raised. Not too many kids from my high school got killed in Vietnam.

I had a very high draft number. I don't remember what it was exactly, but I was in no danger of being drafted. Still, I volunteered for alternative service, in part to shore up my CO application. And I thought it would be interesting to do the service.

I was living in Berkeley, where I looked around for something to do for my alternative service. But I found nothing, and so instead took the first job I found — as an accountant for the Alameda County Assessor's office.

Just as I began that work, the Huey Newton Black Panther trial was taking place across the street. Once, when some demonstrators from the trial entered our building, the chief administrator turned off the power, so people had to march up and down the frozen escalators. At one point, an old man fell down and couldn't get up by himself. The response of the people in my office was, "Screw him. Let him take care of himself." I helped him up and I took my lunch hour to drive him home. It was the normal, human thing to do, yet in those circumstances, at that time, politics often got in the way of being human.

Eventually, the draft board told me that my job as an accountant wouldn't qualify for alternative service. I ended up working as an X-ray file clerk in the emergency room at Mariott Hospital in Oakland. Mariott was a private, 350-bed hospital that had a contract with the Oakland police department to handle police emergency cases. We got some of the victims of shootouts between the Black Panthers and the Oakland police. It was fascinating and exciting to stop being angry with one another and get on with the task of helping a human being survive, instead of treating him like a piece of scum — either pig scum or nigger scum.

There was a lot of violence then. The Zebra killings were occurring, where a couple of blacks from San Francisco were capturing whites and Asians and whaling their faces with machetes. I was fairly uptight, especially about walking to catch the bus late at night after work. One night, a rumor swept my block that one of the Zebra killers was on our street. Everyone, including me, came out with weapons. I stood out there in the street with a bayonet that my brother had sent me as a gift. My God, I was involved in mass hysteria. It could have been a lynching. The rumor was probably started because some poor black guy was walking down our street. It was a bad time.

I lived with several other resisters in Berkeley. Although my status was settled, theirs was not. Among war resisters, there was a sense of being on ice, of having lives shut down, of not knowing what to do, except wait for an indictment. One of the resisters in my house got so tired of waiting to go to jail that he made a paradoxical leap, the kind of psychological shift you sometimes see in people who take extreme positions. He joined the Marine Corps and volunteered for combat duty in Vietnam.

———

My trial took place nearly a year after I refused induction. During that time, I began working in the office of the American Friends Service Committee.

At my trial, I testified about being a pacifist, about not getting into fights in high school, and about the difference between individual violence and war. There were six or eight people in the gallery. It took only forty-five minutes. I felt I had a fair chance to defend myself and to explain why I was doing what I was doing.

About a week or two later, the judge gave me three years' probation on the condition that I do alternative service. I felt that I got in court what I had wanted all along. In essence, the court said I was a conscientious objector. My draft board in Reno was furious. I got angry letters from Martha, the clerk, but she couldn't touch me.

The sentencing had taken place a few weeks before I was supposed to go to Europe for the American Friends Service Committee. My probation officer, who was very understanding and sympathetic, approved my work in Europe. Before I left, he gave me a stack of forms to send in every month — my probation reports.

In the summer of 1967, I went first to central Yugoslavia, where I worked for a month in a student camp digging a ditch for a freshwater line to a small village. Students from all over the world were there. Then I got a job through the Yugoslav Red Cross at a children's hospital. I maintained buildings and worked on new roads. I stayed there for a year, until the end of 1968.

When I returned to the United States in late '68, things had really changed. There were more violent antiwar demonstrations. More people were going to jail or leaving the country. The judge who had sentenced me had been reprimanded by the Justice Department, so he had stopped giving suspended sentences.

I finished my alternative service at the Goodwill in Portland. There were a lot of COs there. I started in the furniture department, moved to antiques, and ended up repairing musical instruments. I bought an old chair there that is still my favorite piece of furniture.

I feel lucky about my service. I traveled, lived in Europe, and did work that wasn't involved in "national security." But I have a little guilt, because other COs were emptying bedpans while I worked in a Communist country. Yet I was glad I wasn't doing it for the draft board.

After my conviction, my draft board had classified me IV-F, unfit for duty, because I was a convicted felon. When I finished my probation at the end of 1969, my board reclassified me I-A and sent me a notice to report for a preinduction physical. They were going to try to draft me again. I figured it was just Martha trying to get me, so I returned the notice to the board and told them they were wasting everyone's time and money. I never heard from them again.

My draft board approved my request for an alternative service assignment to a three-year term with the Mennonite Central Committee's Teachers Abroad Program. I had two choices — English-speaking Africa, where I would spend three years teaching, or French-speaking Africa, which meant a year studying French in Belgium and then two years in Zaire. That attracted me the most, so I applied for Zaire.

A short time later, I received a letter saying I had been accepted for Algeria. I knew very little about Algeria, except I had a generally negative impression that it had some kind of radical revolutionary regime. But I thought, "Why not? A year in Belgium sounds pretty attractive." It became even more attractive when I learned that, rather than studying French in Belgium, I would do it in Grenoble, France.

I spent my year in France studying intensive French and Arabic at the University of Grenoble. That year was wonderful, very comfortable and beautiful.

After Grenoble, I went to Sidi-bel-Abbès, an Algerian city of about 100,000 that used to be the old headquarters of the French Foreign Legion. I taught English in a public high school there. The first year was very difficult, adjusting to a new language, religion, and culture. Most of my contact was in French, because anytime I tried to speak Arabic, people assumed I was French, and addressed me in French. But I continued to study Arabic with a Syrian tutor.

When I finished my alternative service in Algeria, I received a fellowship to do doctoral study in the African Studies Program at Northwestern University, where I focused on North Africa and the Middle East, and eventually received my Ph.D. So alternative service not only gave me a chance to do something positive during the war. It also totally changed my life.

■

It was the summer of 1969. I was a counselor at a local camp run by the Brethren Church. At night, after the kids were asleep, all the counselors sat around the fire and talked about the war.

One of the counselors was waiting for the FBI to pick him up because he had burned his draft card. Near the end of the summer, he was arrested at camp. Another counselor planned to enter West Point in the fall. A third was a Green Beret, on leave after nineteen months in Vietnam, and planning to go back for another tour of duty later in the summer. He was a demolitions expert who had literally blown up children in the war. Our discussions that summer helped refine and crystallize my opposition to the war.

Even though the Peace Corps wasn't officially designated as alternative service, I considered it to be equivalent. If I wasn't going to be in the military, I still wanted to give some service. The Peace Corps was an acceptable way to do it.

I went first to the Dominican Republic for a year and a half as a geologist. Then I went to India. When I completed my Peace Corps service in 1971, I applied for CO classification. The board accepted my application right away. I'm sure my Peace Corps service helped pave the way.

■

It wasn't like God told me, "Never go to war." People my age went through a chapter in our country's history that changed us and made us different from people just a few years older than us. Perhaps I had some thickheaded courage to do what I did, yet in a way I was just going along with others of my generation when I decided in 1971 that going into the military was the wrong thing to do.

I had started fishing when I was thirteen, so by the time I registered for the draft, I had five or six years of job experience, a full share in a commercial fishing boat, and a good paying job. I couldn't see giving that up for $100 a month as a soldier. And being a fisherman meant I had learned to be free and independent. I wasn't about to have a gung-ho, right-wing type who hadn't even finished high school ordering me around.

My oldest brother had gotten out of the draft by faking high blood pressure. He had gotten drunk the night before his physical, and when he saw them coming to take his pressure, he got himself totally enraged so his heart was pumping hard. When they rechecked his pressure, he was smart enough to be ready for them again. I decided to try the same tactic.

It was the summer I graduated from high school — 1971. I was eighteen. The night before my preinduction physical, all of us from out of town were put up in the Mayflower Hotel. I drank heavily and got real wild that night. I remember throwing a bed out of the top floor of the hotel and later getting stopped with a group of guys walking down First Avenue with open beer cans. We told the police we were there for our draft physical, and they said, "Well, take it easy, boys," and let us go.

The next morning at the physical I had a terrible headache and I was determined to be so obnoxious that the army wouldn't want me. On every form, I just filled in all the squares without paying any attention. Eventually, I got sent to a psychiatrist. When he came in, I was already sitting in his chair with my feet on his desk. I really made a general asshole of myself.

I got myself psyched up, and sure enough, my blood pressure was 180 over something. So I felt pretty good. But then someone snuck around a corner and took my pressure again, before I had a chance to work myself up. It was much lower that time. Given how obnoxious I was, they were only too happy to say, "I-A. Let's send this asshole off to war and hope he gets killed."

So I passed the physical. I considered myself a CO, but I wasn't willing to work in a hospital or pick up garbage or do whatever COs had to do. I didn't feel any devotion toward my country or any responsibility for it.

I enrolled in school that fall, but someone told me there were no more student deferments, so I dropped out. I should have had counseling or something to make sure I knew what I was doing, but I didn't. Anyway, they drafted me in the fall of '71.

The draft notice came to my parents' house. I just ignored it. My wife today says that's my typical coping style: ignore it, and hope it will go away.

137

The Strength Not to Fight

Patty Hearst had the right idea when she hid out in San Francisco. There is no better place to hide than right at home in a familiar area. So I continued fishing that fall, staying at a friend's house right near my parents. My friends knew my situation, and so did my family. My mother thought I should go in the army because she didn't want me to get in trouble. But my father supported me. He didn't want me to get shot.

Until that time, I had lived a real wild life, always getting pulled over in my car for traffic tickets and drinking. Frat house type of stuff. But I realized then I had to clean up my act. I knew I couldn't get pulled over by the police.

After about a year living that way, I was at a friend's house one night drinking beer with his father, who was some sort of local political boss. He read one of my poems and said he saw a crossroads there in the poem. He warned me that if I didn't make the right decision, I'd go down the toilet. He said he could help me the way he had helped his own son — by getting me in the National Guard. My reaction was typical of the way I did things then. I didn't talk to a lawyer or a counselor. I just blindly went with him to the National Guard recruiter.

The recruiter said my arrest was imminent, because I hadn't reported for induction. It may or may not have been, but he scared me so much that I decided to go ahead and sign papers to join the Guard.

National Guard training was in the real army. So I got sent to Fort Polk, Louisiana, for basic training. As soon as I arrived there, I regretted my decision. I should never have signed up.

On one of my first days at Fort Polk, a Complaint Committee was formed. I volunteered and went down to the meeting to complain that the food stunk, it wasn't a free country, and I hated everything about the army. A little while later, I read in the camp newspaper that the Complaint Committee had met and there had been no complaints. I realized too late that the committee was a way for our sergeants to pick out the troublemakers.

So I got assigned to the platoon with the biggest, meanest sergeant you ever saw, straight back from Vietnam, and charged to the max. He was calm on the outside, but he always seemed ready to explode, and we heard that he put people in the hospital. Everyone shook in fear of that guy.

I fought back psychologically by being uncooperative. I'd often get twenty-five push-ups as punishment. When you were finished, you were supposed to say, "Permission to recover," but I'd forget, and get twenty-five more, again and again. Pretty soon, I was in good shape, and the push-ups didn't faze me.

One day, I met a guy who asked me to bruise him all over his back. I did it with some pretty hearty slaps and punches and I left some large black and blue spots. That night, I was on firewatch when he pretended to fall down the stairs. I called the sergeant, who believed his story that he was injured. I realized then that you needed an angle. That guy was smart enough to get out. But I was never smart enough or had the right kind of counseling to figure out an angle for myself.

It was 1972. The sergeants and officers were testy, tight as wire, because they were afraid of the guys they were training. Every so often, someone would lose it and kill a sergeant. We knew that was happening in Vietnam. The army was losing control over its troops.

On our first practice under live fire, I was crawling on my stomach along the ground, when a sergeant told me to crawl around a log. I turned over onto my back and swung my fully loaded M-16 up in the air, so it pointed toward the back of the range, where our sergeants were standing in a line on a hill watching us. The entire line of sergeants dove in the mud to get out of the way. It was totally innocent on my part. I was just turning around. But they were afraid I was going to shoot them.

One sergeant ran down to me and ordered me to immediately shoot off all my rounds. Then he dragged me to a truck where a captain started screaming at me. He was a little guy from Texas. He kept yelling, "What are you on? What are you on?" He probably meant drugs, but I didn't understand him at the time, so I just said, "I'm on this truck. I'm on this truck." Which just made him madder.

Another time, I was in line at the drinking fountain when a big guy walked in front of everyone and just pushed a kid away and started taking a drink. Nobody said a word. I walked up and knocked his helmet off, and we ended up fighting. My sergeant soon had me in his office doing push-ups, when he told me that I was nothing but trouble. I said it was just a basic difference of political opinion. I tried to go into some college-kid explanation, but that made him so mad he almost squished me on the spot. He screamed, "Damn you, college kids." And all his animosity toward war protesters came pouring out. He was quivering with anger. Another sergeant rushed in and got me out of there. I was on the verge of tears, I was so angry. But I managed to survive until the eight weeks of basic training was over.

Next, I went to Fort Sam Houston for medics' training. Ninety out of a hundred people in my company hated the military. Morale was really low, from the bottom to the top. Everybody felt our friends were back home protesting the war, and there we were getting trained to fight it. Were we stupid, or what?

I made my bed, but as a matter of principle, I never once shined my shoes or did anything else to look like regular army. Everyone smoked a lot of pot. Once, on a march, I was in the back of the company pretending to limp, like I was hurt, when a sergeant came up behind me and caught me. He told me I better get my ass moving, so I limped a hundred miles an hour to catch up with the rest of the company. They never did anything to me.

When I finished at Fort Sam Houston, I hitchhiked back home and reported to my National Guard unit. It was summer, so I immediately had to go to California for the two-week summer training. It was easy. I had my own jeep. There was a big swimming pool. We played army awhile each morning. That was it.

When I returned home, I was supposed to go to one Guard meeting a month. But for a year I didn't go. I missed so many meetings that I was finally ordered to report to Fort Benning, Georgia. Fort Benning was an officers' training school, so it was hardcore army, with a ton of brass and everybody saluting everybody all the time. I arrived wearing a wig and a coonskin cap to cover up my short hair.

At Fort Benning, during off-duty hours, I was kept under house arrest for having missed so many Guard meetings. And I was shifted from being a medic to being a tank soldier. During my second week there, a sergeant put me in a foxhole and ordered me to fire an M-16. I said, "I'd prefer not to." It was a line I'd gotten out of a book, *Catch 22*.

The sergeant said, "We don't care what you prefer."

I repeated, "I'd prefer not to."

We went back and forth.

"We don't care what you prefer."

"I'd prefer not to."

"We don't care what you prefer."

"I'd prefer not to."

Suddenly, I took the gun and started firing madly, trying to melt the barrel off. When M-16s get hot, they usually jam up, and that's what happened to mine. The sergeant grabbed me and dragged me out of that hole. He never gave me a gun again.

By the time I left Fort Benning a few weeks later, I was so mad at the military, I told my National Guard captain back home that he had to let me out. I tried to appeal to his intellect, but of course he didn't have the authority to release me from the Guard. So I said, "This is the last you'll ever see of me." And that was it. I never went to another National Guard meeting.

Instead, I hitchhiked to Mexico. I spent the next several years in Mexico and Guatemala, and summers fishing in Alaska. After about a year, I heard from my dad that registered warning letters had been arriving because I wasn't reporting for National Guard duty, and that finally I had been activated into the regular army. Worse still, because I hadn't reported for duty, I was charged with army desertion, which was pretty serious. But I still didn't go back.

I had many fortunate experiences over the next few years. Like when I arrived in Guatemala City from Mexico one evening, planning to stay in the city for a while. I think it must have been '75 or '76. I ran into a friend who was just leaving for Lívingston, out on the coast, so I went along. We took a bus and arrived after many hours on the road. I hung my hammock between two trees on the beach and immediately went to sleep.

While I was sleeping, the huge Guatemalan earthquake hit. Twenty thousand people were killed around Guatemala City. I slept right through it. If I had been back in the city, I could have been killed.

I was isolated out in Lívingston, and didn't know how bad the earthquake was, so I didn't contact my family. But soon after the quake, I was interviewed by a visiting journalist, who wrote a story about meeting an unemployed fisherman who had slept through the earthquake. My parents read the story and figured that sounded like me. So they took hope that I was still alive.

While I was in Lívingston, a Canadian from Vancouver dove into the river and cut his knee very badly on some metal. Because I had medics' training, everyone thought I was like a doctor, so I stitched him up. It was a big cut, about thirty stitches. I warned him to fly straight home and take care of his leg, but he didn't. A few weeks later, I was in Yucatan, where a friend told me that he had gotten gangrene and died.

After several years of sneaking between Central America and Alaska, everything finally came to a head in 1978. I was working on a halibut boat out of Seward, Alaska. We had an eight-day lay-up in Seward, so I decided to go on a hike for a few days. I was afraid of the bears, so I took a .30-30 rifle off the boat with me.

After three days, I came walking out of the woods into town, carrying the rifle. It was summer, and the days were very long. I had lost track of time. It turned out to be four o'clock in the morning, so a Seward police car pulled over to question me. In Alaska, driver's licenses have Social Security numbers on them. I didn't have a license, but I was foolish enough to tell him my real Social Security number. He let me go, no problem.

On my way back to the boat, I stopped at the harbormaster's office for a can of pop. Meanwhile, the cop had checked my Social Security number, found a federal warrant on me for desertion, and put out a call for backup, calling me armed and dangerous. As I walked out the door of the harbormaster's office with my can of pop and my rifle, there was the full TV "Police Story" — a line of cops standing behind the doors of their cars, guns drawn, one cop shaking as he yelled at me to surrender. I screamed, "Man, don't shoot. I'm innocent."

After they handcuffed me, I stupidly asked if I could go back to the boat to get my belongings. They just threw me in the back of their car and drove me off to jail.

That night, I slept like a baby. All the years of pressure and the fear of getting caught were finally over.

The next day, the military police arrived to drive me to Anchorage. They were real mean when they put me in the car. I was handcuffed behind my back so hard my circulation was cut off. But we started talking on the two-and-a-half-hour drive. Morale was so terrible in the military at that time that they identified with me, and we ended up having a great visit all the way to Anchorage. After a while, they even took off my handcuffs.

In Anchorage, they didn't put me in a cell, but instead in a room with an open window. I could have gone out the window, but I was afraid I was being set up. So I stayed.

I expected to be flown to Fort Leavenworth, Kansas, but they checked my records, and eventually learned I had never signed for any of the registered letters from the military. So they couldn't prove that I even knew I had been activated into the army. That meant they couldn't prove I was a deserter. All they could prove was that I was AWOL from the National Guard. So the MPs let me go. I just walked out the door. They even gave me back my gun and my ammunition.

Because I had been arrested right out of the woods, I had only a little money and hadn't had a bath in days. How would I get back to Seward? I had a blank check in my wallet and decided to try to cash it. I bought a toothbrush, brushed my teeth, and washed my face. And then I went into a bank, where I told a teller my story and she agreed to cash my check. With that money, I went back to Seward and finished the fishing season.

When I got home, there was a letter waiting for me, telling me I had been dropped from the National Guard rolls.

I often laugh at the fact that people who went to Canada got pardoned, while I managed to put myself into a special niche, where there is no pardon. And I've never been officially discharged.

Almost every Mennonite in the Freeman-Marion area of South Dakota got CO deferments easily. You'd just say, "Hi, I'm Joe Blow from Mennonite Church 248," and they'd say, "Fine. CO." But I hassled my draft board by sending all sorts of things I'd written. Mostly poems and articles. The idea was to load up my file to make sure the board knew I was serious. I was a little angry and probably went overboard, but at least I didn't send a Xerox copy of the encyclopedia or statements written on bricks and two-by-fours like some people did.

The draft board responded by denying my application, saying I was political rather than religious. That was okay with me. I liked the challenge. I felt it gave me the chance to harangue the draft board further.

I don't remember much about the appeal hearing, except one interesting question that has stuck with me ever since. The board wanted to know if I had been responsible for the other antiwar material coming into the draft board from the surrounding county. Their question made me realize a lot of other draft-age kids were sending in material. I began to wonder, who were all the other antiwar people? What was happening to them?

143

After the hearing, I was granted CO status. But I did not have a good attitude. I considered alternative service to be a form of conscription. So at that point, I traveled to Canada to plan my move there.

Just then, 1973, President Nixon ended the draft. It seemed unfair, in a way. I had prepared for the big test, and just when I was ready, they called off the game: "Go home. We don't need you anymore."

With the end of the draft, the Mennonite Alternative Service Program shifted to voluntary service. I thought that was great. Saul, the King of Israel, was a volunteer. My parents had done service. The concept of service was completely normal to me.

So, along with two friends from Bethel College, I applied as a volunteer with Friends of the Earth. It was an opportunity to apply my environmental studies degree. And Friends of the Earth was identified early on as the environmental group most willing to take on military issues. For me, that fit well with my philosophy.

I stayed two years with Friends of the Earth, all the while trying to incorporate the environmental ethic into my life-style. It was forced monkism, and worked great if you were single and didn't have any other demands. After two years, I went to a Church of the Brethren house in Washington, D.C., for one year. Then I spent two more years at Friends of the Earth. Altogether, I did five years of voluntary service. Ever since, I've wanted to work in jobs that don't support war.

———

It's difficult for many people to face how their job may support the military. I once wrote some thoughts about this in a short poem:

Daughters, Sisters, Fathers, Brothers
Cousins, Uncles, Aunts and Mothers
It isn't really what it seems
Working for the war machine.

It's just a job, it is no sin
It pays the rent, it sucks you in
It's just a paycheck, times are lean
Working for the war machine.

While contracts come and profits mount
The payroll doesn't keep account
Of whether blood is red or green
Working for the war machine.

Please don't stop the funding flow
Our jobs are on the line you know
It's not our fault we're in between
Working for the war machine.

Not every one can go and fight
Or pull a trigger in the night.
Or drop napalm like gasoline.
We're small cogs in the war machine.

Chapter 4

A Country
Not My
Own

Borders promise change. There is a time on the Orient Express, deep in the Balkans, when people begin to shake their heads when they mean "yes" and nod when they mean "no." For the traveler, accumulated change signals the exotic. But for the refugee, there is the subversion of order, a disjunction that may last a lifetime.

All borders hold secrets. Approaching them, one sees the flowing line of cars or boats or people on foot, silhouettes funneled through narrowed international arteries. Possibilities of adventure, enchantment, or romance lie ahead. And yet, hope in what lies beyond borders rests not only in what they will bring to our lives, but in what they will help us leave behind.

On this midwinter afternoon near Blaine, Washington, I roll down the window for a breath of cold air. Most cars in line display British Columbian plates. The crowd is returning from a weekend of filling tanks with cheap American gas and shopping for bargains in the malls surrounding Bellingham. This crossing — at Peace Arch Park — is the westernmost end of what is often called the world's largest open border.

The invisible line that divides Canada and the United States stretches for more than three thousand miles, from the rocky coastal islands of the San Juans in Washington, across towering

146

mountains and through vast plains, on to the densely populated eastern cities, where Canadians and Americans alike seem to be pressed together for warmth against the deep winter cold. Scattered along that boundary are more than a hundred highway outposts, crossed each year by millions of people, who wait sometimes in two-mile-long lines of cars, inching forward toward the gated border.

For thirty thousand to fifty thousand young Americans during the Vietnam War, this border opened one way only. These young men called themselves draft dodgers. When they crossed that border to Canada in the 1960s and 1970s, they hoped they were leaving behind forever their struggle against the people and the institutions that tried to make them go to war. Most made the journey alone.

We meet first in the front seat of a car in a parking lot on the edge of the city of Vancouver. We exchange pleasantries, comment on the ever-dreary rain, and talk briefly about our jobs. As the windows steam, I begin to wonder why we are waiting here, the engine of his car not yet running.

Trying to turn our attention to the reason for my visit, I ask what year he came to Canada. His answer is imprecise. "During the war." I press, from a different angle. "I'm glad you agreed to do the interview. It's important that I hear from people who decided to stay in Canada." His answer once again seems evasive. "There's a lot of us here."

Wiping the fog from the windshield in front of me, I worry for the first time that the interview may fail. Then he laughs tensely.

"You know, even after all these years, waiting for you in my office this morning, I thought, 'How do I know this guy's not from the FBI?' "

I turn in my seat to face him, then answer with forced humor. "You don't know. I could be from the FBI. That would be just like them, wouldn't it, to send an agent to talk to someone about a twenty-five-year-old case of draft evasion!"

His tension reduced for the moment, he turns the ignition key and we drive to a building where he knows we will find an unused office.

The events of that remembered time took place with such speed and with such intensity that he is hard-pressed to reconstruct his journey. At first, places and people seem to have faded from his memory. Yet, as we talk on into the evening, he begins to remember, much as, on a quiet, sleepless night, one can slowly retrace steps taken in some far-off, much-loved place. Vietnam remains encapsulated, an interim in his life that has shaped everything that followed.

He tells me of years in which he lived cheaply, invariably running out of money, while fighting bedbugs, terrible food, and hostile police, and he shivers with the memory of cold nights covered only by thin blankets. He was in exile. But, for this survivor, these memories are a peculiar satisfaction.

There were times, he tells me, that he never had any wish so strong as to be at home again. When, after the amnesty of 1977, he finally made that journey back, he found an aged and changed family, unwilling to hear his story and unable to offer refuge. His voice is clenched with emotion as he tells me that he returned to Canada, never to go home again.

In this chapter, COs describe their migration from the United States to Canada and elsewhere. They explore their reasons for abandoning efforts to gain draft deferments at home, even when that meant they had to leave their families and friends for what they believed would be forever. They describe living underground, secretly crossing international borders, and working with war resisters' organizations. Draft dodgers who remained in Canada recall the amnesty offered by Presidents Ford and Carter, and they describe their continuing struggle to integrate into Canadian society.

▬▬▬

Some guys are dead. Others went to jail. I came to Canada.

▬▬▬

If I fled to Canada, I would never again be able to see the Redwoods, or the coast of California, or the other beautiful places that mattered so much to me, or the friends I had grown up with. And most of all, I would never be able to see my home again.

I didn't have the foresight to know that there might be an amnesty. I thought leaving would be forever.

148

I have to admit I had a rather low opinion of the army. I was raised in a navy town — Alameda, across the bay from San Francisco. Along with three thousand other baby boomers, I got a good dose of authoritarian education at Alameda High School. In the fall of 1963, in protest against the way the student paper was controlled by the principal, we put out a pirated edition with "Censored" printed across the front. Our principal believed in one thing — football. We never saw him except when the football team won the league championship, which it invariably did.

My father was part of the opposition Left in the United States in the days before World War II. He was always suspicious of politicians — especially LBJ. He was also more aware of moral questions than I was, and he talked about the draft and Vietnam in a way that tested me and challenged me. I was active in the Episcopalian Church and thought of going to divinity school, but instead I decided to go into teaching. I entered San Francisco State University in the fall of 1964.

San Francisco State was a hotbed of student activism. The Free Speech Movement had begun in Berkeley across the bay. Alternative student papers and antiwar speakers were everywhere. There was so much information available. I remember Bertrand Russell and Jean-Paul Sartre in Europe issuing bulletins about plastic antipersonnel bombs made of material that wouldn't show up on X rays. It seemed to me mindless that our country had such enthusiasm for spending so much money to kill so many people for no apparent reason.

Partway through my first year in college, my father passed away. That was in 1965. I had gone straight from high school to San Francisco State because he had wanted me to go to college. With his death, I realized I agreed with Mark Twain when he said: "Don't ever let an education get in the way of learning." So I studied less, and became more involved in political activities. I went to antiwar demonstrations. I carried a coffin down Market Street in San Francisco in the spring of 1966.

I gradually came to see the draft as a means the government was using to stifle opposition. Many student leaders of the antiwar movement were harassed by their draft boards; some were drafted while they were students. A good friend of mine from high school, a student at Berkeley, was drafted even though he had a student deferment. He went to his draft board, Local Board 50 in Oakland, where a clerk told him there had been a clerical error and he needed to apply for renewal of his student deferment. But they didn't have the form he needed. He returned a second time to get the form, without success. I went with him as his witness on a third visit. On the fourth visit, his father, his lawyer, and I went together. They still refused to give him the form. Finally, a TV station sent a camera crew, which filmed him as he walked into the office demanding the form. This time, he got it.

By the spring of 1966, I thought my country had gone insane. The Selective Service System was drafting fifty thousand young men a month and shipping them off to Vietnam. Strange things were happening in California. Ronald Reagan was running for governor. Politics was going toward the extreme Right. People in sit-down protests at the Oakland induction center were savagely attacked by the police, maced, and beaten to the ground.

I was determined I wouldn't go in the army, but I didn't have the money for a protracted legal battle. Just then, I met a guy who had been in prison for protesting the war. He gave me a good idea of what I could expect in prison, through his marvelous stories about what the guards did to him. I knew I wasn't prepared to end up there.

I had just married, and I wanted to start a new life anywhere I could live in peace. Just about that time, I read an article in the San Francisco State student paper written by a guy who had moved to Canada to avoid the draft. I had never considered Canada before, but the idea appealed to me, so I called the Canadian consulate in San Francisco. The consulate officer was astounded that an American would want to immigrate to Canada. It was usually the other way around. It was only later that large numbers of draft dodgers went to Canada. I didn't mention Vietnam or the draft to him. He sent the application forms and instructions for the medical exam. My wife and I applied and we were accepted in two weeks.

When I went to tell my mother I was leaving, I wondered how she'd react, especially since my dad had recently died. My mother was a lifelong Democrat, and while she wasn't openly opposed to the war, she didn't think draft resistance was wrong. When I told her I was going to immigrate, there was a long pause, then she said, "But they have a queen in Canada." I was so taken aback by her reaction that I could only say, "But she's a very nice person."

For the rest of the school year, I looked forward to going north and starting a new life. Immediately after I finished classes in June 1966, we headed to Canada. We took the train from San Francisco to Vancouver. At the border, a Canadian immigration official sat down in the seat next to me to check my papers. He told me about job opportunities. We had a lovely conversation.

Soon after crossing the border into British Columbia, I saw out of the train window an old building, quite amazing and beautiful, built before the turn of the century. It looked like an old fortress. I asked, "What is that building? A castle?" No one knew.

In Vancouver, we got a permanent address and I quickly found a job in the library at the University of British Columbia. I sent a letter to my draft board with my new address, telling them I had immigrated to Canada and that I intended to stay there permanently. A few weeks later, I got a notice to appear for a preinduction physical in Oakland. No way I was going to do that. So I contacted a Quaker lawyer who fortuitously had just returned from a conference in Seattle about Canada and draft evasion. His advice was not to report for the physical and to renounce my American citizenship. That's what I did, in the fall of 1966. Soon after, the draft board sent me a new draft card with a IV-C classification — undraftable alien. Then I spent four years as a stateless person before becoming a Canadian citizen.

It was through my lawyer that I met other draft resisters, who gathered at a meeting at his house in late fall 1966. There were about two dozen of us there to plan some kind of concerted action against the war. We knew there were two kinds of people coming to Canada. One, like myself, had decided to leave the States and immigrate to Canada. The others were AWOL deserters, often on their way to Sweden. At that time, it wasn't clear whether deserters could stay in Canada. I think the Canadian government hoped the problem would just go away. But of course it didn't. It got bigger and bigger.

The group that met that day decided to form the Vancouver Committee to Aid American War Objectors. We filed papers so we could legally solicit funds, we got a little office, we set up a counseling service, and we began to publish information about resisting the war by moving to Canada. We developed a network with draft counseling offices in the United States and we found places where people could stay until they got settled or moved on to Sweden.

Eventually, we handled thousands of people, literally thousands.

Later, I asked someone about that beautiful castle I'd seen after crossing the border into Canada. It turned out to be the British Columbia penitentiary in New Westminster.

━━━

I'm the first-born son of intellectual Jewish parents. I was born in New York in 1950, but we moved to Los Alamos when I was six months old. My dad's a physicist. He worked in the labs that designed and built atomic bombs.

I don't know how my father felt about his work at the time, but later in life, I know he felt badly about it. By the time I was in high school, he was active in the movement against antiballistic missiles. I remember seeing the *Bulletin of Atomic Scientists* lying around the house, with the doomsday clock on the front, showing how close humanity was to nuclear annihilation.

When I turned eighteen in March 1968, I was living in Minnesota, attending Carleton College. I registered as a CO, and then quit school, so I lost my student deferment. Canada seemed like my only choice. At the time, I didn't know what my father thought. He could be a difficult and demanding person. We didn't talk much about the war.

It was only years later that I found out that my dad applied for jobs in Canada, and actually went there for job interviews. He did it to make sure that he would be able to move the family there if I had to flee to Canada. He wanted to keep the family together. I wish I had known. It was a side of him that I didn't see much then, a side that I admire and love.

━━━

During its investigation of me in late 1966 and early 1967, the FBI interviewed everybody, even my kindergarten teacher, who didn't remember me at all. All that time, I imagined cars following me while I was walking down the street. I had been religious through high school, but I began to see religion as hypocritical after I learned that my priest told the FBI that I should join the army and kill people. I was a pacifist, but my beliefs became based on humanism rather than religion.

I was involved with the SDS and a Quaker group at the University of Missouri at Kansas City, where I was taking a double major in math and physics. Just before Christmas, 1969, during my senior year, the draft board revoked my student deferment.

Going in the army was completely out. I would have died there. I had heard stories from people who had been in the army and I had read in the papers about drill sergeants who beat people in the head with rifles and abused them. I was sure that would happen to me if I went into the army.

At first, Canada was out too. Canada was unknown in the Midwest. It was to me, anyway. I had hardly ever heard of the place.

So I began to prepare myself to go to jail. I went to see a counselor to talk about how to survive in prison. He told me I'd probably end up in Leavenworth and would be raped the first week I was there. "Oh, great," I thought, "I can hardly wait." Soon after that meeting, a friend casually asked, "Why not go to Canada?" When I looked at the alternatives, it sounded like a pretty good idea.

I didn't really debate it much in my mind before I wrote to the Vancouver Committee to Aid American War Objectors. I got back a book, which I still have, that told about living in Canada, what to expect there, how to become a landed immigrant, and the best places to cross the border. When I finished reading the book, I decided right then that I would go to Canada.

I figured I had three choices: Montreal, Toronto, and Vancouver. I didn't speak French, so I believed Montreal was out. Toronto didn't impress me, and Vancouver looked nice. So that was it. I decided to go to Vancouver.

I have two sisters. One of them was real right-wing, a member of the John Birch Society, who gave me brochures from the Minutemen describing the ten steps the Russians were using to take over the world. She considered me a traitor and thought I should be lined up against the wall and shot.

Most of the rest of my family supported my decision. My father was a World War II immigrant from Yugoslavia. He was very antiestablishment, a railroad union member who didn't believe anything politicians said and who assumed they were all crooks.

On the day I left, my other sister and my mother came with me to the bus station to say goodbye. My father couldn't come because he had to work. One of the images forever engraved on my

153

mind is sitting on the bus and staring out the window, seeing my mother and my sister standing there, looking at me as the bus pulled away. That was June 1, 1970.

My mother was forty-two when I was born, so she was in her sixties the day I left for Canada. She and my father thought they'd never see me again. For my mother, that turned out to be true.

I took the bus from Kansas City to Omaha to say goodbye to my girlfriend, who was a student at the University of Nebraska. Then I caught a train from Omaha to Seattle. The book from the war objectors' committee recommended taking the train into Canada because it would involve the fewest questions at the border. I also liked the idea because my father was a railroad engineer.

For the train from Seattle to Vancouver, I wore conservative clothes and I cut my hair. I had packed everything I owned in just three suitcases, but I left two of them in a locker in the train station in Seattle. With only one suitcase, I wouldn't look like I was moving to Canada. I planned to tell the border guards that I was on vacation.

On the train, the immigration agent asked how long I planned to stay. I said, "A week." He asked how much money I had. I said, "Two hundred dollars." Then he went on to the next person. It was only then that I realized there were fifteen to twenty male passengers in my car, and all of them were my age, with freshly cut hair and conservative clothes.

As I crossed the border, I believed I would never be able to go back to the United States. I felt like I was breaking all my ties with the past. I was sure that my draft notice was already in the mail to my Kansas City address.

It was nighttime when the train arrived in Vancouver, so I went to the St. Regis Hotel downtown. The next morning, I called the war objectors' committee, which had moved, and so it was a bit of a hassle locating them. But I finally did, and I walked to their office. I was lucky. Earlier that same day, a doctor and his family had offered to take in a couple of draft resisters. So somebody from the committee drove me out to their home.

Meanwhile, a friend of a friend offered to go to Seattle to pick up the bags I had left at the train station and bring them back to Canada. I had never met him before, but I gave him the key to the locker, figuring I might never see him again. But he brought the suitcases back to me.

The doctor I stayed with was local chairman of the Physicians for Social Responsibility, the organization that works against nuclear weapons. His wife was involved in peace demonstrations at the Peace Arch at the U.S.–Canada border. They let me and another guy live in their house for free. I stayed there from June until November. The other guy, who is now my best friend, was an army deserter from Indiana. He arrived the same day and ended up staying at their house for more than a year.

Within a week of my arrival, I wrote to my draft board, thumbing my nose at them, saying, "I'm now in Canada and you can't do anything to me." I think I told them to go to hell, too. About a month later, I got a draft notice ordering me to report for induction. At that point, I knew that was it. I couldn't go back.

In September 1970, while I was still living with the doctor's family, I met a woman, a Canadian citizen, and fell in love. In November, we were married and I moved in with her. Soon after that, I went to the immigration office to sign papers making me a landed immigrant. It took about five minutes. At that point, I could work, stay in Canada forever, do everything but vote. Unfortunately, my marriage didn't work out, and we were separated the next June.

Not long after I was divorced, I received the news that my mother had died. I wanted so badly to go to the funeral in order to be there for my father and my sisters. But I assumed I would be arrested if I tried to go back. I went through weeks of deep anger at the draft, the war, and my government, but finally I accepted the fact that I just couldn't go back. That was a very difficult time for me. I missed my mother's funeral.

I was going to school at East Los Angeles College in the fall of 1965. The war in Vietnam was escalating, but there wasn't yet an antiwar movement on the junior college campuses. Yet there was a counterculture. I was involved in that — smoking dope, growing my hair long, reading the *Los Angeles Free Press*.

I had a student deferment, but midway through my second semester, the rules changed. At the beginning of the term, the draft rules said you had to have twelve and a half units per semester to maintain your deferment. By the end of the term, the rule was fifteen units. I had only twenty-six for the year, so I lost my deferment and became I-A.

I was determined not to be drafted, and so in 1966 I applied to be a conscientious objector. My father was a patriot and strongly opposed my decision to be a CO. He was IV-F in World War II, and had this idea that he had not paid his debt to his country. So he argued with me that I had a debt to pay.

I was getting draft counseling from the Unitarian Church in Whittier and from the American Friends Service Committee in Pasadena. But I wasn't part of any movement. I had never even been in a demonstration against the war. In East LA, there wasn't any antiwar movement. Chicano Power was just starting, but mainly we were counterculture. So I was very isolated. For me, being a CO was personal. It was just that there was this military system and this war, and I individually decided what I would do with my life in relation to them.

At that time, you had to have some religious affiliation to get CO status. I went to see my rabbi, who was a right-wing son of a bitch whose son was in the Marines. I explained that I was a CO and needed a letter from him. He wrote, "Tommie's a very nice boy and if he says he's a pacifist, I believe him, but he didn't learn it from me." It was the kiss of death with my draft board.

At my draft board hearing in San Gabriel, two men and a woman asked me questions about my religious background. I said I was Jewish. One of them said that he knew several Jewish people and they were very patriotic. Given the rules at that time, I never had a chance. They turned me down, and soon after, I was drafted.

I tried to flunk my draft physical. What an amazing experience! Four hundred guys standing in line in their underwear! The guy in front of me had a scar from his knee to his ankle and a letter from his doctor saying he couldn't stand for more than twenty minutes without acute pain. I thought, IV-F. Right? Wrong. I-A. It was 1967, and the body count in Vietnam was so high that they were taking everybody. It was a meat market.

I told them I was a drug addict, so they put me into the psychologist's line. He asked what drugs I was addicted to, and I named as many as I could. He said, "The army will cure you of that, boy." So I passed. I-A.

Jail terrified me. It seemed horrifying, and I couldn't imagine being able to stand it. So with my CO application turned down, my only other choice was Canada.

I left for Canada on a Monday in December 1967. On the Saturday before I left, I got together with my girlfriend and two other friends to see Janis Joplin and Big Brother at the Shrine Auditorium. I was really into San Francisco bands — the Dead, the Airplane, Big Brother. Big Brother was my favorite. I saw them two other times, at the Fillmore in San Francisco, and at a club in Huntington Beach with about thirty other people. What a great experience! Anyway, that Saturday night before I left was a great concert, terrific. Janis was fabulous. We stayed up all night.

On the next morning, Sunday, I was in a postconcert depression when all my relatives came over to say goodbye. My uncles, who were all patriots, said they couldn't understand how I could leave my family. My father moaned, how could I do this to them? It was a nightmare. I felt depressed and unsupported.

Then one of the guys I had hung out with on the streets in East LA pulled into the driveway in his big red chopper, this same weird Sunday morning. We'd grown up together and were real close, so I figured he'd understand why I was leaving. I didn't expect him to be like my relatives. But then he said, "Oh, man, you can't leave like this. You're gonna leave your family. You're gonna leave your friends." It was surreal. Nobody supported me. I felt really alone.

The next morning, my grandmother packed me a lunch, my parents gave me some money, and we all headed off to Union Station. My girlfriend was there, too. She planned to join me later when the school year was over. But in the end, she never did.

It was pretty heavy at the station. Everybody said goodbye. Everyone felt I was leaving and never coming back. It was sad and very dramatic. I loaded myself on the train, I waved goodbye, and that was it. I left.

I sat next to a Jewish guy and his girlfriend. He seemed sort of hip, and it gradually became clear to me that he was doing the same thing I was doing. But if he wasn't going to tell me, I wasn't going to tell him. We were both too paranoid to talk about it.

At the border, I told the customs guys what I had rehearsed — that I was going skiing for a couple of weeks. And I showed them my $300. I was nervous, but it went smoothly. No questions about the draft or Vietnam. After we crossed the border, the guy next to me finally confided what he was doing.

When we arrived in Vancouver, I called a telephone number someone at City College had given me. I said I needed a place to stay, and I brought the guy from the train and his girlfriend with me. The three of us went out to an apartment in the West End. It was very weird. We met a girl we had never seen before, and she gave us, three strangers, a place to sleep on her floor. It was 1967.

The next day, I went to the Committee to Aid American War Objectors. The office was very well organized, very supportive, and quite businesslike. A man from their office took me in a car to a house in West Vancouver, to the home of some Unitarians. West Vancouver is on the side of a mountain. It's the Beverly Hills of Vancouver. The streets are listed alphabetically, and the higher up the mountain you go, the later in the alphabet the street name, and the more expensive the view. This family lived on Palmerston Avenue — a "P" — so they lived way up there. They were very different from me culturally, very straight and rich.

But they were also very kind. The family fed me and took care of me. They let me stay for two weeks. I never gave them any money, and they never asked for any.

The most important step for getting landed-immigrant status was to get a job. There was a fraternity of draft dodgers in Vancouver. One of them told me to go to the Jewish Community Center. Two other draft dodgers were already working there, and the director, who was Canadian, was antiwar. They interviewed me and gave me a job. It was only ten hours a week, but that was all I needed to get landed status. Not only that, but two of them needed a roommate in the house they were sharing, so I moved in with them.

The best place to get landed status was at the border, but I was afraid a warrant was out for my arrest, so I didn't want to enter the United States. But I heard there was a turnaround at the Peace Arch. You leave Canada, and then you can turn around before you hit U.S. customs, and go back to Canadian immigration. I got someone to drive me, and that's what we did. Canadian immigration interviewed me right there. And that was it. I was a legal immigrant.

Within two weeks of arriving in Canada, I had a job, a place to live, and landed-immigrant status. And I soon got a girlfriend, too. A sociology student at UBC doing a study of American draft dodgers came to interview me. Pretty soon we were going out together.

The next summer, 1968, my brother, who was in high school in LA, came to visit me. He met the sister of that UBC student, and decided to move in with her. So my brother moved to Vancouver, and we all lived together. It was like a family, and I felt I had a real support system. But my father was really distraught. He felt he was losing his sons. And we didn't see eye to eye on the war or much else.

The first time my parents came to see me, they drove up from California in my uncle's Cadillac. We were living in this hippie slum at Seventh and Oak, a famous building in the history of Vancouver counterculture. It was a ramshackle structure, falling apart, ten or twelve apartments with hippies living in all of them. I remember my aunt and uncle and my parents walking through the door, seeing mattresses on the floor, my brother and me living there. Tears came to my mother's eyes. "Oh, you're not living here?"

For years, my father felt he had lost his sons. But my parents never stopped coming to visit.

I remember my first trip back to the States. I went back illegally because I wanted to see my family and friends. I borrowed a guy's Canadian ID and got a ride in a VW through the ride board at UBC. The U.S. border guard was a real pig. He went through everything we had. I was with my girlfriend, who was carrying our money, about $200. I had ten dollars in my wallet. The guard asked if we were married, and when we said no, he said, "Then that's her money. You have only ten dollars." It had nothing to do with the draft. It had to do with being a hippie. It was 1970. You got hassled all the time.

I stayed in Oakland with a friend's sister and her boyfriend, who had just gotten out of the army after two tours of duty in Vietnam. He was there with a buddy from Nam. He wasn't sleeping at night and kept a gun under his pillow. He talked about not being over the fear of being in the jungle, but he didn't really talk about the war. There was a lot of tension, and I felt that they were violent and unstable. So we left to see my parents in LA.

When we got near my parents' house, I hid in the backseat until we were in the garage. I was very paranoid that someone would recognize me and turn me in. I was tense the whole time I was there, and I stayed inside with the curtains drawn. After a few days, I left.

During Ford's presidency, the U.S. Council of Churches had a network of lawyers helping draft dodgers in Canada. I signed a letter authorizing a lawyer in California to check into my case. He got my file and charged the government with violating my rights, like they hadn't informed me of the right to appeal. I don't remember all the things he cited. Eventually, he got a letter from the state attorney saying they had dropped all charges against me. That was it. I was legal. It felt great, and I was very happy. So were my parents. A lawyer I never met, who never charged me a thing, had cleared me. I could cross the border legally. And I've never been hassled since.

———

After my uncle told me he planned to turn me in to the FBI, I knew I had to leave Chicago. But my financial resources wouldn't get me to Sweden and I wasn't getting any help from anyone. So I contacted one of the priests who had been my teacher in the seminary. He was at a monastery about forty or fifty miles from Chicago. He agreed to help.

One evening, I slipped away from home. I took a small bag I had been squirreling away with clothes and a few personal things. My family didn't know I was leaving for good. I didn't say goodbye to anyone.

I went to St. Catherine's, an inner-city church where I had been a VISTA worker and I had friends. I spent three days there, and then got a lift to the monastery. During my three weeks at the monastery, I got a suit and prepared myself emotionally to leave. I read a lot, prayed a lot, and tried to clarify my beliefs, my values, and my ethics. I didn't want to make a snap decision. I looked at the decision I was about to make and I knew it would affect me for the rest of my life.

I had to develop a plan for getting into Canada. While looking through a Canadian newspaper, I saw in the religion section an ad for Notre Dame Church in Montreal. The ad included the pastor's name. So I practiced a story for Canadian immigration: that I was going to visit my father confessor at Notre Dame Church in Montreal.

After three weeks at the monastery, I took an Air Canada jet from Chicago. I wore my suit and tie, I was clean-shaven, and I had a new haircut. I carried a small briefcase and about $300 in my pocket. At Canadian immigration, I told my story, including the pastor's name and the church. They let me through. No problem.

As soon as I arrived, I made contact with the draft resisters' group in Montreal, but it was very depressing, a lot of depressed people crowded together in a small building. It was like a refugee station. I felt very vulnerable there, so I spent only a few days, and decided I'd do the best I could on my own.

I found a place to live for twenty-eight dollars a month. I ate a lot of hot dogs and I panhandled for spare change. I knew I needed to find a job, but I had no credentials, no transcripts, and I couldn't have an identity because I was there illegally. I was constantly worried I'd get caught and be sent back across the border.

Then one day I was reading Buddhist writings in a shopping mall. I hadn't eaten in quite a while, and was trying to convince myself I was fasting. A guy named Roy came by and invited me for a meal. We soon became friends. He had access to files at a social service agency, where he pulled a birth certificate of someone close to my age who had recently died. With that birth certificate, I got a driver's license and a security number. I kept a low profile for a couple of months, sold my suit, and then took on that new identity — Paul Washburn. I was Paul Washburn for most of the next two years, and then I became Steve McHenry. I also used a couple of other names for shorter periods of time.

I lived underground in Montreal because the Royal Canadian Mounted Police and the FBI were looking for me. Once, my landlord told me that two men in suits were asking about me, so I picked up my bag and left immediately, leaving no forwarding address and not going back to my job to pick up my last paycheck. Just leaving right then to search for a new place to live and work. Several times, I disappeared like that, then resurfaced later at a new job, with a new home.

I considered going back to Chicago several times, but I always decided to hang on. Canada was very different from what I had expected — which was dog sleds driving through the streets. I didn't feel I should socialize too much with other draft resisters. Guys from Texas and North Carolina had pretty heavy accents, and I was trying to lose my American accent to sound more Canadian. I didn't want to be identifiable. I wanted to be anonymous.

I saw so many people like me in draft resisters' offices and crash houses. Many of them, from the pressure they were under, had checked out of life, deciding to "leave" one way or the other. For some, that meant heroin. I remember especially one guy in a wheelchair who had been in the war. He was a psychological mess. I felt like everybody was displaced. It was hard to hold on.

I was quickly losing my self-respect. I started shoplifting a lot

161

because I couldn't get enough money panhandling. Stealing was against my religious upbringing. But how hungry must you get before you steal food? How desperate must you get before you steal a clean pair of underwear so you can feel a little more confident applying for a job? One day, I lifted some spray deodorant, but decided I wanted stick instead. So I put the spray back, took the stick, and a store detective caught me. Besides the deodorant, I had hidden under my coat a pair of undershorts, a razor, and some toothpaste — a total of $1.49 worth of merchandise. The detective said that most people go for cameras, but there I was stealing underwear and toiletries. He felt sorry for me and let me go.

The only member of my family who was willing to keep in touch with me was my grandmother. I called her and I wrote to her, but without a return address, so she could never write to me. Once, I put a different name and my real return address on the envelope, hoping she'd send a letter back to me that way. Soon after, I received notification that there was a parcel waiting for me at the post office. I had been warned never to pick up parcels, so I asked a friend to get it for me. It was a package full of Communist literature — pamphlets and brochures, Communist party papers, and a membership application. I was sure it was some sort of trick by the FBI, and I concluded that my family's mail was being monitored.

Another time, I got a telegram saying my mother had died and that I should go home quickly. I arranged for a flight, figuring I'd go back and face whatever legal penalties would be waiting for me. Thank God, someone suggested I call home first. I phoned, and my mother answered. I hadn't talked to her in so long, I just blurted out, "Mom, I'm so glad you're not dead." I'm sure the FBI was trying to trick me into going back so they could arrest me.

For a short while, I was the star of the town of Westmount, the upper-class, English-speaking part of Montreal. People there had heard about this American who was resisting the war and who had unusual ideas about God, flag, and country. So I got invited to a lot of dinners. Instead of panhandling, it was suddenly roast beef and Yorkshire pudding. I'd sit there and say, "Pass the potatoes, please. Yes, I'll have another slice of roast beef. Thank you very much." I went to dinner at the homes of people who owned the Molsen Brewery and who had controlling interest in the *Sun Life* and *Montreal Star* papers. They were curious about me.

Once, I stayed overnight at the home of a wealthy family with a son named John. When I went to bed, he took me to my suite, which had a bed as big as my own room back at the rooming house where I lived. When I came out in the morning, John was lying on the floor in the hallway, wrapped up in a coarse wool blanket. I said, "John, didn't you sleep well? What's going on?" He said, "I'm trying to experience what it's like for you, what you're going through living underground." I thought it was sad. He wanted something I couldn't give him. I said, "If I could give you my identity, I'd gladly hand it over right now."

After nearly two years of living underground, I was tired of moving around and hiding. I wondered if it would be easier to go home, face the consequences, and get back to my old life. In Chicago, I had done well in school, I had been a successful musician, I had had a good life. But all that was gone. It had become part of a past that could get me into trouble.

Despite the dangers, I decided to sneak back to Chicago to visit. I wasn't sure what I hoped to accomplish. Partly, I wanted to explain to my parents what I had done. I also felt a combination of curiosity, sentimentality, and a desire for excitement.

I crossed the border hidden in the trunk of a car. Pretty risky. Just after I arrived, I was standing outside the Palmer House in downtown Chicago, waiting to take a city bus to my parents' home, when I saw a Chicago Transit Authority detective I had known when I worked with the CTA three years earlier. We locked eyes for about two seconds, I recognized him, he recognized me, and then I ducked into the subway.

It took me about forty-five minutes to get home. When I arrived, I stood outside the house for a minute, thinking, "I've really done it. I got away, I've been gone two years, and I survived." Then I went in. I was hoping to see my father, but he was at work. My mother was shocked to see me and very upset. She told me my father was taking it very hard and hadn't said my name in two years.

Within minutes of my arrival, the phone rang. I heard my mother say, "No, I haven't seen him, officer. I don't know where he is." The CTA detective had called the FBI. Family loyalty is pretty strong. Even though my mother was opposed to my leaving the country, she was covering for me. When she put down the phone, I said goodbye, walked out the door, went downtown, and hopped a bus to New York. I crossed the border back into Canada by hiding under the backseat of a car driven by a friend who was returning to Montreal.

When I got back, I knew I needed to get out of the pressure I was under, constantly changing rooming houses, working at odd jobs, always on the move. I had reached a point where I wasn't sure I really cared whether I would be grabbed and arrested. Perhaps it would be easier to return home and face the music. I was tired of always moving, always hiding. On top of everything else, my girlfriend was pregnant, but I wasn't sure we could make it together. I couldn't make a commitment to raise a child with her while living as a fugitive.

Just then, the summer of 1970, I decided to go with three other guys to chart a river in northern Quebec and Ontario. The government was planning a hydroelectric project in the wilderness area. We heard Indian stories about the region, strange tales about falling off the end of the earth. The four of us decided to see the river before it was flooded. I left even though my girlfriend was pregnant. I wasn't sure whether I would come back in time for the birth.

That trip turned out to be a turning point in my life. The four of us spent two months on a canoe trip, paddling for the whole summer on the Harricanaw River. We took photos and kept journals, and we compiled reports on everything we saw, the birds, the plants, and old trails dating back to the last century.

It was a very difficult trip physically. About two hundred miles into the trip, our canoe hit white water, with three- or four-foot waves. The boat tipped over and I went under. Even with my life jacket on, I couldn't get back up. For about forty-five seconds, I was trapped under water, and then suddenly I got loose, bobbed to the surface like a cork, and swam to shore. They say that when you flirt with death, everything condenses, and you get an out-of-body experience. That happened to me. In my life in Canada up to that point, there was not a lot of hope in sight. But after that experience on the river, for the first time in a long while, I was glad to be alive.

We lost a lot of our supplies in that accident. We had to carry our canoes for thirty miles through swamps, until we finally arrived in Moonsonee, a town way up in northern Ontario. We walked into town as if we were right out of a Clint Eastwood spaghetti Western like *The Good, the Bad, and the Ugly*. We were dirty and gaunt, thin from eating a spoonful of rice and granola and dried apricots for many days. When we told the people in town where we had been and what had happened, one woman said, "We don't do those kinds of things."

We spent five days in Moonsonee. On our last day there, we rounded up some instruments and put on a dance for the locals. One of the guys was a fiddle player, I played bass, another played guitar, and another washboard. We had a great time.

Three days after I came back from that trip, my first daughter was born. By having my first child and deciding to stay with my girlfriend, I was able to begin to replace some of what I had lost. It wasn't easy, but building a family was a beginning. Up to that point, I had been a fugitive. But after that trip, I gradually began to regain a sense of myself.

Later, my girlfriend and I got married.

The period from about 1966 to 1968 was the draft-dodger boom in Canada, while '68 to '70 was the deserter boom. The draft dodgers were middle-class white kids going to universities, from families with some money, who knew how to dress and how to act properly in polite company. A little long-haired, but clean long hair. Your average deserter was a working-class or poor kid, white or black or Latino, from the South, from a farm, or from a big-city ghetto, who made many of the people who welcomed draft dodgers feel uncomfortable on a personal level. You might want to have a draft dodger over for dinner, but probably not a deserter.

The deserters couldn't legally work or immigrate, and so they tended to survive as individuals in a much more underground existence, doing odd jobs under the table, dealing drugs, petty crime. They always had to live with the fear of being arrested, which would mean they'd be deported. The draft dodgers were more likely to go to a university, get a graduate degree, get married, and have a house and family. Like I have.

When I arrived in Montreal to attend McGill University, I was still seventeen. I defined myself immediately as a hippie student radical. I carried a guitar around. I could sit down on a university campus and suddenly there would be people passing around marijuana. When I turned eighteen and I had to register for the draft, I planned to follow the advice of my draft counselor back at Columbia University by listing a home address in Montreal. That way, I would get assigned to Local Board 100.

On the day I went to register, I was in the midst of occupying a university building in a protest. I left the occupation and wandered down the street to the U.S. consulate. Unbeknownst to me, someone else, knowing where I was going, had written in chalk on the back of my coat, "Fuck US Imperialism." I went into the consulate, walked up to the counter, and said, "I'd like to register for the draft." There was a hushed silence. This didn't happen every day — an American in Canada walking into the U.S. consulate to register for the draft. After a moment of approval, I walked behind the counter to a desk to fill out forms. Everything then got very icy, but I didn't know why. It was because they could now read the back of my coat.

The U.S. consul looked at my application and said, "Don't you have a home? Don't you have an address in the U.S.?" If I had said, "Home address, Newark, New Jersey," I would have been assigned to my New Jersey local board. Following the draft counselor's advice, I'd written down on a three-by-five file card the relevant subsection of the law, which said, if I failed or refused to enter on line two of this form any address within the jurisdiction blah-blah-blah, then I'd get Local Board 100. So I announced to the consul, "According to subsection 100.4A of the 1967 Selective Service Regulations, I am failing or refusing to enter on line two . . ." I was a little snarky. Later, I got a letter from them saying that, under current regulations, I would not be subject to induction unless I resided in the United States or any of its territories.

When they put in the lottery system, I got number 56, which meant that I would certainly be drafted if I lived in the United States. I was classified I-A, but I had this wonderful letter which struck me as a real catch-22. It meant that as long as I lived outside the United States, then American law considered me legal and I wouldn't be drafted. But if I moved back to the United States, then they'd draft me. If that happened, then I'd move back to Canada. So as long as I didn't go back to the U.S. to live, then I could go back to the U.S. to visit, but if I did go back to the U.S. to live, then I wouldn't be able to visit.

I soon began to work closely with the American war resister community in the city. My legal status allowed me to drive through the border, pick people up, and bring them across to Canada. For some months, I ran the hostel, which was a house in a poor section of the city for newly arrived people avoiding the draft and people who were AWOL. We solicited donations, usually getting things like stale bagels. Once we hit the jackpot and got a closetful of Spam.

While I was there, most of the people coming through were deserters, often blacks and Latinos, working-class kids who were not likely to immigrate successfully to Canada because they didn't have the education and skills that Canada wanted then. Some deserters survived on petty crime, some got arrested, and others drifted back to the United States. A few built successful lives in Canada.

I was in Canada on a student visa, but eventually I decided to change my status. Upon returning from a visit to see my parents in New Jersey, I applied for landed-immigrant status right there at the Montreal airport. I had proof of a job offer, I filled out the forms, I took the medical exam and got the X rays right there, and I was approved on the spot. It was quite a lovely system.

In 1971, I was in a group of war resisters from Montreal that went back to the United States, to Washington, D.C., for the May Day demonstrations. The slogan for the demonstrations was, "If the government won't stop the war, we'll stop the government." The plan was for fourteen thousand people to shut down the city of Washington by sitting at major traffic thoroughfares at six in the morning and keeping people from getting to work. It was really highly developed sixties lunacy. It would make a great movie.

We knew there would be mass arrests. Our group from Montreal decided our role would be to try to free prisoners. Our biggest success was when we saw a city bus that had been taken over by D.C. police. It was filled with prisoners and was about to be driven off. We pushed a parked car in front of it and then ran back and pushed another car behind it. People inside kicked out the windows and escaped.

At one point, we saw a young woman tied to a lamppost being guarded by a police officer. Four of us surrounded them and tried to look menacing. I was five feet eleven, I weighed a hundred and thirty pounds, and I hadn't slept for three days. As we closed in, the woman shouted, "No! No! I'm a pacifist. I *want* to be arrested." We thought she was crazy.

I saw plain-clothes police mingling with protesters suddenly pull out billy clubs and attack people, so I decided I needed a club, too. I managed to get a police officer's club and hold on to it for about three seconds by running up to an officer on a slow-moving motor scooter and pulling his club out of his holster. Bad thinking. The next cop to come by — about two seconds later — jumped off his motorcycle, pulled his gun, and politely suggested that I drop the billy club before he blew my motherfucking brains out. Suddenly my sanity returned and I did as he suggested. And then I was arrested.

I was one of about eleven thousand people arrested that day. It was totally chaotic, with no arrest records for anyone. I was thrown into a paddy wagon. Nobody knew why I was arrested or who the arresting officer was. Most people were taken to the Robert F. Kennedy Memorial Stadium, but I was driven to the Washington, D.C., jail, where I joined about three thousand other people being held outdoors in the exercise yard. We were just unloaded and marched in. No paperwork at all.

Inside, there was a rock festival atmosphere, a huge party. Eventually, the police tried to strike a deal with us. Anyone who volunteered to be processed and fingerprinted would pay a ten-dollar bail, sign a promise to appear in court, and be let out. That led to a big debate. Was it better to stay in jail in solidarity with the mostly black prisoners inside the rest of the building, or should we get out and rejoin the demonstrations? Remember, we're talking late sixties, early seventies quasi-insanity here. I opted to get out, while some people stayed for as long as two weeks. I was processed with hundreds of others in a long line by four cops sitting at tables. Each cop would arrest the next person in line. The arrest times were written down as 8:01 A.M., 8:02 A.M., 8:03 A.M. and so on. They were mass-producing fictitious arrest records.

We hitchhiked back to Montreal after the demonstration with someone who was AWOL. He said he was "taking the weekend off." He had already served two months in the stockade for desertion, and they couldn't control him. What could they do? Throw him in the stockade again for a few days? So what?

I returned to Canada and never went back to appear in court on the charges. Sometime later, I read in the *New York Times* about a class action lawsuit on behalf of the fourteen thousand people arrested over the three days of the protests. The suit charged false arrest, which was true for many people, since police had rounded up anyone who looked like a protester. Although my arrest was probably for good cause, nobody knew why I was arrested. I sent my name and a twenty-five-dollar retainer to a Maryland lawyer in the hope I would make big bucks from the U.S. government. Later, I heard that the people who initially filed the suit won an average of $10,000 each. I never got anything for my twenty-five dollars, except some amusement. But I still have my appearance notice. I was supposed to appear in court in Washington, D.C., in August 1971.

By staying in Canada, I had the power to recreate myself. Like many draft dodgers, I became a Canadian nationalist. In my politics, I'm usually anti-American.

I'm like other American draft dodgers too in that I'm a little pushy, a little brasher than Canadians. If you drop your average American draft dodger into a Canadian context, you'll find that he talks too much at parties.

━━━

In 1970, I left Canada to visit my parents near New York. One night in New York City, I was tripping on acid. For a few hours in the middle of the night, I felt that not being a part of the U.S. Army in Vietnam meant that I was missing the existentially defining experience of my generation, and therefore I should enlist. Otherwise, I would be alienated, psychologically crippled for the rest of my life.

Luckily, I could find nowhere to enlist in New York at two in the morning.

━━━

At the Vancouver Committee to Aid American War Objectors, we collected draft cards from everybody who came through our office. We had one whole wall completely covered with the cards. That wall often got photographed by the news media. I kept my regular job at the university — I was respectable. And I liked to talk. So when the media started showing up, more often than not, I was the one they talked with. I had Bob Trout of CBS at my kitchen table, asking why I had left the United States and why I was opposed to the war. He seemed sympathetic, not hostile in any way. That interview ended up on the nightly news with Walter Cronkite. I also talked to people from the *Los Angeles Times*, the *New York Times, Ramparts Magazine,* and the *Ladies' Home Journal.*

The *Ladies' Home Journal* interviewed me and my mother back in California for a story about mothers whose children had gone to Canada. I wondered, "What would a reporter from the *Ladies' Home Journal* be like?" I expected a sixty-year-old grandmother with a cane. Instead, when we met in the lobby of a downtown hotel, a woman only a year older than me came bouncing out of the elevator in a miniskirt. We went to dinner and she asked all the standard questions. Her angle was the effect of my decision to move to Canada on my mother. I never knew whether I ended up in her article.

Working at the war objectors' committee, I met a lot of people fleeing the United States. Those avoiding the draft usually were well versed in their opposition. They knew what they were opposing and they had a political analysis. In contrast, the AWOL people were very nervous and often in a state of shock. They were basically honest young men who had thought it was honorable to go in the U.S. Army. But when they got to Southeast Asia, they discovered the war was something entirely different from what they expected. And inhuman. I was often shocked by their paranoia. They thought they were being pursued, and were quite frightened that something would happen to them before they could make it to Sweden. I remember one guy named Ken. To be honest, I never knew if he used his real name. Ken had been in Vietnam, where his lieutenant had ordered him to kill bound captives. When he refused, the officer did the job for him and then threatened him by saying he'd have a little "accident" because they didn't want cowards in his unit. It sounded like a bad Hollywood movie. Ken had fled Vietnam in fear for his life.

The picture we got of Vietnam was horrible. I especially remember the Tet Offensive in 1968. My wife and I had been invited to a friend's house, one of the other members of the war objectors' committee. We were just about to sit down to dinner when we saw on TV the chief of the South Vietnamese secret police blow a man's brains out, right there before our very eyes, without trial, without appeal, without anything. It ruined our dinner, I'll tell you. It wasn't a joke. Apparently the guy who did it is now operating a pizza joint somewhere in southern California.

Because I had renounced my U.S. citizenship, I had not technically broken U.S. law by being in Canada. So I could legally visit the States. On my first trip back, the immigration official typed my name into some sort of computer, and apparently nothing showed up. I've visited several times since, and never been stopped.

This may sound absurd, but I think of myself as a law-abiding person. It was important to me not to violate the law. Even a law I consider ridiculous, like the Selective Service Act.

I began to consider leaving the war objectors' committee in 1968. I was having trouble with my marriage, and the radical Left had begun to be involved in the committee. We had started out as a group of people, like the Quakers, trying to extend a helping hand. Our first concern was peace. But gradually we got more Maoists and Trotskyites. They worked very hard, but I felt they had political axes to grind. We had horrendous meetings, arguing about what the committee should be doing. The radicals felt we should begin an educational effort to radicalize people. I was still a new fish in the Canadian pond and didn't really know what they were talking about. And it seemed to me the incorrect direction for the committee. So, at the end of 1968, I moved away from Vancouver out to the countryside and ended my work with the war objectors' committee.

▬▬▬

In 1972, the head of the Vancouver Committee to Aid American War Objectors called me to suggest that I write a letter to my draft board asking to see my file. He said that I'd probably find that my file had been lost. So I wrote the letter and received a reply saying that my file had been lost in a catastrophe. An army deserter friend was told the same thing, that his army records had been lost. Eventually, he went to Philadelphia, where he was discharged from the army in one day. Everybody I know of in Canada, from the West Coast of the United States, the East Coast, and the Midwest, found the same thing — that their files had been mysteriously lost. Most of us think the army and the Selective Service had their own amnesties to clear their records and get Vietnam over with. But no public statement was ever made about it.

▬▬▬

I met Donald Duncan, the ex–Green Beret and antiwar activist, in Vancouver around 1967. He said that the antiwar movement in western Canada was not as well organized as in the east. He was in Vancouver on January 1, when thousands of drunken British Columbians jump into English Bay, many while wearing absurd outfits. On January 1 in the east, the Great Lakes are frozen and the St. Lawrence River is a solid block of ice, while in British Columbia, we're drinking beer and jumping in the ocean. Duncan was kind of disturbed by that. He wanted to see a strong political organization. Instead, he saw some people jumping in the bay, and everyone else on their boats out fishing.

We used to have a town fool in Vancouver. His name was Joachim Foikis. He was a sixties phenomenon. He wore a court jester's outfit, and on important civic occasions he'd show up to make pithy comments. He said he had a vision. An angel came to him and announced that he should go to the far end of the earth and be a fool. So he came to Vancouver. Most of us here thought, "That makes sense." We understood.

In the spring of 1975, I was on a high school field trip in the Queen Charlotte Islands, on the north coast of B.C., just south of the Alaskan panhandle. One night while we were there, we heard a radio report that the American forces had withdrawn from Saigon and the U.S. embassy and the whole city had been taken by the National Liberation Front forces. For years, I had been anticipating a big party when the war ended. Instead, I was isolated on a faraway island with a group of high school students. It would have been a lot of fun, finally celebrating peace. But I also felt a big sense of regret. Wars are such a waste. So many people died for the ego of a madman from Texas.

I thought the Carter amnesty in 1977 was long overdue, though it seemed narrow and half-hearted. My mother was very pleased by it. Among most Americans in Canada, the reaction was cynical. We didn't take it seriously because it didn't affect us. Most of us were here simply because we didn't want to kill anybody because of their politics.

Although the amnesty was as much as I would expect the American government to do, I wanted to see more. I wanted war crime trials. I wanted punishment for the officials responsible for the war. And I wanted reparations for Vietnam.

━━━

The amnesty was an insult. I don't know anyone who took advantage of it. It required that we admit that we did something wrong, and then we were to be forgiven. I didn't do anything wrong. I don't want forgiveness. When the program was announced, everyone I knew laughed about it, like it was a big joke.

━━━

In the mid-seventies, I was tutoring high school kids on an Indian reservation up in northern British Columbia. My wife got sick with hepatitis and the medical facilities were not equipped to care for her properly. We felt we needed to move back to the city, but we wanted to be safe from the FBI. Right then, the amnesty was offered. I didn't believe I had done anything wrong, but it was a chance to finally be free from worrying about being arrested. So I took the amnesty.

━━━

Altogether, I lived underground for seven years. I figure that the charges against me would have resulted in about seven years in prison. Yet I would do it again. No question about it. No hesitation at all. Because I believe in life. I know that my father went to World War II for reasons that were fine for him. Perhaps if I had grown up in the thirties, I would have ended up in the infantry like him. But I was a product of the forties and fifties. I will defend my family. But I will never go to war.

I have certain regrets. I'm not glad that I've been unable to live near my family. Or that I have a brother I see only occasionally. We're not strangers. But we certainly have missed a lot of our lives together.

Until Vietnam, America never experienced a mass emigration of its citizens because of their political or moral beliefs. America has always been the mother of refugees, the place where people come for safety. But during Vietnam, it was the place people were fleeing. The forces that led to that exodus shaped my life forever.

Chapter 5

Making Peace

It was my final interview. We had been talking for nearly two hours. The hands on the plain round clock showed it was nearly eleven. A work night, time to put an end to our talk. I asked my last question. Could he reflect on what Vietnam had meant to him in his life?

Terry's gaze, long fixed on me, now drifted, unfocused, into the distance, as he sifted through twenty years of memories.

"Prison was such a total experience. After I had been there for a few months, I began to lose touch with how it felt to be on the outside. I could no longer remember what my life had been like, before prison, before Vietnam. For me, Vietnam changed everything."

He paused, taking a deep breath before going on.

"For years after I got out, I had a recurring dream in which somehow I violated parole and suddenly was back in my cell. The same guys were still there. 'Never thought you'd show up again,' they'd say.

"My dream faded over time, and I hadn't had it for eight or ten years. But last night, after thinking about this interview, I had that dream again."

Yet this time, he tells me, the dream was different.

"Like before, I was back in prison for violating parole. But I

was also somehow in the present time, and I needed to talk to a friend. I desperately wanted to figure out why I was in jail. What had I done wrong? Why were they doing this to me? When I woke up, I didn't know where I was. Was it then, during Vietnam, or was it today? The past and the present seemed combined into a single moment."

His story over, we shook hands and said goodbye, and I left, walking alone to my car through the quietness of the late night. On my drive home after that final interview, I thought about Terry's dream. It was a reminder of how recent, how alive, Vietnam sometimes seems. And it reminded me as well of the first interview I conducted, a year and a half earlier.

Lynn had just come home from working the graveyard shift and hadn't slept. As we talked through the afternoon, fatigue and coffee loosened his control.

"My prison cell is inside me now," Lynn said. "I still see it in my dreams."

Lynn had suffered a great deal from his imprisonment. "I don't know what got me through. I don't know how I survived. I remember once in prison I met a priest who had been jailed for civil disobedience against the war. I knew he was one of the truly holy people, someone who had lost all his social status, power, and influence, yet remained a pure, burning spirit. When we truly need them, people like that will always emerge."

As Lynn's words came back to me, I felt I understood a little better what had gotten him through. He had wanted deeply to be one of those "pure, burning" spirits himself. But the experience of conscientious objection and imprisonment had been too painful and too humbling for him to accept his own holiness. Still, his fundamental faith in the potential for human goodness was there nonetheless, under the surface. His burning desire to act with righteousness had helped him survive.

"Sometimes I dream about that priest. I would like to thank him. He helped to get me through."

The dreams of the Vietnam generation take us back to the time that made us who we are.

As the years passed, conscientious objectors were released from alternative service, the military, and prison. Those who fled to Canada were granted amnesty. Many returned home to families they had not seen for years. As the crisis of the war faded, COs faced a disturbing peace. In this chapter, they talk about their efforts to reconcile themselves with their parents, with their country, and with themselves, and to find their way in a future after Vietnam.

Felons

Everything can be forgiven. Everything can be healed.

———

I remember as a kid riding with my parents in downtown Indianapolis, near the war memorial. I asked my dad what the old military guns were for. He said, "They're for shooting and killing people."

I'm grateful he gave me a straight answer. I never forgot it.

———

In retrospect, prison was my rite of passage for manhood. True, it was a long adolescence, and true, it wasn't over until my middle twenties. But I made it. I made it.

Toward the end of my time in prison, I really started to push the limits. I was a short-timer getting cocky. I hadn't been beaten up. I hadn't gotten raped. I had survived. Prison was going to be something I would remember for the rest of my life.

Just before my release, I let my hair and my sideburns and my mustache grow out to the max. I didn't want to walk out of prison looking like I had just come out of military drill camp. The prison authorities had to keep telling me to keep my hair within acceptable parameters.

I was bucking to get out early on work release, even though the rule was that anyone convicted on Selective Service charges had to do all their time before getting out. I was known to be involved with the prison activist circle. I was also suspected of being one of the guys who brewed alcohol in the walls of the building. We actually chiseled out a wall and built a still around the heating pipes. We collected fruit and berries and made our own alcohol. Because I was suspected of all these things, I was starting to piss people off. But they couldn't pin anything on me.

Then one day, an associate warden and two of his goons grabbed me, put me against the wall, pulled out a ruler, and measured my mustache. It was one-eighth inch beyond regs. They finally could bust me for something concrete.

At the hearing to take away my good time and deny my request for work release, I laughed and mocked them. At the end of the meeting, I said, "You chicken shits. After all this time and all the heat you put on me, you can only get me on this chicken-shit charge." Snip, snap and my mustache was back in compliance. But the hearing officer ruled that I couldn't get out on work release.

So I went over his head and contacted the associate warden I had given the hockey-puck turkey pieces to. He overruled the hearing officer and let me apply for work release. So I had a minor victory. That felt good.

My first work release interview was at a community mental health center. At that time, patients were being deinstitutionalized and the community centers needed people to handle them. My interview went well. The staff at the center supported my antiwar stand.

When I returned to prison after the interview, I was walking back through the main joint when a new guard I had never seen before started walking toward me. A lot of the guards were lifers back from Nam who really gave me a lot of shit. So I immediately put up my shell, hunched up, and got really guarded, thinking, "This one's going to give me shit, too."

He walked up, poker-faced, and asked, "Are you Johnson?"

"Yeah, what of it?" I said, sounding like the real tough guy.

"Are you really here on draft resistance charges?"

"Yeah." I was still guarded.

"So you're against the war in Vietnam?"

I thought, "Okay, okay, how long ago did you get out of the army?" I just said, "Yeah, so what?"

But instead of giving me shit, he said, "Can I shake your hand? I just got out six months ago. And it sucks. We're in Nam for all the wrong reasons. You're here for the right reasons. I would understand if you told me to fuck off, but I'd be honored if you would shake my hand."

I almost cried and hugged the guy. I felt at that moment there was a reason for everything that had happened to me. Everything made sense. Everything seemed worth it. I shook his hand, slapped his back, and thanked him for approaching me. I never saw him again.

The last place you muster out of prison is the storeroom, where they keep the civilian clothes of everyone who has come in, all cleaned and hung in racks. You get to pick out a snappy outfit — a suit and a pair of shoes. The majority of stuff was three-piece suits, none of it appropriate for how I wanted to dress. No bell-bottom jeans. No fringed leather vests. But at least I could pick out my own clothes, and they didn't look like prison issue. I could walk out looking like I was becoming something other than a prisoner. In a small way, I began to regain my individuality. That was a great feeling.

On the day I left, my buddies threw a party for me in the back of the tank. We smoked three kinds of hash and two types of marijuana and drank two types of wine, literally having a get-down, fucked-up party. The last day in prison, you give away to your best friends any of your possessions — a favorite book, a pillow, a blanket. You have very few material possessions that are yours, so everything has great value, especially if it's one of a kind. People brought presents, like little pieces of jewelry they had made, a ring, or a necklace, and books to exchange. I had commissioned paintings from prisoners who were artists and hung them at the foot of my bunk. I gave away all of them except one, which I still have. It's a painting of the Tibetan word "om."

Our cell block was a three-mile drive away from the landing for the boat to the mainland. The driver of the van was outside waiting for me, beeping his horn. He couldn't believe that I wasn't there at the door, waiting to go. The guard had to come back and break up the party. "I don't believe it, you stupid shit," he said. "You're going to miss the boat." Then he said, "I'll walk out of here as if I haven't seen what you're doing, and you'd better be on the van in two minutes or you'll spend a lot more time here." I thought, "God, let me out of here," and I ran out in a cloud of smoke. I hopped on the van, and the driver and I laughed all the way to the boat.

The ride across the bay to the mainland was great. The skipper let me captain the boat, so I got to work the wheel and toot the horn and pull up to the dock for my very last time. It was wonderful, commanding an eighty-five-foot boat on my release.

My girlfriend's father, my future father-in-law, was waiting for me. He was active in the Lutheran Church and worked for the homeless a decade before it became a topical issue. He took me back to his family for my first dinner of freedom. He didn't know me well, but he respected what I stood for and he was proud of his daughter for loving me. I remember how good it felt to be accepted by him.

Society puts the squeeze on prisoners. We are at the bottom of the pile, suffering the most pressure. I came out of prison angry and raw, and I was very class-conscious and race-conscious. Being in the pressure cooker of prison and seeing American society from that perspective had changed me. I was no longer the loose, hippie peace freak I had been before I went in. I never got to the point of condoning violent actions, but now I could understand why others would be so appalled at the horrors of what our country was doing that they would resort to violence. I understood the anger and frustration and rage that could be acted out destructively. It wasn't right to have riots and burn Watts, but I understood why people would do it.

But, thank God, I didn't come out hating. I didn't hate the guards. I didn't hate the prison administration. Some of them were rotten SOBs. But you can't hate people for their institutional roles. To hate is to trap yourself in a way that perpetuates and gives power and recognition to what you are hating. To not stay stuck in a stifling cycle of embitterment — that's the lesson I learned in prison. The challenge was: could I survive a truly alien environment, a different culture and a different set of societal rules that nothing in my prior background had prepared me for, and still land on my feet and keep running and survive? I could. I did.

A year after I got out, I pulled into a hamburger stand near home. Inside was one of the prison guards, a little Napoleon with a chip on his shoulder, a cocky bantam rooster, who had always been on my case. He was there with his wife and kid. When I walked in, he looked at me, grabbed his kid with one arm, his wife with the other arm, and ran out the door, peeling out in his car, laying rubber as he left — out of fear for how much I would hate him and give him shit for all he had done to me in prison. I just smiled and thought, "Instant karma." You get back what you put out. I hadn't even frowned at the guy.

For a long while, I was sure I would never forget my prison

number. But one day, a few years after my release, I realized I knew some of the digits, but not the exact pattern. I was amazed, because for so long, nothing could happen in my life unless I used that number.

But I haven't forgotten the feeling of being in prison. In my job today, I go in and out of jails a lot to do mental health evaluations. Every time I hear the sound of the large metal gates clang shut into the concrete walls behind me, I feel a deep reverberation inside myself and I want to yell, "Let me the hell out of here!"

I burned the files on December 24, 1970, and I was released on May 11, 1973. During that time, I spent twenty-eight and a half months in federal prison.

If you want to find out what it's like being in jail, get a board, go into your bathroom, put the board over the tub and some kind of mattress on top, leave the light and the radio on all the time, and have somebody stick your meals through the door. Try it for a weekend. You'll have a little better understanding of prison.

On the day of my release, I went into the dressing room to finally take off my prison khakis, the uniform I had worn for more than two years. I was given an old pair of blue jeans. Because of the sensory deprivation in prison, the jeans seemed like the brightest blue I had ever seen. Then I looked over the shirts and I picked out a bright red one.

My friends met me at the gate. I remember we went to a grocery store. It was incredible, seeing the stacks of food. I could get anything I wanted to eat. It was stunning. I was in a state of shock.

On my second day out of jail, Dan Berrigan coincidentally was not far away, giving a speech. We got together to visit. We did a radio interview and talked at his hotel. Later, Dan invited me to the University of Manitoba, where he was teaching classes in religion. I remember getting on the train in California and waking up the next morning in Klamath Falls, Oregon, with snow all around. Then we were in Vancouver, and then traveling across Canada. I had never before been out of the States. Or that far north. It was like a slap in the face, entering a world that seemed to me very different. The accents were different. The color of the money was different. From the train, I remember seeing herds of elk in the open fields.

Dan treated me like royalty. He's a gourmet cook, and stuffed me with food and wine. I spoke to his classes about my experiences. I relaxed. And I met a woman there and fell in love. It was wonderfully healing, everything my soul needed.

I finally felt, "I'm out of prison. I'm out. I'm really out."

I never forgot the tearful juror who held her hand out to me as I was being taken away to jail in handcuffs and waist and ankle chains. While I was in prison, she mailed a prayer card to me that said, "What do grace and glory mean except that we can endure in the midst of absolute fire, in the midst of incomprehensibility."

About three months after my release, I contacted her to see if she would be interested in talking about the trial. I wanted her to see that I had gone to prison and that I had survived. I wanted her to understand that I did not blame her. I wanted her to know I believed I had been imprisoned because of what I had done.

Eventually, I met at her house in the Bay Area with five of the jurors. We talked about things we hadn't been able to talk about during the trial, especially the war, which was still going on, and how we might respond to it. We talked about how juries were used to give legitimacy to a process where the defendant was essentially already guilty when the trial began. They talked about how the trial had made them more aware of the war, and of their own responsibilities. They told me how the trial had changed their lives.

Several years after my release from prison, I met a woman who told me that her son had gotten a letter from the draft board saying his files had been destroyed, and so he was not drafted. Because people like me burned draft files, perhaps he didn't have to die. Perhaps he didn't have to kill.

For many years now, I've been active with the Catholic Worker Movement. I cofounded the Family Kitchen, its feeding program. I helped start the Pacific Life Community, which undertook the campaign against the Trident submarine. Since Vietnam, I've been jailed about a dozen times for civil disobedience, the longest time for three months.

In the early 1980s, I was arrested for cutting some of the fences at the Trident submarine base and was sentenced to ninety days in jail for destruction of government property. Unlike my incarceration for burning draft files, this time I decided not to cooperate. I went limp and was dragged down the stairs from the federal courthouse to the county jail, and then through the halls to my cell. I decided not to eat or to leave my cell, and to do nothing except my bowel movements, which, with a little fasting, would not be an issue for long.

But there was one guard who took it as a personal affront that I wouldn't leave my cell. He made up his mind I was going to obey his orders. Every day, he came into my cell, threatening me. Finally, one day, he cranked the cell door open, grabbed me by the shoulders, and forced me up against the wall. He was probably expecting me to resist or to struggle with him, perhaps throw a punch, and then he could do whatever he wanted to me. But I did nothing. I just looked down at the floor. He became ashamed at what he did, let go of me, and left the cell very hurriedly. He came back later and apologized.

Arrest has never been important to me. Burning the draft files was important. Cutting the fence at the Trident base was important. Trespassing at the Trojan Nuclear Power Plant was important. When I took those actions, it was good to say "no" to death, and it was good to say "yes" to life.

———

One day, I opened up *Life* magazine and saw a photograph of what was billed as these crazy people called hippies living in San Francisco in a strange place called Haight-Ashbury. The article condemned them, but when I saw that picture, I realized there were other people in the world who felt just like me. I had never thought about growing my hair long, I didn't know anything about dope, and I was in the army. But there was something about the people in that picture that made me feel for a moment as if I was not alone.

When I was in medics' training at Fort Sam Houston, one of the COs had a poster of Jesus carrying a rifle slung over his shoulder. The message was that it wasn't good enough just to refuse to be personally complicit in the war. If your country has gone crazy, then you must act — even if you sacrifice your own path to heaven by being violent. The crimes of the country were so great that it wasn't good enough just to be an individual pacifist.

I settled down in Leavenworth prison to do my time. I didn't know then that the Presidio 27 was held in such high esteem by other GIs. A lot of the soldiers knew about us. All the while, our support committee on the outside kept pushing and pushing and pushing, and never let go of the issue.

Finally, with all the publicity, the government decided it was better to release us. One day, an official came to me in prison and said I would be paroled. I was sure they wouldn't do it. "Forget it. I don't want it. Only suck-butts get parole."

They tried to make me go through the prerelease ritual of taking classes about readjusting to society, but I refused. I figured they were going to dangle parole on a string in front of me and make me jump for it and jump for it while they laughed. Fuck that. I had gotten tough enough in prison to protect my emotions.

But, sure enough, within a couple of weeks, they released all of us. My wife, who had moved to Kansas to be near me, was waiting for me. It was winter 1970, and they gave me a little car coat, a suit, a bus ticket to Kansas City, and twenty-five dollars. Of course, everybody in the town of Leavenworth knew I was just out of jail, because I had the same stupid car coat that everybody else had. I figured the first thing I needed to do was to get rid of that stupid coat.

I was officially on parole, but I never did any of the parole classes or met any of the other requirements. The military just cut me loose.

I was still a pretty gentle person, but after being in prison, I was definitely down for the revolution. I drove to San Francisco with my wife, where I immediately began working with the Pacific Counseling Service, which was made up of people who had organized support for the Presidio 27. At Pacific, I worked against the war and helped GIs who wanted to become COs. We differed from the traditional CO organizations because we were perfectly willing to help people who didn't really fit the CO rules. We figured if someone applied for CO status, that helped to clog up the system. We offended some of the other CO organizations, which were concerned that the CO law might be eliminated if it was abused.

I stayed in San Francisco for six months, and then I left to open a new counseling office near Fort Lewis and to work on an underground GI newspaper, the *Lewis-McChord Free Press*. I worked there for a couple of years, but by then I was in my mid-twenties, and I felt I was getting a little old for GI work. That sounds silly now that I'm in my forties. But the GI movement was made up mostly of young GIs. So I left and got a job in a factory.

Most of the Presidio 27 were working-class guys. Our actions didn't help us a bit personally. We couldn't use the GI Bill. We didn't get any veterans' benefits. But none of us, as far as I know, has ever expressed the slightest regret. We were the government's worst nightmare, individuals within the military who followed orders on the basis of conscience. That's what Nuremberg was about. Even though we did the confinement, Uncle Sam was the loser. We helped to end the war. I have no regrets whatsoever. Absolutely no regrets.

I remember during my medics' training feeling very inspired by a photograph of Dr. Howard Levy, an army officer who refused to train Green Berets. In the picture, he was being hauled off to jail, this little shrimp of a guy carted away in handcuffs by big, beefy MPs. The picture was obviously taken to denigrate him, but I found it inspirational and stuck it on my locker at Fort Sam. I also had a poster of a reservist from the Bay Area who refused to be activated. In the background of the picture were three guys called the Fort Hood 3, some of the earliest GI resisters to the war. The caption said, "I followed the Fort Hood 3. Who's going to follow me?" Well, I was the one who followed. And many more followed me.

Years later, I met a guy at a party. I had never seen the guy before, but when he heard my name, he suddenly started pumping my hand. It turned out that he was the army's company clerk who had read my CO application. He hadn't cared one whit about the war, but across his desk came my application, and when he read it, it turned him around. He became a GI resister.

In the sixties and seventies, my generation was going to make a new society. We thought we would hand the torch to the next generation, and together we would march toward a better future. Well, we looked back, and that next generation wasn't there. It went into yuppiedom.

Once you step in shit, you always recognize the smell. When *The Deer Hunter* came out, several of my buddies and I thought the movie smelled. We figured it was trying to rewrite the history of Vietnam and would help lay the basis for another war. So we passed out leaflets in front of movie theaters, saying the movie reversed the good guys and the bad guys in the war. Most people thought we were just being stupid veterans who couldn't lay Vietnam to rest. "Put it behind you, man. It's over. The United States isn't doing that shit anymore." Several of us went to the Academy Awards in Los Angeles, where we got our heads caved in by the

LAPD. I was charged with two felony counts of assaulting their clubs with my head. The charges were later dropped.

During the 1980s, I worked against the use of white phosphorus in El Salvador. I know what white phosphorus does, because as a medic I took care of people who were burned by it. White phosphorus takes the moisture out of your skin by sucking the oxygen from the water molecules. So when that stuff spews out of an antipersonnel weapon, you can cover the burn, but you can't extinguish it. The phosphorus will use the moisture from your flesh to fuel the fire. It will burn down to the bone, and beyond, until it's exhausted. I knew it was being used in El Salvador, but we couldn't convince the American people that they needed to speak up. That was a very lonely time for me.

Like many guys, I have had to fight with one hand against the military, and the other hand against my family. My father was a career military officer, who couldn't handle the fact that I went the opposite way. So he cut me off completely. He literally wrote me out of his will. When my children were born, he refused to recognize them as his grandchildren.

I no longer have much contact with my parents. Twenty-five years after I refused to fight in Vietnam.

The Crusade for Justice kept up the community pressure around Denver for my release from prison when my period of observation was up. My prison counselor told me I deserved to be released, and that he would recommend it to the judge. But he heard that the judge wanted to sock it to me, so I was prepared for the worst.

By that time, my counselor had become disillusioned with the prison system. He told me he was angry that I was being singled out and that the feds were having meetings to discuss how to keep me in jail. He said, "That's not how the prison should be run."

My hearing before the judge had to be held within ninety days of my initial incarceration. One day, the counselor told me my court date and asked that I not tell anyone. He also said I would be going early in the morning. I was worried that the judge wanted me there early so he could throw the book at me in private. So when my wife visited me in prison, I told her to let the Crusade for Justice know I would be in court on that day.

I arrived in court early that morning and was taken to a back room by two U.S. marshals. We sat there for three or four hours and then walked back to the car and returned to prison. I never saw the judge. When I asked what was going on, the marshals were tight-lipped.

Back in my cell, I was steamed, I was really pissed, I was boiling with rage. I had my hopes up, but I was back in jail with no explanation. If a guard had said the wrong thing to me then, I hate to imagine what I might have done.

My counselor called me into his office. "Calm down, calm down. Don't blow it. I just found out you're going to be granted probation."

It turned out that the courtroom and hallways had been packed with my supporters, mostly with Chicanos, also SDS and other antiwar people. My counselor told me that the judge wanted to throw the book at me, but he felt he could not do it because the media were paying attention to my case. So he was going to give me probation. But he wanted an empty courtroom. He didn't want to do it in front of all those people.

A few days later, on short notice, I went before the judge in an almost empty courtroom. He said virtually nothing, and gave me three years' probation. When the hearing was over, I walked away, free. That was in March 1971.

During my probation, I was arrested in antiwar protests, but I was never convicted, and so my probation was never revoked. After three years on probation, my record was expunged, and so I'm officially no longer a convicted felon.

There are three interesting footnotes to my case. The first is about the U.S. marshal I was convicted of assaulting at my preinduction physical. For several years after my release, he sent me a card every Christmas. In one of them, he wrote, "I feel some remorse and regret about the circumstances of our meeting. Merry Christmas and Happy New Year." Someone told me he was not a redneck at all, but a well-meaning family man who had real misgivings about Vietnam. Testifying against me during my trial had brought him face to face with his conscience and with his real turmoil about the war.

The second footnote is about the federal judge in my case. In

1968, the year I was arrested at the induction center, a white antiwar radical from Colorado was charged with bombing power lines. The feds claimed he was part of a radical underground group that was knocking off banks for cash to fund their radical activities. He was on the FBI Most Wanted list for several years, and finally got caught in 1975 or '76. After his arrest, he was shipped back to Colorado. And who does he go up against? The same judge I faced. But by then, Watergate had blown open, Nixon had resigned in disgrace, the Vietnam War was over, and it was clear that everything the antiwar movement had been saying was true about the crooks and the criminals in the White House, and what they did in Vietnam.

At the sentencing, the judge gave this eloquent speech about how Vietnam had wrought divisions in the country between young and old, and how the wounds must be healed. Then he let the bomber go with a slap on the wrist. Sentenced him to probation. So maybe the judge had a change of heart. Maybe he finally looked more deeply at the issues I had raised. Even my judge ended up jumping on the antiwar bandwagon.

The final footnote concerns my prison counselor. He stuck with his job for a few months after I was released, but he was so disillusioned with the prison system, the war, and his country that he soon quit his job, moved to Boulder, grew long hair, and started an alternative newspaper. That's the last I ever heard of him.

———

I spent two and a half years in prison, the last year and a half at Danbury in Connecticut. As my release date neared, I decided to apply for admission to the Boston University graduate school in political science. Out of the blue, I wrote to a radical professor there, saying I liked his books, and asking if he could arrange to have an admission application sent to me in prison. Two weeks later, I got a letter saying I was admitted to the graduate program with a full fellowship.

I anticipated release for months, making little calendars and checking off the days. When I finally got out, a friend picked me up and took me to stay at the home of a Quaker woman who visited draft resisters in prison. The first thing I did was to get roaring drunk. And sick. I started school the next day. I should have gone to Bermuda for a couple of weeks.

For months, I was paranoid about being followed, about being grabbed and taken back to prison for the rest of my life. I still have recurrent dreams that I've just been let out of prison, but suddenly I'm grabbed and they say I have five years left on my sentence.

After finishing my Ph.D. in political science, I was hired as a researcher by the law firm defending Daniel Ellsberg for the release of the Pentagon Papers. I attended the lawyers' meetings and was fascinated. So one day, on the spur of the moment, I decided to apply to Harvard Law School. My application had two letters of recommendation — from Alger Hiss, who had been convicted of spying, and Howard Zinn, a noted radical. I was admitted to Harvard.

I was concerned that I couldn't practice law as a convicted felon, so I went to see the chairman of the State Bar Committee. I told him I didn't want to spend three years in law school if I couldn't practice law. He asked me, "What were you convicted of?" I said, "Draft resistance," and he said, "We don't care about that in Massachusetts." It turned out that there was no rule in Massachusetts barring convicted felons from practicing law.

After entering Harvard, I wrote to the judge who had sentenced me. I said, "You may not remember me, but when I testified at my trial, you were extremely hostile, and asked me sarcastically what law school I had gone to. Well, I'm going to Harvard."

While I was a law student, I wrote for my FBI and Selective Service files under the Freedom of Information Act, which had been passed in 1975. The FBI files were heavily censored, but the draft files were virtually intact, including a letter from J. Edgar Hoover saying I was a troublemaker who should be put in the army. From the files, I discovered that I had been drafted out of turn, almost a year early.

There is a procedure called a writ of *coram nobis*, by which someone who has already been convicted and served his sentence can revive the case on the grounds of government misconduct. I filed the writ, representing myself, arguing that I should never have been drafted because my draft notice was punishment for my antiwar activities.

An assistant U.S. attorney in Cincinnati told me, "very, very confidentially, just between you and me," that he had dodged the draft, too. And he said that his office would not contest my petition. In court, the judge ruled that I had been drafted out of turn, and so he overturned my conviction for refusing induction. But he upheld the lesser charge of not showing up for my physical, ruling that if

I had shown up, I might have flunked, in which case the whole issue would have been moot.

I also applied for amnesty under the amnesty program, but I was told I was not eligible because my offense had occurred before August 1964. I complained to the chairman of the Amnesty Board, who suggested I apply for a presidential pardon. I did so, and in December 1976, I got a presidential pardon. It did not wipe out the conviction, but it wiped out the civil disabilities, like not being able to vote.

I promptly sent the judge another letter to tell him my conviction had been overturned and I had been pardoned. By now, he had been promoted to the Court of Appeals. He responded to me by saying it was his policy to answer all letters, but he had no interest in me. He said mine was an unremarkable case, and he had no regrets about his handling of it. He also said I had been extremely rude because I had addressed him in court as "Mister" rather than "Your Honor."

I never regretted going to prison. I'd do it again. But I resented the petty bureaucracy, the dehumanization, and the psychological harassment. I remember how resentful I was for being referred to by my number instead of my name — 25930.

I think everybody, even Supreme Court justices, should spend some time in prison to see what it's like. Lawyers should spend thirty days, to understand the consequences of locking somebody up, what it's like to be psychologically abused and treated like a piece of shit.

Today, I'm a political science and law professor. I never intended to be a full-time lawyer. I just wanted to be able to work on occasional cases that interested me. But my first case became my biggest — the Japanese internment camps.

I started out to write a book about the internment, but during my research, I uncovered documents in which the government's own lawyers admitted lying before the Supreme Court in the original hearing during World War II. As an attorney, I realized I had found evidence of misconduct. From my own draft case, I knew about the writ of *coram nobis*. So I decided to contact Gordon Hirabayashi and the other Japanese Americans involved in the original case to see if they were interested in reopening their cases. They agreed, and I recruited a team of lawyers to work on their appeal. That work ultimately lasted ten years.

The outcome of the case, after ten years, was that all of the convictions were overturned by the federal courts, and Congress passed a bill providing monetary redress to all the survivors of the internment camps. When the lawyers who worked on this case get together and reminisce, we agree that we'll never have another case like that for the rest of our lives. It was one of the most successful grass-roots political-legal movements in history.

That work was enormously satisfying for me. And the case was very meaningful to the Japanese-American community. Today, I spend a lot of time traveling around and speaking about the case. After my talks, Japanese Americans often come up to talk to me about the case. Sometimes, they're crying, and they thank me for what I did.

▬▬▬

When I went to get a driver's license, the form had a question asking if I had ever been convicted of a felony. I marked, "Yes." When the examiner asked me about it, I told him it was a draft charge. He smiled and said, "That might hold up your license. Here's a new form."

Veterans

The army catches you when you're fresh and dumb and eighteen. Not many eighteen-year-olds have deep-seated beliefs. That's why they don't draft twenty-five-year-olds.

I'm glad I didn't take the easy way out. I was put under fire and forced to develop and mature. It was my proudest moment.

▬▬▬

Looking back after twenty years, it's hard to identify what turned me against the war. I have an answer, though I don't know how accurate it is. For the record, what hit me more than anything else was how backward Vietnam was. I don't mean that in a derogatory way. I mean, the technology there was so unadvanced, compared to what I was used to, growing up on Maryland and Virginia farms. It seemed to me that if we were there to help the Vietnamese, there was much more we could do besides military

190

action. Everything we did seemed to cause massive destruction. I flew on helicopters a lot and saw the countryside peppered, everywhere you looked, with artillery holes. We just bombed and bombed and bombed without end, and devastated vast areas.

The other thing was the way we treated the Vietnamese. Like calling everyone "gooks." That's the term I used throughout my tour. It applied to everyone, including the people we were supposed to be helping. And prostitution was all over the place. I was certainly deeply involved with that, like hundreds of other guys I knew. We just saw it as a normal part of life, that women were forced into selling themselves.

I served with the 101st Airborne Division in the southern part of Vietnam, around Phuoc Binh and Cu Chi. I arrived there in '68, just after the Tet Offensive, after being trained at Fort Bragg, North Carolina, and Fort McClellan, Alabama. When I first arrived in Vietnam, there wasn't much for me to do, except go down to the nearby village, which had a lot of prostitutes and places to drink. I got high a lot, and hung out. Later, I was sent up north around Hue, where I worked on a big truck with a tank on the back that was supposed to be used to decontaminate us after nuclear war. We put water in the tank and gave guys showers when they came back from the field. It was nothing deadly or dangerous.

Most of the time, I got up in the morning and smoked pot all day. When you're stoned all the time, you don't question things. You're satisfied and more willing to go along with the program. Some people think that the military actually promoted drugs in Vietnam to keep us under control, so we'd be more cooperative. Later, after I left in '69, the marijuana dried up, and heroin appeared on the scene. That was a whole new ballgame.

I returned from Vietnam in 1969 very angry and very bitter, and convinced that we should kick our leaders out of government. Many GIs returned from Vietnam with the idea that we could actually overthrow the government. After seeing the force of arms in Vietnam, and realizing we could use guns at home just like we could use them there, we thought violence made sense. So many of us gravitated toward a revolutionary perspective.

I came from a farming family, not working class, but I was like a lot of other GIs who felt such bitterness. We were guys who never had shit in life, got sent off to fight a war, and then came back to nothing. I wanted to strike back, to overthrow the parasites at the top who sucked the blood of working people and caused such murder and destruction.

But I had a year left in the army, so I got involved with an underground antiwar newspaper called *Left Face,* at Fort McClellan. Most of us who worked on the paper had been to Vietnam. *Left Face* came out monthly, around a thousand copies. We did a feature called "The Lifer of the Month." We picked out some professional soldier, some asshole lifer, and told what he had done to his men during the previous month. We printed his picture and mocked him. It was a powerful way to defy the army's authority, and a vehicle for GIs who otherwise couldn't communicate with one another. The paper represented a way to empower people who didn't have another way to speak out. We'd sneak into the barracks, put copies on bunks, and run and hide before the military police came.

Those of us who put out the paper were soon identified as antiwar, and so the army tried to fuck with us every way it could. I was a sergeant, so they couldn't restrict me to barracks and assign me KP duty like they did some of the other guys. But I got court-martialed just for driving through a stop sign. I got a lawyer to fight it, and I worked out a deal. But that experience showed that speaking out was not okay and that many of my ideas about constitutional rights were an illusion.

When I left the army in February 1970 I was barred from the base because of my work on the paper. In May of that year, I met a friend in town, in someone's yard. Unfortunately, the owner came outside with a gun and I got arrested for trespassing. I had never been arrested before, and so I didn't know shit about what to do. Another guy in my jail cell told me, "No problem, man. You just go in there the next day, plead guilty, and they'll charge you twenty bucks. You'll be out in an hour."

So that's what I did. But the minute I pleaded guilty, some men who had been sitting in the courtroom went up to talk privately to the judge. I didn't know who they were — probably military intelligence or FBI agents — but the judge then sentenced me to six months on an Alabama chain gang. For trespassing. I realized I had made a big mistake and got a lawyer, who eventually got me out of it, but that experience radicalized me even further.

In 1971, I left Alabama and went to Cuba for six months to cut sugarcane. After returning, I eventually joined Vietnam Veterans Against the War, becoming a full-time office worker in New

York. I worked on vets' issues like unemployment, job training, and educational benefits, always hoping that the GI and vets movement would be the foundation for broad social change. But the ground war was the basis for the movement, and when the ground war came to an end in 1973, the movement quickly began to collapse. The United States was still ferociously bombing Vietnam, but the American people, including most GIs and veterans, lost interest in what was going on there.

Eventually, like many vets, I got a job in the post office. We got extra points on the screening test. I got involved there in a group called Outlaw, a name that referred to strikes being outlawed in the post office. I was elected shop steward at the Thirty-fourth Street branch, the biggest one in Manhattan. At first, the union hierarchy welcomed radical vets with open arms. We were new blood, fresh blood. Automation was really getting going then, and a lot of jobs were threatened. Our union president advocated a strike, so Outlaw said, "Sure," and we shut down the place for four days. I got arrested on the picket line.

Our strike was illegal, but since our president had asked for it, the union had to support it. But when the strike was over, the union went after us, to get rid of us. We were too radical for them, and they couldn't control us.

In 1974, I quit the post office, got married, and went off to West Virginia to work in the coal mines with others from a group called the Revolutionary Union, which had grown out of SDS a few years earlier. I was from Virginia and had some kind of southern accent, so our leaders figured I'd fit in there.

When I arrived, it was the height of the oil crisis, so everyone was talking about a hundred years of prosperity coming to the coal mines. People who had left during the layoffs of the 1950s were returning from the plants up north, and there was a lot of activism. Although strikes were illegal, miners often protested grievances at local mines in wildcat strikes, without the official sanction of the United Mine Workers Union. Soon after I arrived, there was a strike at one of the mines in the next county. The company got an injunction in federal court, and a couple of the miners went to jail rather than obey the judge's back-to-work order. We spread the strike to four other counties, and within a matter of weeks, miners in four other states joined in. Ultimately, the walkout involved eighty thousand miners.

193

The conflict in the mines culminated in a national coal strike in 1977. We went out in December and stayed out for 111 days. We voted down two contracts that our union leaders negotiated for us, but ultimately we accepted the company's original offer. There were very powerful forces working against us. It was a real watershed for the mine workers to accept the contract, to accept defeat. That experience taught me that the struggle for change can only go so far. When the road forward is bleak, most people give up.

I stayed in the mines until 1980. All that time, I couldn't figure out why the miners didn't become revolutionaries like me. Shit, the government was against us, everybody seemed to be against us. What was wrong with the miners? Gradually I figured out that despite the oppression and exploitation that coal miners experience, they have a tremendous amount of privilege. As fucked up as their lives might be, they still had steady work in union jobs paying ten dollars an hour, while millions of other workers had no job security, no high wages, and no benefits whatsoever. So I left the mines to continue my work elsewhere with the Revolutionary Union.

My work with the RU culminated in 1980 in a May Day event in West Virginia. A group of us spent months organizing for a May Day demonstration in Charleston. The purpose of the demonstration was to try to make May First an international workers' holiday. Our goal was to polarize the society around the need for revolutionary change.

I guess we did, in West Virginia for one day, anyway. Ten of us had a demonstration in Charleston, the capital. Our plan was to march down the street with red flags. We arrived together in a truck, started marching, and saw five thousand people coming toward us, every one of them ready to kill us. One of our group fell down and got knocked unconscious, and everybody else ran away, except me. I kept walking toward the crowd. Then I got arrested. The cops saved my life.

After that experience, I left the Revolutionary Union, which by then had changed its name to the Revolutionary Communist party. I figured that if I was alienating ninety percent of the people, most of whom would like to kill my ass, something wasn't right. There ought to be a better way to win people over to the revolution.

Looking back, I think I never really saw pacifism as a viable alternative to the power relationships that matter in the world. Personally, I was so angry and bitter from my experience in Vietnam, I wanted revenge. I felt that the only way the country would change was by having a gun jammed up its ass. I figured that's what they'd do to me, and if I didn't do it back, they would kill me. But also I realized that the use of violence can be the seed of your downfall. If you advocate change based on the use of violence, you're buying into a system that in the end will be absolutely corrupt.

In the seventies, you didn't see many GIs or veterans supporting the war. We had many opportunities to march and to speak out for the war, but we didn't. In '72, Nixon tried to organize Vietnam Vets for Nixon, but he got nowhere.

When the war was over, Vietnam vets were angry and bitter. Like all soldiers, we had been used and then thrown away. We had massive unemployment and drug problems. Many of us were screwed up by what we did in Vietnam. The American Legion and the VFW and the Veterans Administration shut the door in our faces. Nixon in particular had nothing but disdain for these veterans who bit the hand that sent them off to war. People forget that vets in the 1970s identified the government as our main antagonist. Vietnam veterans felt betrayed by their government. We felt it was the government that was shitting on us.

Since the seventies, a lot of effort has been directed toward reconciling the veteran back into American society. With the Vietnam Veterans Memorial, there was a shift away from the issue of why we fought in Vietnam. Instead, the attention shifted to the forgotten Vietnam vet, and increasingly to duty to country, patriotism, going along with the program, and my country, right or wrong. I think the effort to rehabilitate those ideas has been pretty successful. Vets have been used for that purpose. And the new story is that the antiwar movement rather than the government screwed the vets.

So in the 1980s we got the creation of the myth of protestors spitting on vets. I never knew anyone who got spit on. At the time, I never once even heard of it happening. GIs may have been confronted by people who argued with them about the war and challenged them about Vietnam. There was nothing wrong with that. Some soldiers might have been upset when challenged on the war. But I never knew vets who got spit on. Yet I know vets now who have begun to believe the myth themselves, and to repeat the story that GIs were spit on by people in the antiwar movement.

The Strength Not to Fight

I've been to the Vietnam Veterans Memorial twice. I really have trouble looking at it. I see it as a political symbol, justifying what we did in Vietnam, rather than condemning the war. I worry that it will confuse kids, like we were confused when we were growing up. I'm afraid memorials only sanction mindless patriotism and the worst kind of nationalism. America needs a lot of things, but not those. I realize that some people see the Wall as an antiwar symbol. The fifty-eight thousand names on it are awesome. But I always think of the two or three million Indochinese who died. A Wall for them would encompass the entire Washington Mall.

▬

"Thou shalt not kill" is not an equivocal statement. It doesn't say, "Thou shalt not kill unless there is provocation." It doesn't say, "Thou shalt not kill unless you're in the military."

▬

War can exist only when people are whipped into a form of hysteria. War is an induced state of mind. That's why it's so important to be true to yourself, to your individual values, so you can call into question the stories about how bad the other guys are and how inferior they are and how important it is to kill them. If you always remember the humanity of the other side, it's much harder to go to war.

▬

I'm a high school history teacher. Each year, I show the film *Hearts and Minds* in my class. It's hard for me to watch because it brings back so much of the emotion of the time.

I especially remember the famous sequence that created so much of an uproar — General Westmoreland sitting on the veranda of his mansion in Georgia explaining how death doesn't mean anything to Southeast Asians. As he speaks, there are scenes of a military cemetery in Saigon, where a nineteen-year-old Vietnamese soldier is being buried. His mother is completely hysterical, tearing her hair out by the handful, leaping into the grave, and pleading to be buried with her son. While General Westmoreland explains how human life means nothing to the Vietnamese. He was the classic southern cracker. Vietnam was a good career move for him.

That scene always has a big impact on my students.

In the last ten years, I've had a lot of anger problems that seem to come from nowhere. I have a good home life, a good family life, I'm healthy, and I'm successful in most of the things I do. But I have flashes of irrational anger, violent fantasies, and frequent bouts of really bad, dangerous driving that don't make sense.

At first, I didn't connect it with being in Vietnam. But then my wife suggested it might be related. I took forever to face it and to get through my defensiveness, but one day, just as clear as a bell, I realized when it began — in 1970. For all my playing with guns as a kid, I never had these violent, angry fantasies before 1970. That's when I went to Vietnam, and that's when I was infected with them. They've been with me ever since.

I have no nostalgia for the Vietnam period. It was vicious and ugly. The American people suffered deep moral and emotional injury. Soldiers came home to a torn, divided country. Half again as many of our soldiers have died of suicide as died in the war. Vietnam was a painful time. It's not surprising that we ended up with the Reagan era. People wanted to forget.

Over the years, I've worked as a medic on emergency relief teams in Nicaragua, El Salvador, and the Philippines. I've tried to use the skills the army taught me to do what I could in situations where families' lives are turned upside down by war. There are so many more victims in the world than there are victimizers.

Four years ago, I went to a weekend retreat with a men's group. We spent much of our time working on grief. For me, that meant the grief and the shame I felt for the men who didn't make it, the guys who died while I was working on them in Vietnam.

I especially remember one particular guy who had been shot through a lung. I worked on him, and all the while he kept saying, "I can't breathe, I can't breathe." I didn't have the knowledge then to realize that his good lung was filling up with blood. I should have turned him on his side, onto the bad lung, so it wouldn't drain into the good one. But I didn't know that. So he suffocated right there in front of me. I had screwed up. No one else knew. But I knew. I knew.

When I was eighteen, *Life* magazine had a story about a guy who had forty different things he wanted to do with his life, like climbing certain mountains and achieving other great goals. He had already accomplished something like twenty of his goals.

It's great to have goals and to achieve them. But today, the forty things on my list would be completely different from when I was eighteen. I still see courage in climbing mountains, but I see more courage in being able to speak your own truth and stand up to scorn. It takes less courage to face a mountain than it does to face the wrath of others. You have to have the courage to stand alone in your convictions, to know what is true for you. That's very hard to do when you're young or old. But I find it easier now, as I grow older.

I remember years ago someone told me that you must speak the truth quickly, because otherwise your fear will make you edit the truth. Today, I try to talk from my heart.

In 1991, I decided to contact my mother. I had not talked with her since my father and my brothers died and I left for Thailand, eighteen years earlier. I wanted to say hello. I needed to hear her voice. I didn't want to hear five years later that she had died without my having made an effort to reach her.

She had moved to the far reaches of Montana, so it took me a while to track her down. Eventually, I found where she lived, and I called her on the phone. Our conversation didn't go well. She wasn't glad to hear from me. We said hello, but we couldn't really talk to each other. She had remarried and had two kids, eight and ten years old. She had a new life. I wasn't part of it.

I remembered the old saying. "Once — a victim. Twice — a volunteer." So I decided not to call her again.

But I did my duty. And if I hear someday that she has died, at least I tried to reconcile with her.

Just the other day, I heard on the radio the old saying, "The ones who hate war most of all are the soldiers." I thought, "That's bullshit." You can't tell me there aren't always a lot of soldiers clamoring to go to war. That's where you get rank. That's where you experience the comradeship. That's where you get your manhood. That's where I felt most alive.

Parts of Vietnam, I really miss.

―――――

I was astounded at the Vietnam Memorial. A memorial to the fifty-eight thousand Americans who got killed. How about a memorial to the hundreds of thousands of children who were killed in Vietnam? How about a memorial to the millions of civilians killed? Let's see about reparations for Vietnam. Let's see about war crimes trials. Let's see the people responsible for the war in Vietnam punished. Let's see about burying *all* the dead.

———

My best friend in high school happened to live in the next county, where there were far fewer Mennonites than where I lived. His draft board was not as sympathetic to COs as mine, so his application was turned down. Around that time, a buddy of ours, a medic, was severely wounded in Vietnam. That had a big impact on my friend. So just after getting married in 1970, he enlisted and volunteered for combat. He became a helicopter pilot, and in 1971, while I was in France preparing to do my alternative service in Algeria, he was killed in action.

I had lived in Harris County. He had lived in Franklin County. I got a CO deferment. He didn't. That was the difference between us.

Years later, when I was living in Washington, I visited the Vietnam Veterans Memorial and found my friend's name on the Wall. It was a very moving experience for me, because unlike other war memorials, this one points out the cost of war. I'm an amateur photographer, and I took a picture of his name that turned out very nice, a kind of monument to him. I sent the photograph to his parents. I included a letter explaining why it had taken me so long to come to terms with his death. And I told them what wonderful memories I had of him. It was the first contact I had with them since his death.

I wasn't sure if I should send the letter. I didn't want to re-awaken unpleasant memories for them. But his father sent me an extremely moving, eloquent response, expressing his gratitude for what I had done and telling me that it had helped them overcome their grief over the loss of their only son.

I'm a historian now. I try to use my skills to understand the origins of war, so that we can work to stop it for the next generation. My study of history tells me that every war is enormously costly to everyone involved. I know we will never draw any laws from the study of the past, but perhaps we can get a glimpse of alternative futures. I continue to believe that we can find a way to build a better, more peaceful world. I'm very much a child of the Vietnam era.

But for my generation, it's too late. We have failed. We have let our children down.

Questions

When I got my CO deferment in 1968, my draft board assigned me to do alternative service at a former minimum security prison in the desert in California. I felt it was a punitive assignment, almost like going to prison, so I refused to accept it.

For four years, I kept the forms flowing back and forth with my draft board, trying to resolve our disagreement and avoid imprisonment. Finally, in 1972, I was ordered to report for a preinduction physical. I was being drafted, but I decided not to go.

Then, on the morning I was supposed to report for my physical, I was sound asleep when the phone rang. It was the director of the state Selective Service System, who said, "Thank goodness, you haven't left yet. Don't go."

It was over, just like that. My draft board was dropping the case. I sat there stunned, dumbfounded, my head spinning. I had been deeply embroiled in the case for four years. I was expecting to go to court and maybe to prison. Suddenly, with one phone call, everything was lifted off my shoulders, without any explanation.

Perhaps because of the odd way my case ended, I have ambivalent feelings now about being a CO. I question my motives. Self-preservation certainly was part of what motivated me. Maybe I just didn't want to cut my hair and live in a barracks with a bunch of other guys. If I had done alternative service in a mental hospital, maybe it would be a little clearer today that I was a pure conscientious objector.

I don't mean I'm bedeviled by doubts. I think I was sincere. I think I did the right thing. But after all these years, my feelings are not sorted out.

I still have a strong interest in Zen Buddhism, as I did in the sixties. I love that cosmic whimsy. I mean, we're all shit sticks, but, hey, an accident could happen and something good might occur. I believe that if I'm attached to an antiwar mode of thinking, then

I'm still attached to the issue of war. And attachment, regardless of what kind, leads to suffering.

So I would like to say that being a CO was an important, courageous, moral stand, but I don't see it that way. When I try to locate myself and the CO issue in some historical or cultural or theological context, as far as I'm concerned, it doesn't mean shit. If being a CO really meant something, then all this constant killing wouldn't be going on all the time. That's how I feel. Being a CO doesn't mean a goddamned thing.

If it had been World War II, that would have been different. I think of William Stafford, the Quaker poet, who was a CO in the forties. It must have taken a hell of a lot of courage to be a CO back then. But for me, it wasn't difficult. It didn't take any courage. I didn't agonize. I just sat down and wrote the application in one night. When I was finished, I felt it was the best I could do, and I felt good about it.

So my story isn't good copy. Other aspects of my life are more important than being a CO.

I'm a writer, but I don't write antiwar poems. Yet sometimes my work seems to have something to do with war. Like this:

O bird
whose throat bleeds
music, who draws religion
from a stone and sings
like water flowing,
who knows a song
knows truth

forgive these dishes
being rattled, the rude indifference
of my bowels broken, a black dog
that barks like a machine.

Here, on earth, at the mercy
of hawks and holymen.

I hear you.

▬

COs were not any big deal. Just a thorn in the side of the military establishment. Being a CO was more an act of individual conscience than a matter of trying to have a particular effect on policy.

▬

After I applied for CO status, I continued working in psychiatric care at Ford Ord while the army reviewed my application. I was offered a promotion, but I turned it down by writing a letter saying it wasn't consistent with my beliefs to be further involved with the military. Turning down a promotion wasn't like standing up in a prisoner of war camp and taking a rifle butt in the face, but it felt good to make a stand.

My dad's best friend — a prisoner of war with my dad during World War II — wrote a letter of support for my CO application. He was a military man and very conservative, yet he had a lot of respect for me and the things I believed. His letter moved me very much, because he was a friend of my dad, and my dad was the one person who was adamantly against me. My father was career military and had suffered a great deal of physical pain and emotional loss as a POW. To see his son take a stand against his patriotism was very hard for him. And to face his reaction was very hard for me.

When I finally got my CO deferment and was discharged in 1971, I moved in with my folks, but my dad didn't even want to talk to me. I got a job driving an ambulance and working in the operating room at a hospital for a month, and then I moved away to Salinas, California, to attend community college on the GI Bill. My GI benefits were prorated for the time I served. It was enough for school and for aviation training.

The only hint that I had other than a normal, honorable discharge was my reenlistment code, which was RE-4, meaning that I couldn't get back in the service.

I don't imagine that having a negative reenlistment code bothered too many COs. But I also don't imagine many COs decided later to try to get back in the military. In 1974, three years after I got out, that's just what I decided to do.

The war was over at that point, at least for Americans. I was taking flying lessons, and nothing sounded sweeter than military flight training, which became a burning passion for me. That's what I wanted to do with all my heart. It was easy to consider the positive aspects of the military when there was no war and my work wouldn't involve dropping bombs. So I took the tests with the air force and the navy, and I passed. Everything was in order, except that reenlistment code.

My dad was thrilled and got behind me by writing letters to congressmen and to officers in the military. I went to my dad's good friend, who had written the letter supporting my CO application, to get his help as well. But now he refused. His feeling was that I had made this big decision to get out of the army as a CO, and it didn't sit right with him that I would try to get back in during peacetime.

I wasn't real proud of what was taking place in my own belief system. Basically, there was something I wanted, and I felt the military was the best way to get it. I guess in some people's minds — and in mine, too — there might be a doubt about how deeply held my beliefs were. I can see the validity of that doubt. It's just that I so passionately wanted to be a military aviator, I would have done anything. In the end, though, my application for reenlistment was turned down. I couldn't get back into the service.

I don't feel at ease today divulging my feelings about those times. I'm still in the process of accepting what I did. I don't think people will respect me. In their minds, I might be wishy-washy. So I don't tell anyone that I was a CO. I can see the validity of other points of view. That's one of my biggest problems. I see too many points of view. Sometimes it's hard to come up with a firm one of my own.

I know only one person who had any negative feelings about what I did. She was a close friend, one of a group that hung out together in Reno in '64 and '65. When I got my draft notice and refused to go, she left our group. Cut off all contact with us.

What she did still bothers me. If she had joined the army and gone off to fight, I wouldn't have stopped talking to her. She's the only one I've ever known who made me feel rejected.

A few years ago, I dug out her picture and put it in a black frame along with my draft notice. I still have them framed together.

———

My family never actually knew I got my CO deferment. I didn't know how they'd take it. My father was a World War II vet. I thought he'd feel funny about it. So I just told him I worked out some legal delays. He never asked any questions. I don't think he wanted to know.

I have a tremendous amount of respect for anyone who was a veteran. I would never want to offend them by telling them I was a CO and implicitly saying, "Boy, were you stupid to wind up fighting when it wasn't necessary. If you had just known how to work the system . . ." I feel some guilt at having manipulated the system when so many others weren't able to. That's the thing that nags me still.

I work for a company today that produces aircraft components. About 30 or 40 percent of our business is military. Originally, I was in employee relations. My role was to make sure that the company treated its employees properly. Now, I work in technical areas like benefits and compensation. The most important issue for me is how the company treats its employees, not whether it does defense work. I'm comfortable with my work in the company.

I don't publicize my CO status to anyone. Just this week, I had a conversation at work with a Vietnam vet. I almost told him I was a CO, but I was afraid it would affect our relationship. Not that he would have the opposite view of the war. In fact, he said he was very much opposed to it. But I was afraid that maybe he would think I was putting him down. So, still, nobody at work knows I was a CO. Maybe that's best.

My company is in the middle of a big layoff. A coworker and I must decide which people will lose their jobs. We pick out the ones to be eliminated. I had a dream recently in which that coworker was a successful fighter pilot in Vietnam. In the dream, she got so close to the enemy plane that she could see the other guys inside the canopy. Then she made the kill. In my dream, she was incredibly shook up. It was the first time she had ever seen the face of the enemy.

Vietnam affects me in a lot of ways. Even my dreams.

———

After the war, I taught school for several years, but it was nearly impossible for me to support my family on a teacher's salary. So I quit teaching and spent six months looking for a job where I could use my background in physics and math. I didn't want to work for a company where money was coming from the Defense Department. During interviews, I had no hesitation about saying "no" to defense work. Yet I needed a job, and if I had been offered one in a company where *some* of the work was defense related, I might have taken it, as long as I wasn't personally working on a military project.

Finally, I got a job in a university nuclear physics program. When I interviewed for the job, they told me the work was funded by the Department of Energy, and military research was in a different department. So I took the job.

I work in experimental particle physics now. Although my department avoids defense funding, the differences between military and other kinds of research are not always clear. For instance, I am currently working on a medical project that involves particle acceleration. That research is also useful for Star Wars. So I'm always dancing on the edge.

Linguistically, the word "pacifism" is hopeless because of its association with "passive." Knowing myself, I suspect that if I saw someone "blanking my blank" — like raping my grandmother — I would kick the shit out of them. I am not a passive person in any sense.

The hypothetical questions COs are always being asked about what they would do in different situations where personal violence is a threat simply do not address the real issues of war and peace. Joan Baez had the classic story that tells how to answer hypothetical questions.

Suppose you're asked what you would do if you were driving a school bus full of kids on a narrow mountain road and suddenly you see a baby sitting in the middle of the road.

You might answer, "Well, I would drive around him."

But no, in this hypothetical situation, the road is too narrow. So you say, "I would hit the brakes and stop."

No, in this hypothetical situation, you are traveling too fast.

So, you might as well answer the hypothetical question with a hypothetical answer. "Okay, I would hit the brakes, they would fail, I would swerve, I would try to miss the kid, I would hit the side of the cliff, the bus would fly off the cliff and land on a school building and the gasoline tank would explode and 350 children would be killed. Now are you happy?"

Exiles

After hearing that my Selective Service file had been destroyed and there was no record of my case, my wife and I decided to take a chance and make our first trip from Canada back to the United States to meet her family in San Francisco in 1973. I was as nervous as could be. I had heard about people being arrested at the border. I wondered if they were lying about my files being lost. Perhaps they were trying to trap me.

The U.S. customs and immigration check took place at the Vancouver airport, where an official checked a huge book. My name wasn't in it, so he said, "Fine, go ahead." I felt a little better, but as I walked down the ramp off the plane in San Francisco, I still worried there might be a trap. Perhaps the FBI would be waiting to arrest me in the States, where I couldn't get away. It was a risk. And exciting. And I wasn't arrested.

From San Francisco, we flew to Kansas City. It was my first trip back since I left in 1970. My mother had died in the time I was gone. After arriving, I called my right-wing sister, the John Bircher who had always opposed my decision to go to Canada. I hadn't seen her in years. "Here I am. This is your big opportunity," I said. But she didn't want to see me. So that was it.

Later, I wrote letters to her, but she never changed her mind. I haven't seen her now in over twenty years. And I've never gone back to Kansas City again.

I made some big choices by coming to Canada. I was lucky. I don't want to touch the past. One little change and who knows what would have happened to me. If I hadn't met the person who mentioned Canada, I might not have thought of coming here. If I hadn't written to the war objectors' committee and if I hadn't found their office when I arrived, I don't know what I would have done wandering the streets. If the family hadn't taken me in and if I hadn't met my first wife . . . if any of those events had changed, who knows where I would be now?

A few years ago, I met a guy who lived on an island way up the west coast of British Columbia. He was an American draft dodger who stayed in that frame of mind. But I don't know anybody else like that. There's no longer an American war resisters' identity. Almost everyone who didn't adjust went home. After twenty years, we've spent as much time in Canada as we did in the United States. By now, most of us are Canadian.

The end of the war contributed to my leaving Montreal. The activities I'd been involved with for years, the circles of people I'd traveled in — all of that was winding down as the war in Vietnam came to an end. Also, Quebec as a distinct culture was really blossoming then. While Vietnam was happening, I could define myself in opposition to the war, and thereby have some legitimacy in Francophone Canada. But as the war ended, I was becoming part of the historical anachronism of English people in Quebec. My life was beginning to feel like another period was coming to an end.

So my girlfriend and I packed our belongings in an old van and drove off. We planned to keep going until we hit the water or the van died. We circled down through the United States and almost stopped in Colorado, but we decided not to stay in the States. We nursed the van all the way to British Columbia, and settled in Vancouver.

Today, I feel that Americans on the whole are nice, friendly human beings, who are fundamentally flawed in their view of the world. Americans don't really believe that the rest of the world has any real existence. They think other people talk funny languages that Americans shouldn't have to learn. Americans think of themselves as kind to dogs and children, and willing to donate to charity and foreign aid. On some gut level, they just can't understand why foreigners are critical of them.

Despite these feelings, I remained an American citizen for twenty years, much longer than I needed to. Some of the delay was laziness, which I justified by saying I wanted to keep my options open. If fame and fortune called me to move to Hollywood to become a famous movie star, I wanted to be able to do it with no problem. Then, once I had children, I wanted to be able to register them with the U.S. consulate as U.S. citizens, so they could choose to move to Hollywood and become famous movie stars.

Another reason for the delay was that I'm really an anarchist. That doesn't mean throwing bombs at banks. It means that I think people in small groups should be able to make as many decisions that affect their lives as possible. Whether I carry a passport from the United States or Canada or Swaziland is irrelevant.

Eventually, though, I ran out of excuses, and applied for Canadian citizenship. From the day I got that Canadian government card in the mail saying, "Yes, you are now one of us," my life has not changed one iota.

But I did call my dad in New Jersey to tell him I had become a Canadian citizen. He was amused. He asked why it had taken me so long.

I'm a high school teacher now. Teenagers today are very prepared to believe the world sucks. The environment is screwed up, nuclear holocaust is a real possibility, and their future seems bleak. Pessimism makes total sense to them. That's the problem. It's difficult to get across to kids that change is possible, and that on the personal level the best response to environmental peril or to war is not to get blasted drunk every chance they have.

In 1968, a CBS news team out in the boonies filmed soldiers refusing to engage the enemy. That was mutiny. In a real army, soldiers could be shot for that. But this was broadcast television and the U.S. Army in Vietnam was no longer fighting the war. Not because the politicians refused to let them fight, but because a mass movement against the war had changed America's consciousness. In 1965, fifteen thousand people came to the first mass protest in Washington. Like a lot of other Americans, I figured they were traitors, Communist sympathizers. But by 1969, in the Mobilization that fall, 2 million people took part in organized protests. In just four years, people who were first considered Commie traitors had turned around the most powerful military machine the world has ever seen. Regular people stopped the war. That's a message of hope.

Today, in my high school teaching, I try in my own little way to give kids the feeling that if you believe the world sucks, okay, then you and other people together can turn it around. That's my lesson from Vietnam.

My politics are less flamboyant now than when I was nineteen. I'm a homeowner with a mortgage and a color TV and two kids and a steady job that I've had for eleven years. I'm much less likely to take on hordes of Washington, D.C., police to try to free prisoners.

Yet I'm still a pacifist. A few years back, I was on a strike picket line when someone crossed the line and punched me in the face. I didn't fight back. My only response was one of stunned bewilderment. Perhaps I just wasn't socialized into proper male hormonal responses.

I play in a band that offers its services for fund raising to political groups ranging from rape support centers to anti-apartheid organizations to the End the Arms Race Coalition to trade unions. I also have a garage full of sound equipment, which I let these groups use for their demonstrations and meetings.

I work with a lot of different groups because change is needed in so many ways, on so many levels. The best part of the antiwar movement came out of the civil rights movement and merged into the women's movement. Stopping the war was just one part of a broader movement against racism and sexism and economic inequality and environmental shortsightedness.

I don't consider it a tragedy that I came to Canada, though I get nostalgic and sentimental about the United States every once in a while. Especially if I watch too much PBS television. When I've visited California in recent years, I've been struck with how many of the problems that frightened me in 1966 have gotten worse. Especially immense overcrowding and crime. Oakland after sunset reminds me of the movie *On the Beach*, after nuclear war. It's completely deserted. With its feeling of individual isolation and alienation, California seems to be under the control of people I can't even identify, let alone support. The people's faith in democracy seems no longer to exist.

The fundamental difference between Canada and the United States is that people in Canada still have a belief that they can actually do something about their problems.

Worse things happened to others of my generation. I've come to Canada and had a good life.

Leaving the States changed everything in my life. Not only where I live and work and the people I know, but my philosophy. Before, while living in LA, I wasn't part of a movement, but when I came to Canada, I got involved in working against the war. The first antiwar demonstration I ever attended was in Vancouver. I studied history and gradually generalized my basic antiwar position into notions of anti-imperialism. My anger at my own circumstances and my anger at the war led to a broader social critique of capitalism. Eventually, I became a socialist and joined an organization called In Struggle, a leftist group centered in Montreal. Later, I became a union organizer.

I feel that I got caught up in a moment in history that set me on my course of life. Except for my own personal relationships, all the things I believe and everything I have ever done that's important in my life have been framed by Vietnam.

Maybe none of it is great shakes. But it's my life. And in that sense it's profound.

━━━

I don't think of myself as an exile. I think of myself as a Canadian who was once an American. I'm a Canadian citizen now, legally and spiritually. I have a family here. I work here. I value the relative tolerance and calm in Canada. I don't think I would be comfortable living in the United States anymore.

When I go to the States to visit, there's a naval air station, with a lot of navy jets, just across the border. Near the gate to the base, there's a sign that says, "Pardon our noise. It's the sound of freedom." I don't ever want to live in a country where I have to read a sign like that. That's why I'm thankful I live in Canada.

I've become quite a Canadian nationalist. My son and I have season tickets to the Vancouver Canucks hockey games. Before every game, they play "O Canada." Much to my son's embarrassment, I sing along. Loudly.

During the Gulf war, we went to a Canucks game and every seat was draped with a Canadian flag, and there was a military honor guard on the ice — which rarely happens. Everybody stood and sang "O Canada." Except me. I stayed in my seat. It deeply violated my sense of what it means to be Canadian. It was the most profound feeling of alienation I've had since the Vietnam War.

━━━

I don't feel like a refugee any longer. But I don't feel Canadian either. I don't know what it means to feel like a Canadian. And I don't remember what it feels like to be an American.

To me, patriotism is not "My country, right or wrong." It's a deep feeling of comfort and safety, linked to a place where your family has struggled and managed to survive. If that's patriotism, then I guess that's what I feel for Canada.

And after all that has happened in my life, I have my honor in Canada.

━━━━

During the Gulf war, I got a phone call from a draft-age cousin of mine who was thinking about coming to Canada. He asked me what it would be like living in Canada, and if I would help him out. His father supported the war. He said, "I hate my father. He's a jerk. I never want to speak to him again. He's never going to see our baby again."

I told him, "Be careful about those 'nevers' and those absolutes. You may find that they come true."

Journeys

Vietnam happened to everybody my age.

━━━━

Einstein said that COs are the warriors for a warless world. There must be people committed to nonviolent reconciliation if the world is ever to mature beyond an eye for an eye.

━━━━

I remember telling my draft counselor at the American Friends Service Committee that I couldn't say with 100 percent certainty that I was a CO. He said he was astonished that people always gave the benefit of the doubt to the government. "Why can't you be fifty-one percent certain?"

I thought, "My God, that's true." Maybe I should use a more intellectually democratic model. One vote more than half and I go CO.

After getting my CO classification and being released from the military, I decided to pay back the American Friends Service Committee for its help. In 1972, I began to volunteer, starting out with work to end the war, and then later with efforts at reconciliation with Vietnam. Eventually, I served on the AFSC national board. That's where I met Dan Seeger, whose Supreme Court case had made my CO deferment possible. We're about the same age. He has a very formidable personality. Rather stiff. I thanked him, and he just said he was glad his case was of some use. It wasn't a big moment for him, but for me, it was a finishing point, the end of my time as a Vietnam CO.

I gradually worked more and more for the AFSC, and in 1980 I was invited to go back to Vietnam with an ecumenical group to explore the possibilities of reconciliation between the United States and Vietnam. My school district gave me the time off from teaching. They knew I'd come back with unique stories to tell my students. Before I left, I went to all the Vietnamese and Cambodian refugees in the district's English as a Second Language program to talk about my trip. They gave me letters to mail to their families in Saigon and Phnom Penh.

I spent three weeks in Vietnam and Cambodia. It was about six months after the Vietnamese invasion of Cambodia that removed Pol Pot and the Khmer Rouge from power. I was impressed with the way we were treated. No one seemed angry at Americans. Vietnam was an especially beautiful place.

When I returned home, I felt very connected to the refugees. We have been in one another's countries. Ever since, I've showed my slides and given lectures about Vietnam. Talking about Vietnam has become part of my life.

━━━

I spent a year in Edinburgh, but I decided I wasn't cut out to be a minister. At that time, you could travel from Europe overland to India. So that's what I did. I went through Turkey, Iran, Afghanistan, Pakistan, and India, countries where there is so much turmoil today. Those travels, those sights and sounds and human faces, helped to affirm what I knew before: that human beings are precious and human life is really God-given.

When I returned, I went into emergency medical relief. I coordinated a planeload of medical supplies to El Salvador after the 1986 earthquake. I worked in El Salvador as a nurse with special training in disaster relief. My work was very connected to my concern with peace and social justice. When I returned home, I became involved in making my church a sanctuary for Salvadoran refugees.

My main job today is as a nurse at Children's Orthopedic Hospital. I have my own children now. I try to pass on to them a respect for human life and a spiritual relationship with God and with others. I'm not in the eye of a storm as I was during my trial, but there are trials in personal relationships where courage and forgiveness and submission are needed. Where you have to be able to forgive and accept the last blow, and in a psychological sense turn the other cheek.

Recently, I heard a talk by one of the conscientious objectors from the Gulf war. He seemed very young. That's probably what I seemed like to people listening to me twenty years ago. He described his refusal to follow an order to get on a plane. His sergeants and other soldiers tried to intimidate him to make him change his mind. He went limp as they tried to carry him on the plane. He described in great detail the people who told him why he should get up and fight, why he should be a man and show his courage, why he should have the strength to go to war. One of the people threatened him, saying he'd come back and find him.

As he talked, I thought of my own experiences. Some people threatened me the same way. As if they could frighten me into doing what I knew was wrong. When you experience those threats, that hostility, just nose to nose with somebody screaming at you, time seems to slow down. I wasn't really ever afraid. I didn't fear anyone hunting me down. I could see that the others were afraid of me.

It's awesome that there's a strength within us to liberate ourselves from fear. To stand up in a courtroom, with all the trappings of authority around you, or to stand up against the military, with all its vestments of power, and to say "no" takes courage. It takes real courage. It makes a grand difference in your life to know that you are capable of taking a stand and doing what is right.

━━━

I've increasingly been able to turn my feelings into song. One of my songs goes like this:

You're eighteen years old, war seems far away
May seem an adventure or honest day's pay
But when innocents die, no victory's won
And you don't have to carry a gun.

Maybe your country says that you should
Maybe the President thinks that it's good

213

But "maybe's" not enough reason when all's said and done
You don't have to carry a gun.
"Maybe's" not enough reason when all's said and done
You don't have to carry a gun.

They might take your father or another someone
Maybe it's your lover or mother or son
When they try to take you, you can fight it or run
You don't have to carry a gun.
When they try to take you, you can fight it or run
You don't have to carry a gun.

It takes courage to stand up for what you think's right
It takes wisdom to know more than one way to fight
It may take many people but it starts with just one
You don't have to carry a gun.
It may take many people but it starts with just one
You don't have to carry a gun.

━━━

In the mid-1970s, I began to have an odd feeling that I was on a conveyor belt moving toward a normal, middle-class life that didn't seem to be what I wanted. I didn't feel able to choose something different. Mostly, I felt sad resignation.

Then one day about seven years ago, I was driving home when I saw a little boy walking alone and crying. At first, I ignored him and just drove past. But then I decided to go back to talk. He was lost. So I took him to a nearby gas station, got his last name from him, and called his home. I remember very clearly the sound of his mother's voice when I asked, "Do you have a son named Mark?" There was a catch in her voice, a signal that suddenly she was very, very frightened. She said simply, "Yes, I do." I told her not to worry, but her son was lost. She came over and got him.

It was a little thing, helping a scared kid and calming an upset mother. But I came out of it with so much. Helping that little boy reminded me that I really can have an effect in the world. It made me think back to when I was thirteen years old and attended a Zionist summer camp. I gave a little speech there, where I quoted from the prophet Micah: "What does the Lord require of you but to do justice, to love mercy, and to walk humbly with your God." Those words didn't mean much to me when I was a kid. But that day, after helping that little boy, I decided I would try to live my life according to the words of the prophet Micah.

So, for the first time since Vietnam, I became involved again in politics. I joined a local collective of about twenty people who worked on political action through consensus planning. With them, I learned about affinity groups and about community. I joined the Pledge of Resistance, a group that promised to resist any U.S. invasion of Nicaragua. I did training in nonviolent civil disobedience and I joined a peace camp at the Nevada test site. I was arrested there several times for trespassing.

All of that work led up to my decision to join the Vietnam veterans' convoy taking relief supplies to Nicaragua in the summer of 1988. Although I had never been in the military, there was a last-minute opening for a truck driver. So I joined. The convoy had a hundred people with thirty-five trucks filled with medical aid and food, mostly oatmeal. Our plan was to drive the trucks through the United States to San Antonio, Texas, then cross the border to Mexico and on to Nicaragua.

At the first meeting of the convoy, some of the guys introduced themselves as our commanders. I argued that the group should be able to ratify their leadership, but they didn't understand what I was talking about. Along with several others, I came from a consensus perspective, while many of the vets thought in terms of a chain of command. The split between these two approaches to making decisions was never really resolved.

When we reached the Mexican border, the U.S. customs police refused to allow us to cross. They said our vehicles violated the embargo against military material going to the Sandinistas. We tried for days to get across, but we were unsuccessful. Finally, our leaders decided to take the convoy to Washington, D.C., hoping that the American people would rise up to support us.

It was a mistake. In Texas, we had been a visible presence with a lot of press coverage, but when we got to Washington, we had a pathetic little demonstration and then vanished from the media. We finally crawled back to Texas with our tails between our legs, by then reduced to about five vehicles and eleven people.

We decided to establish a long-term presence at the border,

still hoping that we could build a movement that would pressure the government to allow us across. We sat there for days, gradually becoming quite discouraged. In one demonstration, the police arrested several of us.

But then one day, one of our drivers simply drove his truck out alone and crossed the border. No one tried to stop him. He came back to our camp on foot and told us what had happened. We realized that if we discreetly drove the trucks one at a time, we could get across. So, that's what we did.

When we finally crossed the border from Honduras to Nicaragua, huge crowds greeted us in the small towns along the way. Nicaraguan radio stations carried reports every day about our progress through the country. When we reached the capital, we had a ceremony in Managua in which President Daniel Ortega came out to meet us. I got to shake his hand. Ortega held up a baby bottle from our convoy and said, "Here's the dangerous weapon that Ronald Reagan wanted to prevent from reaching Nicaragua."

For me, one of the most important aspects of being on the convoy was that I got to ride in a truck with a guy who was in the Marines during Vietnam. We graduated from high school the same year. I was a resister. He ended up in combat. The two of us, every day in this pickup truck, got to talk about Vietnam. I told him I was one of those during the war who thought that people who went to Vietnam were awful. I never spit on anyone, but I could have. He talked about the resistance that existed in the military and how much GIs hated being in Vietnam. From him, I learned that people went to Vietnam just as unthinking and oblivious to the real issues as I had been. Being able to talk to each other showed us how much we had in common.

In my job today, I work with a Vietnam vet. We sit at desks next to one another. We know each other very well and we talk about all the minutiae of our lives. But we've never talked about Vietnam. I've hinted at it, saying, "I had a few rounds with my draft board," but I've never said I was a CO. It's not that I think it would jeopardize our relationship. But it's something that's left open and unresolved. I feel sorry for that.

For me, the war with Iraq was the death of my illusion that mass protest can matter. Thirty, fifty, a hundred thousand people marched in various American cities, many more than in most of the demonstrations against the war in Vietnam. But it was ineffective. It's much more difficult to affect policy today than in the 1960s. My belief that a mass popular movement will matter to people in power has died forever.

Today, I feel thoroughly and completely alienated from the political and cultural mainstream of this country. I no longer feel, as I did during the sixties, that I'm a good American who simply disagrees with the policies of my government. I've crossed over some kind of chasm that is irrevocable and complete. I have the feeling of looking back across a wide gulf. I can see my previous self on the other side. I can see some of my old friends. I can wave. But I feel an irrevocable separation between who I am now and what I used to be. I am sad and weary with how much there is to do politically.

I told my social studies class that I thought George Bush paid attention to the critics of the war in Vietnam. Before attacking Iraq, he went to the United Nations, he got a declaration of support from the American Congress, he made sure he got the backing of NATO, and he used only volunteers in the combat force. Perhaps without realizing it, our government learned its lesson from what went wrong in Vietnam. This time, we fought a war with wide popular support. I certainly supported it.

When GIs first went into Kuwait, they drove their tanks around the bodies in the road. But at a certain point, there were so many bodies that the soldiers got callous and just drove over them. Some day, it will dawn on those guys that they drove over human bodies as if they were rocks in the road. Those are the guys who will have nightmares. The same nightmares a lot of us Vietnam veterans have had.

▬▬▬

I remember writing on my CO application that letting Hitler overrun Europe without confronting him militarily probably would have cost 6 to 10 million lives, and when the United States and Russia confronted him militarily, the death toll was 28 million.

But that's just a numbers game. It doesn't mean much. The great challenge is to figure out what on earth you do when people with a lot of power run amuck. There are no easy answers. But if we put as much energy into developing nonviolent national defense as we do violent national defense, we could save millions of lives.

▬▬▬

The great German sociologist Max Weber put it classically in his famous essay "Politics as a Vocation": Who really is the ethical person? The one who says, "Here I stand. I can do no other"? Or the one who first carefully weighs the consequences of any action? The Catholic Left started out its civil disobedience campaign against the war by saying, "Here I stand. I can do no other." But as the war ground on, our failure to stop it kept being thrown in our face on the nightly news: the body count, the body count, the body count. So it became apparent that something had to change, and the decision was made not to stand around any longer waiting to be arrested. Our efforts changed from public, highly visible acts of civil disobedience against draft boards in broad daylight, to covert, underground activities against the police, the military, and the military-industrial complex. And thereby the Catholic Left began to move, step by step, underground.

One raid was against the AMF factory in York, Pennsylvania. AMF made a lot of sports equipment. Their television commercials said, "We make weekends." Most people didn't know that they also made bombs. One assembly line was making bowling balls, another was making Mark-82 five-hundred-pound bombs. A group of the Catholic Left got inside, removed a critical portion of the fuses from those bombs, and sent one to every member of Congress with a note saying, "We are doing our part to stop the bombing. Now you do yours."

In draft board raids, the total number of draft records destroyed was in the millions. That was in the days before computers, so if you got the paper, you got everything. Sometimes we sent stolen draft files back to the individual men, saying, "You've got another chance. If you want to send this stuff back to your draft board, go ahead."

The government's response to us was very swift and very heavy-handed. People who burned down entire neighborhoods in 1968 weren't hit with the long prison terms some of us got for torching a few pieces of paper. At first, we thought we could use the courtroom as a platform for our views and we could convince a jury of our peers to acquit us. But we soon learned that judges blocked meaningful testimony and instructed juries so that they had no choice but to deliver guilty verdicts. I've talked to many jurors in the Catholic Left cases who left the court in tears afterward, saying they were for acquittal, but feared being cited for contempt of court if they didn't vote for a conviction.

Usually, we clumsily translate the Hindu term "satyagraha" as "nonviolence." But it really means "clinging to the truth" that nonviolence is the way of truth as much as it is the way of love. The decision to change from overt to covert actions confronted the Catholic Left with the issue of the relationship between nonviolence and truth-telling. Once you begin to operate underground, then the need for secrecy quickly leads to lying. And lying eats away at you, producing distrust and paranoia that undermine nonviolence.

Finally, the point of contradiction was over the issue of informers. What does a supposedly nonviolent movement do when it uncovers an informer? That is the final question in any kind of underground activity. An informer represents a fundamental threat to the life of the movement, and we all know what happens to informers in underground movements throughout the world. You kill them, usually in a grisly way to send a message to anybody else who might be thinking about trying to infiltrate the movement. But being the nice, nonviolent folks that we were, we decided that when informers showed up at our parties, we wouldn't talk to them anymore. As if that was going to end the problem.

As the Catholic Left went underground, it played into the strengths of the other side. The authorities wanted us to drift toward violence. That way, nobody would support us and they could do anything they wanted to us. So the FBI, using informers, turned us on ourselves, friend began suspecting friend, and eventually the FBI broke the back of the movement.

The experience of the Catholic Left during Vietnam led many

of us to conclude that nonviolence and covert, underground activities are incompatible. So the nonviolent movement has, since Vietnam, shunned underground activity. It is now the right wing in this country that is known for violence and for underground action.

The Vietnam experience marked me indelibly for life. And so did the commitment to nonviolence. Around 1977, I realized that my calling from God is to spend the rest of my life working directly on the issues of peace and justice. I did so first, for ten years, as the staff person for the Peace Task Force of the Ecumenical Church Council, and as a member of the local chapter of Clergy and Laity Concerned. For the past three years, I've been research director of an institute that does research on demilitarization, human rights, and sustainable development, with a focus on the Asia-Pacific region. So, for me, the experience of Vietnam was not only a matter of personal commitment. It became my life's work.

In 1982, I was one of forty-two people who attempted to blockade the arrival of the first Trident submarine. That episode is one of the amazing stories of the antinuclear movement of the 1980s. It was written up very well in a chapter of *Hope in Hard Times* by Paul Loeb.

We attempted our blockade under the threat of a ten-year prison term. By that time, I was enough of a veteran of civil disobedience to know that if the government said ten years, it meant ten years. Nevertheless, my wife and I made the decision to be involved in the Trident blockade, even if the time in prison meant we wouldn't have children.

The Trident base is down a narrow inlet called Hood Canal, so the submarines have to come a long way from the ocean. At one point in the canal, there is a narrow passage under a major bridge, where the submarines must pass. During the Vietnam War, ammunition was shipped to Vietnam under that bridge. Some people who had tried to slow those munitions ships by blocking them with canoes came back to help us try to stop the Trident at that bridge.

To counter our actions, the government resurrected a 1951 national emergency statute enacted under the Truman administration to prevent dockworker strikes during the Korean War. A national emergency was declared in Hood Canal, which enabled the government to invoke draconian laws governing the waters of Puget Sound. In effect, the government declared martial law. We fought it in court, but the judge ruled that the declaration was legal, which made it a felony for a homeowner to walk out on his or her dock into Hood Canal. The navy argued that this was necessary because a thrown object might seriously damage the Trident submarine. One conjures up images of somebody winging a beer bottle, taking out the sonar on this $1.2 billion, 600-foot-long dreadnought.

The judge's ruling made it impossible for us to go out into Hood Canal to establish the blockade at the bridge. So we decided to take our protest to more open waters, in the Admiralty Inlet, where larger boats would be needed. We got help when boats came from Australia, New Zealand, and Canada to join in our protest.

We had a former Poseidon nuclear submariner advising us on the navy's likely strategy, and someone else watching the Panama Canal, so we would know exactly when the sub would arrive. For a week in advance of its arrival, we had training sessions on the waters. Assembled against us was a huge Coast Guard and naval armada. Every Coast Guard boat on the West Coast was brought in, and some arrived even from the Great Lakes. The navy thought there were going to be thousands of protesters, so they set up a huge prison camp, complete with barbed wire and television cameras to monitor prisoners.

For several days before the sub arrived, the two fleets circled each other warily. We made practice feints in our little boat, the SS *Plowshares*, an eighteen-foot runabout. Most of the protest boats were little putputters, but our runabout had a real good motor. One day, a Coast Guard boat came roaring toward us with its machine guns pointed. I looked at our captain and said, "Let's show them what we can do," and suddenly, zoooooommmm, we easily pulled away from them. I imagined them later that night, back at the drawing boards, figuring they would need PT boats to stop us.

I must confess that the part of me that has always been fascinated by military strategy was greatly fulfilled by what happened next. Finally, I was in a naval battle.

On the morning of the sub's arrival, we were up at the break of dawn. The government's plan was incredible. They activated an entire regiment of the National Guard to close down the Hood Canal bridge. Armed guards were stationed on the public ferry boats. You'd have thought we were the PLO. In our little boat, we had a prominent Lutheran minister, known for his community work and his large family, which included several adopted, handicapped kids. We also had his mother, who was a former Mother of the Year. And two nurses. We were completely committed to nonviolence. We were not crazies. I was probably the shadiest character of all, a nice Ph.D. working for the Ecumenical Church Council.

When Native Americans up north at Point No Point warned us that the submarine had entered the straits, we pulled out in our boats. But just then, the government pulled a brilliant tactical maneuver. Even though at that point we had not done anything illegal, they launched a preemptive strike. They swooped down on us with water cannon boats, 50-caliber machine guns with live ammunition, helicopters, and soldiers in combat uniforms carrying M-16s. They stopped nearly every boat we had before we could get into open waters. One Coast Guard boat came alongside and was about to tie a line on our runabout when suddenly their radio squawked and they zoomed off somewhere else. That gave us an opening, so we slammed on the throttle and became one of the few boats to escape the Coast Guard ambush.

We went after the submarine, and got within five hundred yards before we were surrounded by three Coast Guard cutters and taken into custody.

A couple of weeks before, I had been on the Phil Donahue show, in a debate about the Trident. As I was being hauled aboard the Coast Guard cutter and handcuffed, a young Coast Guardsman looked at me and said, "Hey, didn't I see you on Phil Donahue? Can I have your autograph?" Then he yelled, "Hey, I got one of the ringleaders. Wait till the guys back at Port Angeles hear about this." I figured he had bragging rights in a bar later that night — "Got me one of the big ones, the guy from the Donahue show."

We were then thrown down in the hold of the Coast Guard ship. And what was plastered on the walls down there? *Playboy* and *Penthouse* pictures. So the former Mother of the Year started banging on the walls until the guards came running down, and she said, "As an American citizen and a taxpayer, I am appalled at this immoral sexist display on my government's ship." The guards just rolled their eyes and went off to tell the captain, who came down and apologized, as he ripped down all the foldouts. So we had a minor case of successful in-custody resistance.

After all the years I had spent trespassing onto the Trident base and getting caught no more than twenty yards inside the fence, the irony was that this Coast Guard ship docked at the pier right next to the Trident submarine. As I got off the Coast Guard ship — under arrest — I was so close to the Trident I could have spit on it.

A couple of days later, I was sitting at home when I got a phone call telling me the government was dropping all charges. I was sure that was phony baloney. But that's what really happened. It was brilliant. First, an overwhelming, preemptive strike. Then drop the charges.

The government has learned a lot since Vietnam. They stomp on us before we can do anything, then they drop the charges and say, "Look at all those crazies. We stopped them, but see how nice we are? We let them go." It was very effective. I am sad to say that the government handled us very well. We made our very best effort, at literally an international level, and they stomped us real good.

My wife is a doctor, we have a nine-year-old daughter, and I'm the primary homemaker, so I have not been involved much in civil disobedience in recent years. The one form I have continued is tax resistance. We began withholding taxes in 1978, which was the first year either of us made enough money to have to file taxes. I started giving talks about tax resistance in the early 1980s, and was eventually invited to talk to local church leaders about tax resistance and the nuclear arms race. Archbishop Raymond Hunthausen was at one of my talks. As always, I gave my pitch on tax resistance, emphasizing the fact that for most adult Americans it's the one area of unavoidable personal connection with the military-industrial complex. Afterward, the archbishop asked me for a ride because his car was being repaired. He said I had given him a lot of food for thought, and we talked a bit more.

Some days later, I was scheduled to address a conference at Pacific Lutheran University. Archbishop Hunthausen was on the program, too. By that time in my life, I had learned that if I showed up on time for a speech, I would sit around for forty-five minutes before going on stage. So I arrived at the last minute. When I came in, the audience was in an uproar. My first thought was one of horror, that somebody had killed the archbishop. That's the kind of reaction I still have from the sixties. But when I asked someone what had happened, he said, "Incredible! The archbishop just advocated tax resistance for Christians. And he pledged to do it personally, by withholding part of his own taxes." The archbishop's speech that day became widely known internationally, as a result of which he came under severe attack from the right wing of the Catholic Church. I became involved in the effort to defend the archbishop.

Let's face it, beating the pope is difficult. But I would say on a scale of ten, we won about a seven. We beat the pope. The archbishop happily stayed in office.

I've come a long way from being a fourteen-year-old boy in the Catholic seminary in 1959.

Families

The questions you face at the age of nineteen are intensely important. How am I distinct from my parents? What authority do I accept? What authority do I reject? I read the gospels a million times, but it was only when I had to face the draft that the word of God took on a deeper significance, and I began to find the answers to those questions.

When I think back over my life, Vietnam defined who I am.

——

My parents have an expression for me: I'm "outside the pale." "Pale" refers to a line or a boundary of things, and I'm outside the normal boundary. But over the years, I've twisted the expression in my mind and see it as a "pail." I see the majority of people inside the pail and a few people like me outside the pail.

You know, a lot of life just creeps along and change comes slowly. But applying to be a CO was a moment of violent change, and to an extent it was out of my control, because other people were rendering the decision. It was one of the few times I've ever had to clarify my thoughts and defend them. As time goes by, I believe it was one of the most important moments in my life.

The family line was that they would respect my choices. But that wasn't really true. My parents didn't support me when I became a CO. Years later, after the war, when they were visiting me, we were talking about the family, and I just suddenly started in about Vietnam. I tried to talk to them about being a CO. I tried to explain to them why I had made my decisions, why I did what I did.

I tried to reassure them by telling them how grateful I was for the Christian values they gave me. But, just like during the war, there was absolutely no response. None. Vietnam was still too threatening to them. I tried to tell them why I did it, but it wasn't enough. There was nothing more I could say.

━━━

The final falling out with my parents came in the fateful year of 1967. When I told them I was applying to be a CO, my father wrote a letter to me. He said that every generation of my forebears had accepted military service gladly as the price of maintaining free enterprise so future generations could profit themselves and humanity. At the end of the letter, he said he wouldn't mention my being a CO to my brothers and sisters — or to anyone else, for that matter. I could see my parents were ashamed of me.

As years passed, I went home less and less. Finally, I stopped going home at all. I haven't been back to visit my parents now for more than ten years.

━━━

In many ways, I didn't know what it was to have a father. My own father was shut down, emotionally incapacitated. We could never talk about my being a CO.

For many years after Vietnam, I desperately looked for father figures of any kind. Even Christianity served that function for a while. When I got engaged, I hoped that my father-in-law would fill that role. But my fiancée's parents didn't want us to get married because I was a CO. We got married anyway.

My father-in-law had been a communications officer in the South Pacific during World War II and served on Guadalcanal. He bought the whole *Victory at Sea* video series when it came out. In his own way, he had deep suspicions of me. My relationship with him was very artificial, restrained within a certain upper-middle-class code of how people should behave toward one another.

Yet there was one moment, six or seven years ago, that I'll always remember. We had gone to dinner, and afterward we were standing outside by the car. We hadn't been talking about Vietnam. I don't know what triggered it. But suddenly he took my hand and said, "I know that your generation and my generation had different things to do. I now understand why you had to do what you did. I understand."

I was overwhelmed by that moment. It was the kind of acceptance I never received from my own father. My father-in-law never made another direct comment to me in his whole life. Yet I treasure that moment still. He died last January.

━━━

The FBI agent who arrested me by pretending that he wanted to speak to me like a father to a son happened to live near some of the members of my church. One day, my brother and my parents went with those people to confront the agent. They told him, "You lied. How can you justify that as a Christian? This sincere young man was trying to live out his faith. Maybe he didn't do the right thing. But he's not the one who lied. You are."

My brother was only a year older than me, but there he was, face to face, eyeball to eyeball with an FBI agent. It was an emotional experience for me to see him and my parents and the leaders of the church community confront this agent in a personal way and hold him accountable for his actions.

━━━

I've still got my draft card. I use it all the time in my university teaching in psychology classes. I pull my draft card out of my wallet and ask whether anyone knows what it is. There are always a few older students who do. I use it to illustrate that adolescents are a surplus population, available to the adult generation when needed, but not given adult status and privilege. One example is when I could be drafted, trained to kill, and kill or be killed in Vietnam, but I couldn't vote.

My main academic research now is on refugees. I'm especially interested in the effects of violence on child development. I spend a lot of time in Central America and the Philippines in settings of gruesome, armed conflict, living among violently displaced people who are terrorized by security forces or vigilante groups.

I ask myself what I would do if I were a villager when soldiers were coming, and it was clear that their purpose was to wipe out my village, my family, and my kids. Perhaps I would take up arms in such circumstances. I cannot say I would never violently resist. My heart wrenches when I wrestle with that one, because it's real to me. I've spent so much time among people who have been cut down, whose villages have been burned, who have experienced horrible mutilation and horrendous violence that goes way beyond the boundaries of policy. I look at their experience, and I'm just not convinced that I would never use violence to defend my family under those circumstances. When asked if I'm a pacifist today, I cannot claim I am. I would use violence to defend my family.

A world without war would be wholesome and good and merciful and compassionate. I wish I could say that war will not be a part of the human condition in the future. But is it realistic? I don't think so. I'm an idealist. But I'm not naive.

If I did an objective assessment of the impact I've had on bringing about social change during my forty years of life, there wouldn't be a whole lot to be happy about. Yet I know my efforts have made a difference in the lives of individual victims of injustice. And I believe there's a purpose in living my life according to a Christ-like value system, regardless of the outcome. There's a strong Anabaptist-Mennonite tradition of trying to walk as Jesus of Nazareth walked. To be honest, I can never picture Jesus picking up a gun and shooting another person.

My original decision to be a CO was very private, but since then, I've developed a public voice and moved into a larger sense of community. That's the most dramatic change in who I am over the past twenty years. I take the life of Christ seriously. There are times for quiet meditation, but much of Christ's ministry was in the midst of crowds. I know now, more than ever, that there is a time for action.

With my children, we make conscious choices about the environment and about bringing peace and justice into all of our relationships. Activism in our community and activism in the world are part of our family's life together. We watch the news together and discuss what's happening in the world. We participate as a family in political demonstrations.

And all the time, we remind ourselves that we are the privileged ones on this planet. Our needs are met. We've never been hungry. We have a home.

Of course, there are times I don't live up to my ideals. Especially when I lose my temper. I'm ashamed when I do, and I apologize. Even though violence is not part of our family life, there are many ways to communicate coercion. Sometimes, I'm not who I should be, but my actions tell me who I am.

I tell my students today that if all else fails, and you can't see a difference for your activism, remember there is value in living a life and advocating a life based on God's righteousness, justice, and mercy. There's a place for prophetic activism that provides an alternative to the use of coercion and violence. Even when I feel hopeless — and there are times that I do feel hopeless — I can still add my voice to other voices on behalf of peace and justice. And that is good.

∎

In order to reduce our income to where we don't have to pay taxes to support the military, my wife and I have been working for a long time at what the world considers low-status jobs. My wife runs a child-care center. I do home repairs for low-income elderly and disabled people. We have a large garden for our food, which we feel roots us to the wholeness of the earth. We live in an old trailer with additions I've built onto it. I build it as I go, rather than making a lot of money and hiring somebody to do it for me. I enjoy it, and I want to save some of it so my son can work with me when he's old enough. Then we'll have a complete house rather than just a piece of one.

I believe in meeting the basic needs of my family and trying to share the rest. But there are some things I do that are wrong. I still eat animals. And I commute to work in my car. I shouldn't use that much gas. So I don't feel my hands are completely clean. I don't feel that my life-style is a great example for people to follow. But for me, it has integrity.

∎

I first met Lan at work, where she was a medical interpreter. In Saigon, her father was a renowned professor and her mother a teacher, so she led a relatively protected life. They left Vietnam by the skin of their teeth in 1975, the day before the collapse of the south. They lost all their worldly goods, everything, when they came to the United States.

In 1983, Lan knocked on my door to tell me about a history of the Vietnam War on public television. I was touched because I had figured that Vietnamese refugees were so bitter that it would be difficult for them to talk to somebody like me, who was opposed to the war, even though my actions were done as much out of concern for the Vietnamese as for anyone.

Lan and I watched the TV series and then we talked about it a lot. Our conversation was a very moving experience for both of us. Afterward, Lan wanted to do something in memory of the war, so she organized a gathering of American GIs who had fought in Vietnam and Vietnamese refugees who had fought in Vietnamese uniform. The meeting was very emotional. Many of the GIs harbored bitter feelings about Vietnamese of any kind, even the ones they were fighting with. The gathering was a chance to begin to overcome the past and to connect as people. It has since become an ongoing affair on Veterans' Day.

My relationship with Lan began because of our mutual interest in Vietnam. Then, slowly, our friendship blossomed into romance. In a million years, it would never have crossed my mind that I would end up marrying a refugee from the Vietnam War. But that's what I did.

Our most intense experience together was seeing the film *Platoon*. It's a rough movie. You see the war through the eyes of an American infantryman. You're right down there in the bush, in the firefights with him. The movie hit me like a ton of bricks. When it was over and the lights came on, I couldn't talk. I was in shock. As we were leaving the theater, we passed a group of Vietnam vets. One guy saw me with Lan and gave me a nod, a sign that he thought I had been in Vietnam, too, and had come back with my Vietnamese wife.

When we got home, as soon as I got in the door, I started crying, and I just couldn't stop. I had never cried for my cousin Bruce, whom I lost in Vietnam. I had never cried for the GIs. I had never cried for my own guilt at not having gone to war. It's not that I thought I should have been in Vietnam, but it was only the privilege of my conscience that kept me out. That night, I cried for the GIs, for the Vietnamese, for my cousin, for Lan, and for myself. It was a moment I had postponed for many years, starting to come to terms with Vietnam and with the feelings I had locked away.

I've made my life with Lan now and become part of her family and the Vietnamese community. Sometimes, Lan and I go to Vietnamese restaurants. When we walk in, people often stare at me. "Here's this American guy with a Vietnamese woman." Maybe they think I was there.

Lan's family lives near us, except for one grandmother and some cousins still in Vietnam. Lan's father never had the heart to recreate a life for himself in this country. The only job he was able to get was working as a janitor. In 1987, twelve years after coming here, he died of a combination of health problems that I think were the result of his despair at having lost his world. His kids have done well, though, gotten an education, and started their own families. They've found their way in America.

In some mysterious way, Lan's fate and mine are intertwined. We feel that we are our reward to each other for the Vietnam War.

―――

I was single and young when I went to prison. Married guys, especially ones with little children, had a much harder time than I did. It was almost unbearable to see their pain at being away from their families. Now that I'm married with two children, I wouldn't want to be away from them for long. My heart is too much with them. I like to think I haven't lost something in courage, but maybe I've lost something in endurance.

As I look back from the comfortable vantage point of twenty years' passage of time, I wish I had done some things differently. For instance, I wish I had poured blood on the files instead of napalm. But you can go through your whole life wishing you had taken this job or married that person or gone on that trip or not said those words. We all make mistakes.

But I don't believe that destroying the draft files was a mistake. We were at war then. Not the weekend wars our country stages now, or the low-intensity, off-the-front-page type in Latin America. It was a serious, old-fashioned war that went on for many years. And there was another war in this country then, a war against the young. Times demanded urgent action. I'm proud of what I did. I don't regret it at all.

Prayer is not only what I say. It's what I do. For me, acts of civil disobedience have always been acts of prayer. I hope much of my life is active prayer. Acts of conscience must be part of a life of conscience.

Alexander Berkman, a turn-of-the-century anarchist writer and activist, said that the phantoms of prison last a long time. For many years, I went back to prison in my sleep. Guards came by, counting me in the night. Even today, I don't like being alone in rooms with the doors closed. I'm okay with another person, but by myself, I feel like saying, "Open it up! Open it up!"

I'm living proof that prison is survivable. Everything I held to be true and important was challenged and mocked in prison. But you can find real freedom there, if you face your fears and go through them. Prison melts the dross away from the gold, and you come out knowing, "This is who I am. This is what I believe. This is real. And it cannot be taken away from me."

———

My father was a lieutenant during the Second World War. Three boats were torpedoed out from under him. Once, he was missing in action, washed up on an island, and rescued weeks later. He never talked much about it. During the Korean War, he was called up again. He was very patriotic.

My un-American ways really pissed him off. We finally had a horrible scene where he began to choke me in front of Mom. So I had to leave. I walked out of the house and didn't return for nearly six years.

When I was on trial, my folks wanted nothing to do with me. My father was mortified that we had the same name. My going to prison was so antithetical to his world view that the only way he could deal with it for a long time was to act as if I didn't exist.

As time passed in prison, I started corresponding with my parents, telling them about day-to-day life there, and injecting a bit of my radical social perspective. Eventually, my mom came to visit me at McNeil Island. I got to pilot the boat that brought her from the mainland to the prison. I deliberately put the boat sideways in some rolling chop, so both rails went under the water and people got sick. I got in trouble, but I sure had fun. And my mom liked the ride. She knew what I was doing.

Finally, my father came to visit me, too. By that point, he had digested my sister's fiancé's death in Vietnam and he realized that maybe there was some validity to the questions I had asked and the choices I had made. His visit was an acknowledgment that I was still a member of his family and I still had his name. He tried, very haltingly and with great difficulty, to communicate that to me.

The fact that my father came to prison, sat next to me, and acknowledged my existence was a kind of reconciliation, or at least an acceptance of why I did what I did. My father was still horrified by my actions, and he certainly wished I wasn't in jail, but at least he came to some awareness of my reasons for refusing to fight. And I could appreciate his point of view, that going to prison was the last thing I should have done. But from my point of view, it was the only thing I could have done.

Sometimes, today, I really get down on myself. Why the hell did I waste my time in prison twenty years ago? At the time, I thought I was doing something noble and good, but maybe I just threw away nearly two years of my life. But usually I get over that feeling and remember that there are many more people today willing to say "Wait a minute" before the first bomb is dropped. So I see a glimmer of hope.

Yet I question myself. Since Vietnam, I haven't done a god-damned thing politically. I'm now a father of two, a tax-paying, all-American working stiff. I was in an official county car, going to a mental health center to evaluate someone for an involuntary commitment, the week before the bombs started dropping on Iraq. I was going to take the freeway, when I suddenly saw a ragtag band of protesters marching onto the interstate. I pulled the car over and was frozen. Part of me wanted to join them: "Fuck being a citizen. My moral principles are more important. My heart is with those demonstrators." Twenty years ago, I was part of a group that took over campus buildings after the Kent State shootings. I wanted to do something like that again.

Yet another part of me thought, "Hey, wait a minute, chump. Your boss will fire your ass if you leave a county car abandoned on the side of the road to participate in an illegal demonstration. Think of your family."

Then I rationalized that my boss knew my background when he hired me ten years ago, so how could he be surprised if I joined the demonstration? Maybe I could get away with it.

But finally I decided, "No, that isn't the way. I'm a county official, on important work, going to see someone who is so crazy he is ready to kill himself. That person needs me. I'm the one with the authority to decide what to do with him. That's my job. So out of my way, assholes." And I drove around the protesters, on to my appointment.

I worry that people may discount what I say because of the interwoven tapestry of being an outlaw, a hippie, and a drug taker. Drugs did influence my thinking and my perceptions. I make no bones about it. It bothers me that some people will discount what I say. Part of me would like to polish up my story and delete portions of it. But I believe I should put out the whole story — warts, blemishes, tarnishes, and idiosyncrasies. Unless I lay out everything sincerely and honestly, there is no real relationship, no real communication. I am who I am, with all my parts.

My wife says there is no greater act of faith in the future of humanity than getting married and having kids. I do have a strong sense of optimism. I think there are many branchings of alternative realities, perhaps one where there is no life because of thermonuclear war, another where feudal city-states are in a constant state of warfare. Maybe I've read too much science fiction, or perhaps I'm brain-dead from too many drugs. But I sure hope I'm on the pathway that ends in peace, where human beings become an enlightened, collaborative species moving out into the stars.

My children are amazed that bad people are arrested and punished by society. And they say, "Dad, you don't seem like a bad guy, but you must have been bad if you were in jail."

"I wasn't really a bad guy," I tell them. "But I wasn't the nicest of guys, either."

Three years ago, when my son was four, as part of my job I had to go to the state hospital, which is just a mile or two away from the boat landing to McNeil Island Penitentiary. I took my son and pointed out the prison where Daddy had been in jail. He said, "You were in that place? They locked you up?" I told him, "Yes, that's where I was locked up." At the time, he didn't say much more about it.

About a year later, he started making up songs. He sang me the first song he made up. It went:

> I'm a jailbird.
> I'm a jailbird.
> They said I was bad.
> I wasn't going to be glad.
> They locked me away.
> I'm a jailbird.

"This song is for you, Dad," he said.

———

When the amnesty for draft dodgers came through, I decided to accept it. I didn't believe I had done anything wrong, but I wanted so much to be able to visit home again.

I made my first trip home on a midwinter Sunday morning in 1977 with my wife and our six-year-old daughter. My parents had never seen them.

When we got off the plane at the Chicago airport, about fifteen members of my family were waiting for us. My younger brother was the first to come up to me. More than seven years had passed since I had last seen him. Then, he had been a pimply-faced, cheeky runt, but now he was grown up. He walked up and said, "My big brother." And then he put his arms around me and lifted me right off the ground. My father was there, too, along with my uncle, my cousins, their girlfriends, and my grandmother.

My daughter was the star of the show. She made the reentry much easier. My parents didn't have to focus on me. They could focus on her. And that was a big part of the healing that went on between us.

There were no parades. It was not a hero's welcome. But it was a beginning.

That was fifteen years ago. After that first trip, my wife and daughter and I went back to visit a lot. Later, we had a son, too. I had some good talks with my parents during those visits, yet I would have liked to have seen my dad more. But when you leave your family, even though jet planes can take you back, life goes on, and your old home is never the same again. So we weren't able to talk as much as we wanted. And my dad passed away last December.

Still, the years we had together after 1977 were a good time for us. The important thing was to have some sort of reconciliation. Not closure, because Vietnam is never really over. But to resolve some of the issues and speak out about our lives. I think we did that. We were able to talk about the war. I came to understand that my parents were part of a tradition that they had known all their lives. My dad and my uncles fought in World War II. They faced the threat of fascism and the Nazis. They saved the world from a great horror. They just couldn't believe that our government could make a mistake like Vietnam.

When my father died, I had no bitterness left. I hope he didn't either.

I will always have strong ties with America. When we crossed the border on our most recent trip to the States, I thought to myself, "This is where my father is buried." That's my connection to America now.

You build yourself a life, and you never know what's going to hold you to a place, whether it's a job or your family or your friends. Three years ago, my wife and I were thinking of returning to Chicago so I could go back to school. Maybe to the University of Chicago. I could pick up where I left off. Try to start over again back home. But just then our son, Jason, was diagnosed with cancer. You set your priorities and do what you must, so we stayed in Canada. It would be impossible now for us to get medical insurance in the States.

I look back and I say, "I wish it could have been another way." But it wasn't. Last December, Jason had a bone marrow transplant. With his treatments and his hospitalization, we're pretty busy now. And I don't know what's next. We've been in a three-year war at Children's Hospital. It's been rough. If I had a choice between that hospital room and a foxhole, I would choose the foxhole.

Endings

I'll never forgive or forget what America did in Indochina.

———

In a way, America is really just an idea in the mind. All countries are. That's all there is.

When I think of the war, the phrase that always comes to mind is, "They took my country away." I can't say the flag salute anymore. I just can't.

Bertolt Brecht said that when you have to be virtuous, the government's gone to hell and things must be really bad. That's how I feel about being a CO. I wish I hadn't had to do it. I can never go back to the innocence and the faith in America I had before Vietnam. That's my biggest loss.

———

It's difficult for me to conclude my story, since the issues that have meant so much to me are still unresolved. The arms race continues and government leaders show no signs of restraint. Nerve gas, weapons in space, and increasingly destructive forces at first stagger and then anesthetize the human imagination.

Either we become mutually interdependent, or we fight and kill each other in a struggle to survive. That's our choice.

▬▬▬

Yesterday, before this interview, I pulled out my old CO application. Form 150. And I read what I wrote back in 1968. Here's what I said then.

> I will always combat the kind of thinking that makes wars into glorious adventures, and pacifists into cowards. Our country is easily led astray by warlike men. My greatest responsibility to my country is to wake it up, before it causes any more destruction and sorrow than it already has. I think this is the social significance of conscientious objectors: They turn their friends, neighbors, and countries away from war, away from unthinking violence. Without these people, the world will someday be destroyed.

I still feel the same today.

▬▬▬

The lesson I learned from Vietnam is that you can never really gauge the strength of people's feelings until there's a crisis. Activists work hard, year after year, without knowing how much support they really have. But when the chips are down, people will make enormous sacrifices, they will put off their personal needs, they will take chances, and they will stand up for what is right. In those rare moments, the strength and the goodness of the human spirit will shine through.

▬▬▬

I don't know if I've given the entire picture of being a CO. I don't have the entire picture myself. I hope I've touched on a few of the highlights and a few of the important details. There's a lot I've talked about that I haven't had the chance to get into for a long time. That's good. That's fine. It was good to talk.

Afterword

Although the shooting war in Vietnam finally ended in April 1975, eleven years after the heavy escalation in U.S. involvement, the suffering was not over. The postwar misery began with the first frantic scenes of Vietnamese fleeing Saigon in 1975. Later, in 1978 and 1979, starving Cambodians poured across the border into Thailand, while tens of thousands of Vietnamese washed ashore throughout Southeast Asia. On the Thai border with Laos, a steady stream of Laotians, mostly highland people who had fought with the U.S. Army, swam the Mekong River to safety.

Like many Americans, I felt a deep sense of responsibility for the tragedy of the Indochinese refugees. In 1983, I decided to go to work at a U.S.–operated refugee camp on the Bataan Peninsula in the Philippines.

In late September 1983 I huddled with seventeen other Americans and Filipinos in the covered breezeway of the Ermita Center Building on Roxas Boulevard in Manila as high winds blasted monsoon rains against the minibus parked fifty feet away. Our transport was the supply vehicle on its regular Friday run to camp.

In clumps of twos and threes, we sprinted through the rain to the bus. Inside, the rear third of the vehicle was stuffed with goods destined for camp: large fans; a couple of IBM Selectric typewriters;

several dozen packs of photocopying paper; and assorted wrapped packages, a mishmash of cardboard, paper, plastic, rope, string, and tape. I checked the overhead racks for bundles that might fall on my head, and tried to relax as the driver ground the engine alive. On the ceiling, where the roof sloped downward to meet the upward arch of the wall, the shiny metallic-green paint had begun to peel in a neat four-inch strip. I reached up and broke off the end. Underneath the hardened paint, I found rotting wood. The bus was made of plywood.

We traveled first across town to the freeway entrance at Balintawak, then west toward the mountains. A winding road near the beginning of the World War II Bataan Death March led to treacherous passes in sparsely populated inland mountains. All along the way, signs marked each kilometer of the Death March. With the passing distance, we seemed to go back in time. Signs of urban life gradually disappeared, as concrete buildings gave way to Philippine nipa houses, and jeepneys were replaced by three-wheeled scooters and then by carabao, the Philippine water buffalo. Everywhere there were children. It seemed that half of the population of the country was under fifteen.

Finally, just after sunset, six hours after leaving Manila, we reached Morong, the last town on the road going nowhere except the sprawling camp. Our final nine kilometers passed in almost total darkness through scrubby forests sprinkled with occasional fires in front of a few huts scattered among the trees. At the guardhouse at the entrance to the camp, a lone soldier slowly raised a wooden barrier, while paying scant attention to the bus or to the dark figures who skulked into camp alongside it. In the distance, I could see nothing but blackness, no lights, no other vehicles, no distant hills on this moonless night, only an occasional human figure illuminated suddenly by our headlights, then vanishing in the night as we drove past.

After unloading my belongings at the central office, I made my way to my assigned room, an eight-by-ten-foot cubicle that I shared with another worker, in a billet housing fourteen people in seven rooms. Our communal kitchen was a sink and a two-burner hotplate. Exhausted by the trip, I fell into the bed, a wooden platform less than six feet long, covered with a single sheet, stiffly starched and decorated with brightly colored faces of laughing puppets.

The next morning, hoping to find something to eat, I asked for directions to the market. On my way there, I noticed a large crowd of several hundred people standing alongside five red buses. The name of the bus company was written in large white letters on the side of each bus: Victory Liner. As I reached the edge of the crowd, I heard a man's voice call out a number through a bullhorn. A boy, no more than fifteen, stepped forward alone. On his shirt he wore a small sign that read "643." As he stood at the front door of one of the buses, a second number was called, and this time a family of four fell in behind him. After a dozen more numbers were called, the bus door was opened, and the people in line climbed silently inside.

Through the windows, I followed the boy as he walked halfway toward the back and took a seat alone. He leaned out of an open window, stretching his hand downward toward two other boys, about his age, standing in the dust below. As the three joined hands, the boy on the bus closed his eyes and began to cry.

Suddenly, there was a loud shout, and within seconds the driver slammed the door and started the engine. The crowd surged forward, an army of hands reaching upward toward the open windows. I heard cries and screams, loud voices calling out in languages I could not understand. The bus lurched ahead, gears grinding as it pulled out into the narrow street and slowly picked up speed. Children raced alongside, while the adults left behind waved and shouted. The boy on the bus leaned farther out the window, his eyes searching the crowd. He did not wave. He did not speak. It was only then that I saw the hand-painted sign in the rear window of the bus: "Refugees — Do Not Delay."

On my first morning at the Philippine Refugee Processing Center, I had stumbled upon two hundred Vietnamese refugees on their way to the Manila airport for a flight to their new home in the United States. As the buses roared off and those left behind quietly dispersed, I said a silent prayer for the boy whose life was about to change forever.

Over the next three years, throughout Southeast Asia, I visited refugee camps with names that echo the misery of a generation of Vietnamese, Cambodians, and Laotians: Khao i Dang, Ban Nam Yao, Ban Vinai, and Phanat Nikhom in Thailand; Jubilee and Lantau Island in Hong Kong; Palawan in the Philippines; Pulau Bidong in

Malaysia; Galang in Indonesia. Driven from their homes by wars and economic hardship, more than a million people have passed through these camps to resettle in the United States, Europe, Australia, and elsewhere. Hundreds of thousands of others have remained trapped, often for years, with an unknown future. As I traveled from one camp to another, I saw again and again and again the consequences of nearly three decades of war in Indochina: malnourished infants, children without parents, legless victims of mines, shell-shocked warriors, and hundreds of thousands of homeless refugees.

"It's always the innocent who suffer most," said one of the last men I interviewed, a medic in the U.S. Army in Vietnam. It was the civilian casualties that finally turned him against the war. For many COs, the continuing suffering in Indochina — almost twenty years after the fighting stopped — is a powerful reminder that the consequences of war can last for generations.

Horace Walpole told the story of a prince who went on a three-year journey, bringing home nothing but a nut. His disappointed family cracked it open. Inside, they found a tightly wrapped piece of silk, painted with images of all the rulers and all the peoples of all the kingdoms in the entire world. After many unfoldings, out stepped a little dog, which shook its ears and then danced a saraband.

History has not been kind to the COs. Like the miraculous gift of the prodigal prince, the COs' stories have been largely hidden from public view, absent from the public memory of Vietnam. But allowed to unfold, these stories offer a rich personal and political history, full of the moral struggles of conscience and the intimate struggles of personal relationships.

The questions raised by the COs from the Vietnam War are still with us. How can a world of increasingly destructive military power be turned toward peace? What is our proper response when government leaders ask us to violate our personal morality? In a violent world, how is it possible for individuals to lead lives committed to peace? COs during the Vietnam era provided no easy answers. But surely the questions they raised deserve to be heard in the public debate over the future of America and the world.

I am one of the lucky ones. In 1987, I returned from Southeast Asia to write about the camps. The war in Vietnam had ended twelve years earlier. My struggle with the draft was nineteen years in the past. During all that time, my parents and I had never mentioned Vietnam or conscientious objection. My father and I had argued bitterly during the war. Since then, we had protected our family from our mutual anger, but we paid a high price in years of tension, conflict, and fear. I worried that we would never be reconciled over Vietnam, and that after his inevitable passing I would carry my rage and the memory of his disapproval for the rest of my life.

Wanting a quiet place to write, I found a rundown cabin on a cliff on President's Point, which juts out into Puget Sound thirty miles north of Seattle. The tiny building offered a dramatic view to the east, toward the Cascade Mountains. But the roof had leaked for years, the old cesspool no longer functioned, and the wallboards had peeled loose from the two-by-fours. When my father offered to help me remodel the cabin into an office, I reacted first with caution. He had been an electrician for nearly forty years and he could build a house all by himself, while I knew nothing about construction. We would have to be together more than any time since Vietnam. I wondered whether we could get along. Despite my fear, I accepted his offer.

For seven weeks, we worked side by side on the cabin, mostly in the rain and mostly in silence. We were together day in and day out, we ate at the same table, and we slept under the same roof. Though we never mentioned the war, our work on that cliff over-looking the sea gave us the chance we needed. Slowly, by working together, we began to overcome the separation that Vietnam had brought into our lives.

When we were nearly finished, we stood on the roof early one morning as the winter sun broke momentarily through the dark clouds to the southeast. The slate-gray Sound stretched out from the sandy cliff at our feet. Forty miles to the north, the Mukilteo ferry glided west toward Whidbey Island. The wind rippling the water from the south meant that rain was less than an hour away.

For a moment we admired the view together, and then my father turned to descend the ladder before me. His steps were slower than I had ever seen. My father had aged. I was now as old as he had been during the war in Vietnam.

Perhaps we will never be able to say the words to express our sorrow for the years of arguments and anger over Vietnam. And perhaps if we were to watch again, as we did nearly twenty-five years ago, the scenes of the police fighting demonstrators at the Democratic Convention in Chicago, he would still side with the police and I would again identify with the demonstrators. Yet now we can also acknowledge the family bonds that sustained us through the years. And we know, in our silence together, that Vietnam, our personal war, is finally over.

Bibliography

Allen, Douglas, and Ngo Vinh Long. *Coming to Terms: Indochina, the United States, and the War*. Boulder, CO: Westview Press, 1991.

American Friends Service Committee. *In Place of War: An Inquiry into Nonviolent National Defense*. New York: Grossman Publishers, 1967.

Axelrad, Albert S. *Call to Conscience: Jews, Judaism, and Conscientious Objection*. Hoboken, NJ: Ktav Publishing House and Jewish Peace Fellowship, 1986.

Baker, Mark. *Nam: The Vietnam War in the Words of the Men and Women Who Fought There*. New York: Morrow, 1981.

Balaban, John. *Remembering Heaven's Face: A Moral Witness in Vietnam*. New York: Simon and Schuster, 1991.

Bannan, John F., and Rosemary S. Bannan. *Law, Morality, and Vietnam: The Peace Militants and the Courts*. Bloomington, IN: Indiana University Press, 1974.

Baskir, Lawrence M., and William A. Strauss. *Chance and Circumstance: The Draft, the War, and the Vietnam Generation*. New York: Alfred A. Knopf, 1978.

———. *Reconciliation after Vietnam: A Program of Relief for Vietnam Era Draft and Military Offenders*. Notre Dame, IN: University of Notre Dame Press, 1977.

Berrigan, Daniel. *America Is Hard to Find*. Garden City, NY: Doubleday, 1972.

Bibliography

———. *The Dark Night of Resistance.* Garden City, NY: Doubleday, 1971.

———. *They Call Us Dead Men: Reflections on Life and Conscience.* New York: Macmillan, 1966.

———. *To Dwell in Peace: An Autobiography.* San Francisco: Harper and Row, 1987.

———. *The Trial of the Catonsville Nine.* Boston: Beacon, 1970.

Berrigan, Philip. *Prison Journals of a Priest Revolutionary.* New York: Ballantine, 1970.

———. *A Punishment for Peace.* New York: Ballantine, 1969.

———. *Widen the Prison Gates: Writing from Jails.* New York: Touchstone, 1973.

Bondurant, Joan V. *Conquest of Violence.* Berkeley: University of California Press, 1965.

Breins, Wini. *The Great Refusal: Community and Organization in the New Left, 1962–1969.* New York: Praeger, 1982.

Brock, Peter. *Pacifism in the United States from the Colonial Era to the First World War.* Princeton: Princeton University Press, 1968.

Brown, Robert McAfee. *Vietnam: Crisis of Conscience.* New York: Association Press, 1967.

Capps, Walter H. *The Unfinished War: Vietnam and the American Conscience.* Boston: Beacon, 1982.

Chambers, John Whiteclay. *Draftees or Volunteers: A Documentary History of the Debate over Military Conscription in the United States 1787–1973.* New York: Garland Publishing, 1975.

———. *To Raise an Army: The Draft Comes to Modern America.* New York: Free Press, 1987.

Cohen, Carl. *Civil Disobedience.* New York: Columbia University Press, 1971.

Cohen, Eliot A. *Citizens and Soldiers: The Dilemmas of Military Service.* Ithaca: Cornell University Press, 1985.

Cohen, Marshall, Thomas Nagel, and Thomas Scanlon, eds. *War and Moral Responsibility.* Princeton: Princeton University Press, 1974.

Cooney, Robert, and Helen Michalowski. *The Power of the People: Active Non-Violence in the United States.* Culver City, CA: Peace Press, 1977.

Cortright, David. *Soldiers in Revolt: The American Military Today.* Garden City, NY: Doubleday, 1975.

Currey, Cecil B. *Self-Destruction: The Disintegration and Decay of the United States Armed Forces During the Vietnam Era.* New York: Norton, 1981.

Curry, G. David. *Sunshine Patriots: Punishment and the Vietnam Offender.* Notre Dame, IN: University of Notre Dame Press, 1985.

DeBenedetti, Charles. *An American Ordeal: The Antiwar Movement of the Vietnam Era*. Syracuse: Syracuse University Press, 1990.

DeBenedetti, Charles, ed. *Peace Heroes in Twentieth-Century America*. Bloomington, IN: Indiana University Press, 1986.

Douglass, James W. *The Nonviolent Cross: A Theology of Revolution and Peace*. New York: Macmillan, 1966.

———. *Resistance and Contemplation*. Garden City, NY: Doubleday, 1972.

Duffet, John, ed. *Against the Crime of Silence: Proceedings of the International War Crimes Tribunal*. New York: Clarion/Simon and Schuster, 1968.

Dumbrell, John, ed. *Vietnam and the Antiwar Movement: An International Perspective*. Brookfield, VT: Gower, 1989.

Ellsberg, Daniel. *Papers on the War*. New York: Simon and Schuster, 1972.

Emerson, Gloria. *Winners and Losers: Battles, Retreats, Gain, Losses and Ruins from a Long War*. New York: Random House, 1972.

Ferber, Michael, and Staughton Lynd. *The Resistance*. Boston: Beacon Press, 1971.

Finn, James. *Protest: Pacifism and Politics*. New York: Random House, 1968.

Forest, James. *Catholics and Conscientious Objection*. New York: Catholic Peace Fellowship, 1966.

Fraser, Ronald, ed. *1968: A Student Generation in Revolt*. New York: Pantheon Books, 1988.

Gardner, Fred. *The Unlawful Concert: An Account of the Presidio Mutiny Case*. New York: Viking, 1970.

Gaylin, Willard. *In the Service of Their Country: War Resisters in Prison*. New York: Viking Press, 1970.

Gitlin, Todd. *The Sixties: Years of Hope, Days of Rage*. New York: Bantam, 1987.

Gold, Philip. *Evasions: The American Way of Military Service*. New York: Paragon House, 1985.

Gray, Francine du Plessix. *Divine Disobedience: Profiles in Catholic Radicalism*. New York: Vintage, 1971.

Hall, Mitchell K. *Because of Their Faith: CALCAV and Religious Opposition to the Vietnam War*. New York: Columbia University Press, 1990.

Halsted, Fred. *GIs Speak Out Against the War: The Case of the Fort Jackson 8*. New York: Pathfinder Press, 1970.

Handbook for Conscientious Objectors. Philadelphia: Central Committee for Conscientious Objectors, 1952 (10th edition, 1968).

Harris, David. *Dreams Die Hard*. New York: St. Martin's, 1982.

Haskins, James, and Kathleen Benson. *The 60s Reader*. New York: Viking Kestrel, 1988.

Bibliography

Hayes, Thomas Lee. *American Deserters in Sweden*. New York: Association Press, 1971.

Helmer, John. *Bringing the War Home: The American Soldier in Vietnam and After*. New York: Free Press, 1971.

Johnson, R. Charles. *Draft, Registration, and the Law*. Occidental, CA: Nolo Press, 1985.

Kasinsky, Renée Goldsmith. *Refugees from Militarism: Draft-age Americans in Canada*. New Brunswick, NJ: Littlefield and Adams, 1976.

King, William M., ed. *A White Man's War: Race Issues and Vietnam*, special issue of *Vietnam Generation* 1:2 (Spring 1989).

Knoll, Erwin, and Judith Nies McFadden, eds. *War Crimes and the American Conscience*. New York: Holt, Rinehart, and Winston, 1970.

Kohn, Stephen M. *Jailed for Peace: The History of American Draft Law Violators, 1658–1985*. Westport, CT: Greenwood Press, 1986.

Lewy, Guenter. *Peace and Revolution: The Moral Crisis of American Pacifism*. Grand Rapids, MI: William B. Eerdmans, 1988.

Linfield, Michael. *Freedom Under Fire: U.S. Civil Liberties in Times of War*. Boston: South End Press, 1990.

Lynd, Staughton, ed. *Nonviolence in America: A Documentary History*. New York: Bobbs Merrill, 1966.

Lynn, Conrad J. *How to Stay Out of the Army: A Guide to Your Rights Under the Draft Law*. New York: Grove Press, 1967.

MacGregor, G.H.C. *The New Testament Basis of Pacifism*. New York: Fellowship Publications, 1954.

MacPherson, Myra. *Long Time Passing: Vietnam and the Haunted Generation*. New York: Doubleday, 1984.

McCarthy, Eugene. *The Year of the People*. Garden City, NY: Doubleday, 1969.

McGill, William J. *The Year of the Monkey: Revolt on the Campus, 1968–1969*. New York: McGraw Hill, 1982.

Meconis, Charles. *With Clumsy Grace: The American Catholic Left 1961–1975*. New York: Seabury Press, 1979.

Merton, Thomas. *Faith and Violence: Christian Teaching and Christian Practice*. Notre Dame, IN: University of Notre Dame Press, 1968.

———. *The Nonviolent Alternative*. New York: Farrar, Straus and Giroux, 1971.

Miller, James. *Democracy in the Streets: From Port Huron to the Siege of Chicago*. New York: Simon and Schuster, 1987.

Miller, Melissa, and Phil M. Shenk. *The Path of Most Resistance*. Scottdale, PA: Herald Press, 1982.

Moritz, Debbie, and Bennett Wine. *Amnesty*. New York: United States Student Association, 1974.

O'Rourke, William. *The Harrisburg 7 and the New Catholic Left*. New York: Crowell, 1972.

Osborne, J. K. *I Refuse*. Philadelphia: Westminster Press, 1971.

O'Sullivan, John, and Alan M. Meckler, eds. *The Draft and its Enemies: A Documentary History*. Urbana: University of Illinois Press, 1974.

Peace, Roger C. *A Just and Lasting Peace: The U.S. Peace Movement from the Cold War to Desert Storm*. Chicago: Noble Press, 1991.

Peck, Abe. *Uncovering the Sixties: The Life and Times of the Underground Press*. New York: Pantheon Books, 1986.

The Pentagon Papers. New York: Bantam, 1971.

Polner, Murray. *No Victory Parades: The Return of the Vietnam Veteran*. New York: Holt, Rinehart and Winston, 1971.

Polner, Murray, ed. *When Can I Come Home? A Debate on Amnesty for Exiles, Anti-war Prisoners and Others*. New York: Anchor, 1972.

Quigley, Thomas, ed. *American Catholics and Vietnam*. Grand Rapids, MI: William B. Eerdmans, 1968.

Reeves, Thomas, and Karl Hess. *The End of the Draft*. New York: Random House, 1970.

Schlissel, Lillian, ed. *Conscience in America: A Documentary History of Conscientious Objection in America 1957–1967*. New York: E. P. Dutton, 1968.

Shafer, D. Michael, ed. *The Legacy: The Vietnam War in the American Imagination*. Boston: Beacon Press, 1990.

Shannon, Thomas A., ed. *War or Peace?* Maryknoll, NY: Orbis, 1980.

Shapiro, Andrew O., and John M. Striker. *Mastering the Draft: A Comprehensive Guide for Solving Draft Problems*. Boston: Little, Brown, 1970.

Small, Melvin, and William D. Hoover, eds. *Give Peace a Chance: Exploring the Vietnam Antiwar Movement*. Syracuse: Syracuse University Press, 1992.

Stanage, Sherman M., ed. *Reason and Violence*. Totawa, NJ: Rowman and Littlefield, 1974.

Stringfellow, William, and Anthony Towne. *Suspect Tenderness: The Ethics of the Berrigan Witness*. New York: Holt, Rinehart, and Winston, 1971.

Surrey, David S. *Choice of Conscience: Vietnam Era Military and Draft Resisters in Canada*. New York: Praeger, 1982.

True, Michael, ed. *Daniel Berrigan: Poetry, Drama, Prose*. New York: Orbis Books, 1988.

Unseem, Michael. *Conscription, Protest and Social Conflict: The Life and Death of a Draft Resistance Movement*. New York: John Wiley and Sons, 1973.

Bibliography

Vietnam Veterans Against the War. *The Winter Soldier: An Inquiry into American War Crimes.* Boston: Beacon Press, 1972.

Viorst, Milton. *Fire in the Streets: America in the 1960's.* New York: Simon and Schuster, 1979.

Waterhouse, Larry, and Mariann Wizard. *Turning the Guns Around: Notes on the GI Movement.* New York: Praeger, 1971.

Wheeler, John. *Touched with Fire: The Future of the Vietnam Generation.* New York: Franklin Watts, 1984.

Wittner, Lawrence S. *Rebels Against War: The American Peace Movement, 1933–1983.* Philadelphia: Temple University Press, 1984.

Zahn, Gordon C. *War, Conscience, and Dissent.* New York: Hawthorne Books, 1967.

Zahn, Gordon C., ed. *Thomas Merton on Peace.* New York: McCall Publishing, 1971.

Zaroulis, Nancy, and Gerald Sullivan. *Who Spoke Up! American Protest against the War in Vietnam 1963–1975.* New York: Holt, Rinehart and Winston, 1984.

Zinn, Howard. *SNCC: The New Abolitionists.* Boston: Beacon Press, 1965.